Scarecrow Studies in Young Adult Literature
Series Editor: Patty Campbell

Scarecrow Studies in Young Adult Literature is intended to continue the body of critical writing established in Twayne's Young Adult Authors series and to expand it beyond single-author studies to explorations of genres, multicultural writing, and controversial issues in young adult (YA) reading. Many of the contributing authors of the series are among the leading scholars and critics of adolescent literature, and some are YA novelists themselves.

The series is shaped by its editor, Patty Campbell, who is a renowned authority in the field, with a forty-year background as critic, lecturer, librarian, and teacher of YA literature. Patty Campbell was the 2001 winner of the ALAN Award, given by the Assembly on Literature for Adolescents of the National Council of Teachers of English for distinguished contribution to YA literature. In 1989 she was the winner of the American Library Association's Grolier Award for distinguished service to young adults and reading.

1. *What's So Scary about R. L. Stine?* by Patrick Jones, 1998.
2. *Ann Rinaldi: Historian and Storyteller*, by Jeanne M. McGlinn, 2000.
3. *Norma Fox Mazer: A Writer's World*, by Arthea J. S. Reed, 2000.
4. *Exploding the Myths: The Truth about Teens and Reading*, by Marc Aronson, 2001.
5. *The Agony and the Eggplant: Daniel Pinkwater's Heroic Struggles in the Name of YA Literature*, by Walter Hogan, 2001.
6. *Caroline Cooney: Faith and Fiction*, by Pamela Sissi Carroll, 2001.
7. *Declarations of Independence: Empowered Girls in Young Adult Literature, 1990–2001*, by Joanne Brown and Nancy St. Clair, 2002.
8. *Lost Masterworks of Young Adult Literature*, by Connie S. Zitlow, 2002.
9. *Beyond the Pale: New Essays for a New Era*, by Marc Aronson, 2003.
10. *Orson Scott Card: Writer of the Terrible Choice*, by Edith S. Tyson, 2003.
11. *Jacqueline Woodson: "The Real Thing,"* by Lois Thomas Stover, 2003.
12. *Virginia Euwer Wolff: Capturing the Music of Young Voices*, by Suzanne Elizabeth Reid, 2003.

THEY SUCK, THEY BITE, THEY EAT, THEY KILL

The Psychological Meaning of Supernatural Monsters in Young Adult Fiction

Joni Richards Bodart

Scarecrow Studies in
Young Adult Literature, No. 43

The Scarecrow Press, Inc.
Lanham • Toronto • Plymouth, UK
2012

Published by Scarecrow Press, Inc.
A wholly owned subsidiary of The Rowman & Littlefield Publishing Group, Inc.
4501 Forbes Boulevard, Suite 200, Lanham, Maryland 20706
http://www.scarecrowpress.com

Estover Road, Plymouth PL6 7PY, United Kingdom

British Library Cataloguing in Publication Information Available

Library of Congress Cataloging-in-Publication Data

Bodart, Joni Richards.
  They suck, they bite, they eat, they kill : the psychological meaning of supernatural monsters in young adult fiction / Joni Richards Bodart.
    p. cm. — (Scarecrow studies in young adult literature ; no. 43)
  Includes bibliographical references and index.
  ISBN 978-0-8108-8227-0 (cloth : alk. paper) — ISBN 978-0-8108-8228-7 (ebook)
  1. Young adult fiction, American—History and criticism. 2. Monsters in literature. 3. Supernatural in literature. I. Title.
  PS374.M544B63 2012
  813'.08766099283—dc23   2011029544

∞™ The paper used in this publication meets the minimum requirements of American National Standard for Information Sciences—Permanence of Paper for Printed Library Materials, ANSI/NISO Z39.48-1992.

Printed in the United States of America

To the teens with monsters in their lives,
To the authors who create them,
To the lives who were changed by them,
And to my BFF, who suggested I get to know them better.

There is darkness inside all of us. . . . [W]e all have it—
that part of our soul that is irreparably damaged by the
very trials and tribulations of life. We are what we are because of it, or perhaps in spite of it. Some use it as a shield
to hide behind, others as an excuse to do unconscionable
things. But, truly, the darkness is simply a piece of the
whole, neither good nor evil unless you make it so.

— Jenna Maclaine, *Bound by Sin* (2009)

Contents

Preface

This book is the result of my passion for giving teens the books that they need and want, my interest in supernatural fiction for teens and adults, and my support of teens' rights to intellectual freedom and privacy. It is also a result of the need that Scarecrow Studies in Young Adult Literature had for a book on the supernatural monsters that are populating YA literature in increasingly large numbers and the reasons they are so popular.

It all started late one November evening at the 2009 National Council of Teachers of English conference in Philadelphia, when series editor Patty Campbell said, "What I'd *really* like is a book about supernatural monsters in YA literature—why is everyone suddenly writing about vampires and werewolves and zombies?" And I, predictably, responded, "Memememe! I'll do it if you'll let me include human monsters as well!" Alas, conforming to page requirements meant the human monsters had to be put off to their own book, which may be forthcoming soon, but the Big Three classic monsters are here.

At the beginning, I wasn't sure I could actually do a scholarly study of monsters and monstrosity, but I soon learned that they have been around for centuries and have been carefully studied and dissected for almost as long as they've been in existence. Soon most of my conversations began with stories and facts about monsters (and some people began to duck and hide when they saw me coming), my foodie magazines piled up unread, and my dining table filled up with books on the who, what, why, and how of monsters.

Then came the YA books themselves, piles of them, well-loved ones from the library that I read for the first time and brand-new ones from publishers or from Amazon that I could scribble in while reading, to make sure I didn't miss any details—or as few as possible. I scoured the SJSU (San José State University) databases for articles on the monsters, the authors, and the series, and sent my graduate assistant off to look elsewhere. What were the monsters? Where did they come from? Why did they come back now? What do they have to say about us, our society, our world? Why do they appeal so widely to teens? Is it a trickle-down effect from the adult titles featuring supernatural characters of all kinds, or something different?

Then once the titles had been decided on, I began to research the authors who'd written them. Why did they choose to write about supernatural monsters? What were their goals for their books? How did they choose the kind of monster to write about, and how did they tweak its characteristics to make it unique? I looked at interviews with these writers; I examined their websites and blogs and the variety of ways that they used monsters to connect with readers, and I read articles written by or about them.

Finally, the writing began, and drafts were written, completed, rewritten, thrown out, and begun again. Hair tearing commenced. Fear of editorial slashing grew and grew, and the first section was sent off with great fear and trembling. I waited impatiently until Patty's pleased response arrived. Huge sighs of relief ensued, and the writing continued and was eventually finished. There was no slashing involved, and my hair is shorter, but still intact.

Why did I select the authors I chose to include? The quality of their writing, the depth and richness of their world or their backstory, the uniqueness of their monsters, and the ways they chose to tweak the stereotypes or the classic forms of those monsters were all parts of it. I also chose books and characters that spoke to me, that flew off the page and into heart and mind, impossible to forget. I looked at the authors, wanting to discover why they wrote these books, and what messages, ideas, and lessons they wanted to present to their readers. And I looked for authors who communicated with their readers in some way outside their books—through their websites, through their blogs, through e-mail—and during their tours and appearances I met them face-to-face. From among the thousands of volumes and hundreds of series that feature supernatural monsters, I wanted to select the very best. You may or may not agree with me about the books and authors I have chosen, but I had to draw a line in the sand somewhere. Page limits are difficult when there are so many excellent and popular titles. If I omitted your favorites—and I'm sure I omitted someone's—I apologize. For those of you who want to look beyond the titles examined here, there are inclusive, but not guaranteed to be comprehensive, bibliographies in the appendix.

You'll notice that some of the monsters you are going to meet look very monstrous indeed, and others not so much. Daniel Waters's zombies look a little pale, and some don't walk so well, but other than the Sons of Romero, they look pretty normal. But to the people who are persecuting them, they are monsters, every bit as frightening as the grown-ups in Charlie Higson's London or the zoms of the Rot & Ruin that Jonathan Maberry created. People fear what they don't understand, and that fear creates the monster, no matter what it looks like to everyone else.

Now, on to the monsters! I hope you enjoy playing with them as much as I did!

Acknowledgments

First, I want to thank Patty Campbell for asking me to write this, for believing in me, and for her patience, silence, and gentle editing style. You used all of them to convince me that I could actually do this, especially when I doubted it the most. I'm looking forward to working with you on the human monsters, now that the supernatural monsters have been taken care of.

I also want to thank my colleagues at the School of Library and Information Science (SLIS) at San José State University. Linda Main, our associate director, was a firm taskmaster, with her consistent nudges, nags, and reminders to get it done, get it done, get it done, don't stop, get it done. It's done. And no, you *don't* have to actually read it—for months, you listened patiently to me telling you more about vampires, werewolves, and zombies than you've *ever* wanted to know, even feigning interest sometimes, so you more or less know it all already! Ken Haycock and Sandy Hirsh, previous and current SLIS directors, made sure I had a graduate assistant every semester to help with research, formatting, and emergencies, and also encouraged me to keep going—although I think they both were glad *they* didn't have to write it! Jane Fisher, assistant director of almost everything, was my local cheerleader, quick with congratulations when each milestone was reached, and ready to sympathize when something wasn't going well, whether it was writer's block or exhaustion. Beth Wrenn-Estes has been a good friend and colleague for years; she listened patiently to interminable and obsessive discussions of all things monstrous—and hauled me away from my laptop every so often for some infrequent but much-needed social life. She is also the first person who said to me, "I can't wait to read it!" Now you can, Beth—enjoy! When I was working on the last section of the book, Stanley Laufer, head of our wonderful IT team, spent several hours trying to recover a file I'd accidentally written over, and was able to retrieve almost all of it, which felt like something pretty close to a miracle! As always, Stan, you rock!

And I also have to thank the authors of these wonderful, insightful, valuable novels and series. You did interviews, wrote articles, created study guides, answered my e-mails, and blogged about everything with your readers, all of which made writing this book a fun and interesting journey. Keep up the good work that you do, writing books and connecting with the teens who read them and who need their message so badly—monsters do exist, but monsters *can* be killed.

Thanks are also due to the publishers of many of the YA titles included here, who graciously responded to my requests for books with review copies and advanced reader copies. Because of them, this book will date far more slowly, since I was able to include all the newest volumes of many of the series.

But my biggest thanks have to go to Casandria Crane, my long-term (and long-suffering) graduate assistant, who is finally about to graduate, now that she's gotten me through this book. While I did the fun part of the research, she did the part that wasn't so fun and never once complained about it. She compiled bibliographies, found and organized information, made sense of confusing citations and references, proofread chapters, and put up with every panicked request to "drop everything and do this NOW!!!"—even though she has a husband, a family, and a life. She even claims it really *was* fun. Every writer should have someone willing to do for them all that Casandria has done for me. Without her, this book would have gotten written sooner or later, but absolutely not within the time frame Patty demanded from me. It simply wouldn't have been possible. There aren't thanks enough, Casandria. And when someone wants a reference—send them to me. I'll make sure they know you can not only come up with the most arcane and obscure citation or factoid at a moment's notice, so quickly it seems like magic, you can also walk on water and even thin ice as well!

Introduction: Here Be Monsters—Who and Why

> You know honestly I think there's a Dracula, a Wolf Man,
> and a Frankenstein's Monster in all of us. They are sides
> of our own character, so that's why I think we can relate
> to them in terms of a "I know how that feels" kind of
> thing.
>
> —Richard Roxburgh

There have always been monsters. They exist in every culture
around the world, and the first stories about them were told about
3000 BC, at the same time that humans became literate.[1] Monsters
emerge from the shadows, and our primitive reptilian brain reacts
with fear, recognizing the danger, the threat to our minds, our emotions, our lives. Our stomachs clench, our muscles tighten, blood
rushes from our extremities to our core as we prepare for fight or
flight. But while we are afraid, terrified, we are also fascinated and
attracted to the monster, peeping around the corner to get just one
more glimpse or to see if it's safe yet. Have we escaped, or does the
creature still lurk, searching, waiting for us to reveal ourselves? As
with a train wreck or a freeway pileup, we don't want to look, but
we can't make ourselves stop. The monstrous is just as intriguing as
it is repellent.

Some researchers have postulated that perhaps our brains are partly hardwired before birth, and the most widely spread fears or phobias, such as those about snakes, spiders, sea creatures, or heights, may be part of that hard-wiring, created to keep our primitive ancestors alive. In other words, there can be an actual, real monster (snake, spider, etc.), but the concept of it in the individual's mind is more intense, important, and fearful because in the past, the thing was so dangerous to primitive humans and needed to be avoided at all cost.

In a passage from *The Descent of Man* describing his work in the monkey house at the London Zoological Gardens, Charles Darwin recorded an incident that would seem to support this idea of the evolution of instincts. He knew that monkeys had an "instinctive dread" of snakes. So he put a large dead stuffed snake in the monkey cage. The monkeys were terrified and wouldn't go near it, even though they did get used to other dead stuffed animals he put in the cage. Then Darwin decided to see how the monkeys would react to a live snake. He put one in a bag and set it inside the cage. When a monkey came up to peek into the upright bag, it saw the snake at the bottom and instantly ran away. But then, reacting very much like humans, the monkeys, over and over, one after another, went and peeked into the very top of the bag to see if the snake was still there, verified that it was, and ran away. They were both fascinated and afraid, just as a human might be when watching the snake pit scene in the movie *Indiana Jones and the Raiders of the Lost Ark*—peering at the screen between fingers, hands over eyes, unable to watch the scene, but also unable to resist peeking at it.[2]

We have the same dual reaction to other kinds of monsters, the ones in the stories we tell, the books we read, and the movies we see, the ones that don't exist in the real world—vampires, shapeshifters, zombies, demons, witches, and more. They fascinate us, but we recognize their danger and we fear them as well. Books and movies let us step into their world for a while, to see how close we can get to them without getting caught. And who hasn't looked up from a scary story to see the twitch of a shadow, the creak of the floor in the hall, and wondered if the monster had escaped from the pages?

When imaginary monsters from every culture are compared, they have several things in common: they are usually tall or large and have a looming, threatening demeanor. They eat or attack humans, and their mouths and teeth are large and used as weapons. Their appearance is frightening and may also be bizarre or gruesome. And they are powerful, destructive, and violent, and that violence is most often directed toward humans. An air of evil and menace surrounds them, making them intimidating, terrifying, even at a distance. Supernatural, they come from the depths of our minds, in the form of that which we fear the most.[3]

The popularity of the monster ebbs and flows, and an intriguing question about those shifts is what causes them and how they affect the population as a whole. In *Danse Macabre*, Stephen King notes that "horror films and novels have always been popular, but every ten or twenty years they seem to enjoy a cycle of increased popularity and visibility. These periods almost always seem to coincide with periods of fairly serious economic and/or political strain, and the books and films . . . seem to reflect those free-floating anxieties."[4]

Columbia philosophy professor Stephen Asma agrees with King. It could be the effects of 9/11, the economic crisis, or the wars the United States is involved in. Whenever a society or culture is facing a crisis, the popularity of supernatural monsters increases, both in print and on the screen. They serve to distract us from current events for a while and let us release some of the pressures of life, giving us a "time out."[5] And today, there is no shortage of pressures—school shootings, bombs, terrorists, wars on many fronts, recessions, and economic chaos. In the last ten to fifteen years, the world has become a very dangerous place, with little that can be depended on. We have begun to realize not only that real monsters exist but that their actions can change our lives forever. That realization set the stage for a surge of imaginary monsters.[6]

The vampires, always the most popular choice, came first, but when they became too familiar, other monsters appeared: werewolves, shapeshifters of all kinds, zombies, demons, witches, evil faeries, and more. Reading about or seeing these monsters and the destruction they can create can make our own problems and our own lives seem not so overwhelming after all and give us a break from reality when it gets too hard to handle. And as long as the world is a dangerous place, we'll need monsters to distract us, to frighten us, to intrigue us, to remind us of their lessons.

The literature of monsters is almost always horror. The author creates another darker and more frightening world, which can be either real or supernatural and has been designed to frighten the reader, to prey on fears that get more and more intense as the story progresses. The atmosphere of horror is more important than the plot, as it invokes the darkest and most forbidden part of our society so the reader can experience the emotions found there or confront the fears it induces, and perhaps even defeat them. And the reader can do those things from a safe place, since the monsters cannot really escape the covers of a book.[7]

We are intrigued by that which we most fear; we want to explore that which is forbidden, to poke a stick at the monster, daring it to attack. The horror story is a chance to examine what's going on behind closed doors that we usually keep tightly locked and bolted. What is forbidden is innately tantalizing, and humans are curious. What's behind the door is a question we can't help but want to answer.[8]

We also want to face those fears, regain control of them, shove them into the light and show them for what they are, not what we imagine them to be in the darkness. Perhaps this is the reason why the popularity of horror is a cyclic thing, more popular in times of stress, when there are more fears to be faced or conquered.

Children today are brought up in a "culture of fear," taught that there are dangerous people out there who are capable of harming them, kidnapping them, or killing them and that they should trust no one. By the time they become teenagers, the chances are very good that they've either experienced something truly evil or know someone else who has.[9]

But while telling children and teens that the world is scary is both important and necessary, teaching them how to defend themselves and how to evaluate risk and danger is equally important. If they don't ever experience danger and don't know what it looks like, they won't fear it and can put themselves at risk and in danger because of their ignorance. To know what danger is, one must experience it, and doing so in a book about monsters can be both safer and more educational than living it. It is also important to know what the consequences of danger are and how to decide what acceptable level of risk (and consequences) is appropriate. Today's children and teens need to know who the monsters are, why they are dangerous, and how to overcome them.[10]

In 2009, an Illinois high school teacher asked her senior English class to complete the following phrase: "If you had to choose a word to complete the phrase "The Age of ___" to describe the time in which we live, what word would you choose, and why?" One boy's response was "This is the age of fear." Asked to explain, he talked about 9/11 and the increased security, both locally and nationally, that concerns him. Another student talked about fears about child safety, teen drivers, and sexual predators. And these two weren't alone. When the teacher asked who else had written down "fear" to describe this age, a number of students raised their hands.[11]

We may think that we are protecting our children, but we are not. Technology gives them access to people and information all over the world in just seconds, and they both talk and read. Teens know what is going on in far more detail than previous generations did. They don't just know that the world is a scary place, they also know why. So it is important to teach young adults not only how to defeat the monsters but how to make use of them as well.

Because monsters do, after all, have their uses. In medieval times, monsters were the gods' punishment for the sin of pride. Greeks and Romans believed they were warnings of impending danger or catastrophes. Freud saw them as a chance to see our unconscious minds, a way to contact the Mr. Hyde, the twisted, dark persona that is inside each of us.[12] But once we have gone where the wild things are and have confronted the monsters that live there, conquered or killed them, we are able to return to our reality, and like Max, we find that our dinner is still warm.[13]

Monsters can teach us about our responses to menace or danger from a perspective that is safe—within a story. We identify with the victims in the story, telling them what to do or not do, and asking ourselves what we would do in their place, inside the story. What weapon would I use? If I heard a noise in the basement, would I go down there? Would I run away or would I stand and fight? What would I be willing to do to stay safe? And what kind of a person does that make me?[14] In a story, we can learn that the monsters, while they are scary and overwhelming, can eventually be confronted and tamed,[15] so we and our loved ones are safe from danger. If the monster can't be beaten by plan A, then we can try B or C, until we are finally successful.

Monsters can also contribute to the development and growth of the imagination and encourage us to confront our deepest fears. They frighten us, but they are essential in helping us face the challenges of life. Psychologists agree that a rich imaginative life helps us experiment with ideas and images, and creative mental play allows us to project our fears and anxieties onto the monsters, which are then defeated or killed. We can then take those lessons back to reality and put them into action.[16]

Monsters can also teach us about how to build our own concept of morality, based on how we relate to the monsters in the story—are we the "good guy" or the "bad guy," acting with or without honor? We learn who we are and what we hold valuable based on our responses to challenges, real or imagined. An understanding of what morality is to each of us grows slowly, as we work through the problems with which both life and literature confront us.[17]

There is no doubt that monsters will always be with us—and that is certainly to our benefit, since they help to protect us from those who would attack and hurt us. They allow us to create stories in our minds, practicing how to confront dangerous problems and situations. "As long as there are real enemies in the world, there will be useful dramatic versions of them in our heads."[18] As William Arthur Ward said, "If you can imagine it, you can create it. If you can dream it, you can become it."[19]

But even though the monsters stay with us, they change over the years, to better fit the society they "live in." What frightened us generations ago isn't what frightens us now. Nevertheless, monsters still have the same usefulness: to help us understand our own humanity by showing us what we are not. From their place at the edges of our world, from the boundaries and the borderlands, they give us a standard to measure ourselves by. Here is the human world, they say, and there is the fantastical, fictional, or gothic one that they inhabit, and the impassable boundary between them.[20]

There are four archetypes of monsters: the bloodsucker, the shapeshifter, the ghost, and the thing. Each culture, across the world, changes these archetypes in some ways to fit that culture, but they are always recognizable.[21] Vampires, werewolves and other shapeshifters, ghosts, maniacal machines, and zombies inhabit the pages of contemporary books written for teens. These creatures are frightening, threatening, dangerous, evil. They are also sexy, attractive, alluring, and tempting. They persuade readers to step onto the roller coaster of their stories, taking them to the heights of imagination and to the depths of fear.

Great horror fiction shows us not only the monster, but also ourselves. Writers drag our fears out of the shadows and force us to look at them and see who we are, the parts of ourselves that we conveniently never examine too closely. The authors of horror fiction and the monsters they create don't just scare us—they haunt us, disturb us, and make us think about the story and our part in it, in different ways. We go down the dark corridor of the story, we confront the monsters on their own turf, we see what has been too horrible to contemplate, and then—we leave. The story is over. We have looked the monsters in the eye—and we have survived! And, soon, we are ready to do it all over again.

Confronting a monster is much easier and safer when it takes place in a story. It's unlikely that we'll ever face a vampire, a zombie, or any of the other supernatural monsters we encounter in stories, but our response to them helps shape our thoughts and actions when we are confronted with a monster that is all too real, a person whose human exterior hides the evil and toxic interior, a human monster who can attack and damage our bodies, our thoughts, and our emotions. Asma states, "Good monster stories can transmit moral truths to us by showing us examples of dignity and depravity without preaching or proselytizing."[22] Monster stories can inoculate us against vulnerability and teach us how to be the heroes, kill the monsters, and reestablish the status quo. Because where there are monsters and stories about monsters, there will always be heroes to conquer them, for they must be conquered—their very existence represents a lack of control, an anarchy that can threaten to destroy all of society.

Most of the stories of imaginary monsters follow the same pattern. The monster appears and at first the reports of danger are ignored, until, for no apparent reason, the monster begins to wreak havoc on the unsuspecting world. The people recognize their danger and come together to fight it, led by a hero. The monster is chased away or killed, there is great rejoicing, and normality returns—until the next time a monster appears.[23]

If we are to be real heroes in life, we must find those heroes first inside our own imaginations. Imagining how we will face an unstoppable, powerful, immortal, and inhuman threat can be eye opening, giving us clues about how to face an enemy in real life.[24] Imagining ourselves as strong and powerful, practicing what we will do when confronted by a monster, will allow us to do it in real life. But practice is definitely required. What you imagine will happen when you confront the monster, what you practice, is most frequently what will happen when you do it in reality. It may be easier to give in to fears and imagine that the monster wins—and if that is what we practice, it is a certainty that the real monsters will win as well. It is our choice, and based on the stories we tell ourselves, we defeat the monsters or are defeated by them.

For many of these heroes the practice needed is found in the literature of the monstrous, the books that titillate us, allowing us to get nearer and nearer the danger, while protecting us from it at the same time. It doesn't matter if the monsters are supernatural or human. Both can be confronted, and sometimes even conquered, between the covers of a book or on a movie or TV screen. In a story, no matter how it is told, the monster isn't able to trap us—we are in control and can always slam shut the cover, change the channel, get up and walk away when the monster or the action get too real for comfort. When our courage is restored, we can return to our examination of what and whom we fear.

Books let us get as close to the monster as we want to and still be safe, still be in control. We can take as long as we want, getting close and backing away from the monster, one chapter or one line at a time. We have time to get to know the monster as completely as we need and want to, learning its weaknesses as well as its strengths, discovering the fatal flaws that will allow us to kill, to control, to know and deceive the monster, or to just ignore it and divest it of its power and control over us. To paraphrase G. K. Chesterton, fairy tales do not tell children the dragons exist. Children already know that dragons exist. Fairy tales tell children the dragons can be killed.[25] The stories of monsters don't tell us they exist—we already know that. Stories of the monstrous tell us that the monsters can be conquered.

That is why it is important to make up horror even when the world already has so many horrible things in it. Reading or seeing horror can help lance the boil, open the infected wound that is the monster, release the pressure and let the poison escape, so healing can begin. Even when the monster is so evil that the process has to be done more than once.[26]

Horror is all about disintegration, falling apart, but the vanquishing of the monsters creates the opposite effect—reintegration, coming together—that brings a feeling of rightness and security, if only for a short while. The monster is dead or defeated and life returns to normal—at least for now.[27]

Horror is an allegory—a symbolic story that represents something else. All monster/horror stories say in symbols what we are afraid to say right out. They allow us to let out emotions that usually we are required to control and to let them be uncontrollable. We can by proxy indulge in violent acts, give in to our fears, and exercise power over others that we can't do in reality. Monster stories take the reader/viewer to an alternative world, where all the rules are different. When we turn to that scary book, we aren't expecting things to work out fine. We're waiting for the twist at the end that shows us it's not as happy as you think it is; the monster is only defeated, not dead, and will return another day.[28]

But why are adolescents so fascinated by monsters of all kinds? Perhaps because they live in the same kind of space that vampires, zombies, shapeshifters, and all the other monsters live in—between the categories, at the boundaries, on the threshold,[29] never completely in one world or another, at the borders between the world of the dead and the world of the living.[30] Teens are standing at the boundary between childhood and adulthood, part of them in each world, creating a duality that they share with the monsters, those who are alive, yet dead; those who are animal, yet human; those who can move from the world of fantasy to the world of reality.[31] Meeting these monsters and recognizing their similar situation allows adolescents to identify with them, and perhaps learn how to be comfortable on the borderlines until they are ready to step forward into the adult world.

While many supernatural monster titles are set in the present day in an alternative world, the gothic horror story also holds a fascination for teens. Gothic horror is all about paradox—it scares us to death, makes us jump back, raises our adrenaline level, and gives us a delicious shiver of terror and pleasure. But what makes a story "gothic"? It focuses on the past, the crumbling, decaying past

that overcomes the present, complete with family curses; dark, cob-
webby dungeons; shadowed graveyards; and mysterious deaths. A
sinister older aristocrat pursues and captures a fragile and vulnerable girl, as family members scheme and plot her demise. It is melo-
drama, melancholy, and passion, and even nature is twisted and
poisonous. The setting is a ruined, derelict mansion, surrounded
by dead, looming trees; poisonous plants; and scattered graveyards
with mossy, listing gravestones marking the final resting places of
those who have gone before and haunt those who remain and dare
to ignore them. Evil triumphs, murderers thrive, and innocence is
lost forever. The hero, as well as other characters, is revealed in all
his or her maliciousness and immorality. There are no happy endings here, no vindication, and no escape.[32]

In horror fiction, the boundaries between good and evil are
clearly drawn, and evil is punished before the curtain falls.[33] It reaf-
firms that bad things happen to bad people or bad monsters. But in
gothic horror, evil sometimes gets home free.[34] Gothic novels turn
our ideas of good and evil inside out—the wicked or evil thrive, in-
nocents perish, malevolence rules.[35]

Why does a literary form that revels in rot and ruin appeal to
teen readers? By its nature there is something gothic about coming of age, subversion, and transgression; resistance, both passive
and aggressive; alienation; the awareness of youth and beauty as
transitory states. Teens are young enough to glory in youth and old
enough to grasp the inevitability of its passing, conscious that they
won't always have the pleasures and benefits of youth.[36]

But not all monsters are supernatural, fictional, and able to be
controlled. They can be all too real and difficult or impossible to escape. The rapist, the murderer, the abuser, those who are toxic and
who poison anyone who gets too close to them; bullies who hide
their own fear by making others fear them; everyone who makes
deals with evil, whether it's spiritual, psychological, or moral—anyone, everyone, has the potential to become a monster.[37]

Reading about supernatural monsters can help teens prepare
to face these real monsters in the real world. These titles encourage
teens to make their own decisions; to own their own power; to decide for themselves what is good or bad, right or wrong; to answer
for themselves the question, "What if?" They put information into
the hands of teens, so they can create their own philosophies, live

their own lives, make their own mistakes and pay the price, achieve their own triumphs and reap the reward. These stories give readers the knowledge that they aren't alone in the world, that someone else understands their feelings and experiences. They suggest new solutions to problems that readers may not have seen or considered. They allow readers to experience vicariously what is too dangerous to experience in reality. A character's mistakes can educate the reader about the wisest choice of action in the future. This literature informs, it educates, it creates change. And those who hate and fear change, especially when it involves teens, also hate and fear the literature that encourages that change.

Books about monsters can help teens survive the "culture of fear" that exists in our world today, by showing teens how to understand the monsters in the books, how to challenge them, how to defeat them, and how to disarm them. To the teens who are increasingly alienated from adult culture, forced to learn on their own how to survive, books that reveal these secrets are increasingly valuable and frighteningly necessary. Fortunately, they are also a lot of fun and wonderfully distracting when it's easier to curl up with a fictional monster than a real one.

Notes

1. David D. Gilmore, *Monsters: Evil Beings, Mythical Beasts, and All Manner of Imaginary Terrors* (Philadelphia: University of Pennsylvania Press, 2009).

2. Stephen T. Asma, *On Monsters: An Unnatural History of Our Worst Fears* (New York: Oxford University Press, 2009), 3–5.

3. Gilmore, *Monsters*.

4. Stephen King, *Danse Macabre*, 11th ed. (New York: Simon & Schuster, 2010), 29.

5. Stephen T. Asma, "Monsters and the Moral Imagination," *Chronicle of Higher Education* 56, no. 10 (October 30, 2009): 11.

6. William Patrick Day, *Vampire Legends in Contemporary American Culture: What Becomes a Legend Most* (Lexington: University Press of Kentucky, 2009).

7. Becky Siegel Spratford, *Horror Readers' Advisory: The Librarians' Guide to Vampires, Killer Tomatoes and Haunted Houses* (Chicago: American Library Association, 2004), 11.

8. King, *Danse*, 419.

9. Casandria Crane, e-mail message to author, January 29, 2010.

10. *Gever Tully: 5 Dangerous Things You Should Let Your Kids Do*, video, Ted.com, March 2007, http://www.ted.com/talks/gever_tulley_on_5 _dangerous_things_for_kids.html.

11. Tom Philion, "The Age of ____? Using Young Adult Literature to Make Sense of the Contemporary World," *Young Adult Library Services 7*, no. 4 (Summer 2009): 46–49.

12. Asma, "Monsters Moral," 11.

13. Maurice Sendak, *Where the Wild Things Are*, (New York: Harper & Row, 1963).

14. Asma, "Monsters Moral," 11.

15. Bruce Handy, "Where the Wild Things Weren't," *New York Times*, October 8, 2009.

16. Asma, "Monsters Moral," 11.

17. Asma, "Monsters Moral," 11.

18. Asma, "Monsters Moral," 12.

19. "William Arthur Ward," http://www.williamarthurward.com.

20. Joan Gordon and Veronica Hollinger, *Blood Read: The Vampire as Metaphor in Contemporary Culture* (Philadelphia: University of Pennsylvania Press, 1997), 5.

21. King, *Danse*, 51.

22. Asma, "Monsters Moral," 12.

23. Gilmore, *Monsters*.

24. Asma, "Monsters Moral," 12.

25. "G. K. Chesterton Quotes," Thinkexist.com, http://thinkexist.com/ quotation/fairy-tales-are-more-than-true-not-because-they/347104.html.

26. King, *Danse*, 13.

27. King, *Danse*, 14.

28. King, *Danse*, 32–33.

29. Asma, *On Monsters*, 40.

30. Kimberly Reynolds, introduction to *Frightening Fiction*, ed. Kimberly Reynolds, Geraldine Brennan, and Kevin McCarron (London: Continuum International Publishing Group, 2001), 7.

31. Asma, *On Monsters*, 40.

32. Deborah Noyes, introduction to *Gothic! Ten Original Dark Tales*, ed. Deborah Noyes (Cambridge, MA: Candlewick Press, 2004), x.

33. Noyes, introduction to *Gothic!*, x.

34. King, *Danse*, 421.

35. Noyes, introduction to *Gothic!*, x.

36. Noyes, introduction to *Gothic!*, xi.

37. Asma, *On Monsters*, 8.

Bibliography

Asma, Stephen T. *On Monsters: An Unnatural History of Our Worst Fears.* New York: Oxford University Press, 2009.

———. "Monsters and the Moral Imagination." *Chronicle of Higher Education* 56, no. 10 (October 30, 2009): 11–12.

Day, William Patrick. *Vampire Legends in Contemporary American Culture: What Becomes a Legend Most.* Lexington: University Press of Kentucky, 2009.

Gever Tully: 5 Dangerous Things You Should Let Your Kids Do. Video. Ted .com, March 2007. http://www.ted.com/talks/gever_tulley_on_5_dangerous_things_for_kids.html.

Gilmore, David D. *Monsters: Evil Beings, Mythical Beasts, and All Manner of Imaginary Terrors.* Philadelphia: University of Pennsylvania Press, 2009.

Gordon, Joan, and Veronica Hollinger. *Blood Read: The Vampire as Metaphor in Contemporary Culture.* Philadelphia: University of Pennsylvania Press, 1997.

King, Stephen. *Danse Macabre.* 11th ed. New York: Simon & Schuster, 2010.

Noyes, Deborah, ed. *Gothic! Ten Original Dark Tales.* Cambridge, MA: Candlewick Press, 2004.

Philion, Tom. "The Age of _____? Using Young Adult Literature to Make Sense of the Contemporary World." *Young Adult Library Services* 7, no. 4 (Summer 2009): 46–49.

Reynolds, Kimberly. Introduction to *Frightening Fiction.* Edited by Kimberly Reynolds, Geraldine Brennan, and Kevin McCarron. London: Continuum International Publishing Group, 2001.

Sendak, Maurice. *Where the Wild Things Are.* New York: Harper & Row, 1963.

Spratford, Becky Siegel. *Horror Readers' Advisory: The Librarians' Guide to Vampires, Killer Tomatoes and Haunted Houses.* Chicago: American Library Association, 2004.

1

VAMPIRES: THE ARISTOCRATIC MONSTER

> Whether we read books and watch films about vampires for psychological reasons or simply for entertainment, each of us keeps the vampire myth alive. While we may be able to understand rationally that vampires do not exist, who among us does not start at the shadow at the window, the squeak in the dark?
>
> —Daniel C. Scavone, author of *Vampires* (1990)

Vampires have been a part of every culture throughout history.[1] Each known culture has an evil supernatural being who is immortal and sucks blood from the living in order to prolong its own existence.[2] These stories began in ancient times, and Greece, Rome, Egypt, and Eastern Europe were the locations of the most significant activities and folktales. The earliest vampires in various cultures were said to drink the blood of children because it was more pure and less tainted by the world's influences, and it would give them extra strength and power.[3] These cultures had just begun to realize that blood and life were irrevocably linked together and that taking someone's blood meant that their life might be forfeited as well.[4] As a result, the vampire has always been marked as a deadly and dangerous creature, because in order to live, he has to kill—kill regularly, kill for no other reason than hunger—and his preferred prey has always been humans.

Many cultures claim to have invented the word "vampire," but its origins remain cloudy. It was used in the 1740s in English, French, and German documents to describe vampires in Russia, Serbia, Poland, and Macedonia. Early users could not point to an earlier word that "vampire" came from, and the word "vampire" itself doesn't appear in any other languages until after it was being used in Western Europe.[5] The word closest to "vampire" is the Hungarian word *vampir*, and many scholars believe that is the source of the word.[6]

There is also no way to trace the idea of the vampire itself back to one country or tribe. Stories about vampirelike creatures seem to have arisen more or less at the same time in several different cultures, creatures with varying features and characteristics based on their originating culture.[7] Even then, each culture was creating the vampire it needed to be the repository of its blame and fear. Nina Auerbach, in her *Our Vampires, Ourselves*, notes that from the beginning, vampires have reflected the culture they were created in, and each culture gets the vampires that it wants, needs, and perhaps deserves.[8] Vampires are very adaptable creatures! We can use vampires as a metaphor and a language to talk about the problems we have to deal with in our own world,[9] and when the problems and the language change, so do our vampires.

But in general, there have been only three types of vampires, shown by two major shifts in vampire mythology as seen in their portrayal in folktales, print, and film. These types are the folkloric vampire or revenant; the classic vampire, created by Bram Stoker; and the modern vampire, created by Anne Rice.

Folkloric Vampires or Revenants

The earliest vampires were "revenants," the recently dead who arose from their graves for some reason and appeared to their family or friends.[10] They were shambling, frightening, decaying, zombielike creatures that came back to right the wrong done to them, or to torment and give warnings to those they left behind. They also had the ability to take life from the living by draining them of their blood.[11] When dawn broke, these vampires went back to their graves, only to return over and over, until they were destroyed. They were said to be particularly prevalent in Eastern Europe, especially in Romania, where they were greatly feared; as a result, a wide variety of methods to control or kill them come from that region. These methods included carrying or wearing crosses and other religious relics, holy water, garlic and other apotropaic herbs—all thought to ward off or prevent evil; driving a stake through the heart, sometimes into the bottom of the coffin to pin down the vampire; removing and burning the heart; decapitating the vampire; burying the vampire's body at a crossroads so he wouldn't know which road led home; filling the coffin with seeds or grain to compel the vampire to stop and count them;[12] and putting large rocks on the top of the body, coffin, or grave to prevent the vampire from rising.[13] Some of these methods took place before death, to protect the living; some when the body was buried, to ensure it didn't rise; and some when the body was dug up, its undecayed condition indicating that it might be a vampire. Vampires were soon being blamed for everything from migraines and nightmares to stillborn children, bad weather, early deaths, and disease.[14]

There were also a variety of reasons why an individual became a vampire after death. People who were evil, who spent their lives tormenting or murdering others, were sure to come back as vampires. Suicide was also a way to become a vampire, since killing the body also destroyed the soul, separating it from God for eternity. Being bitten by a vampire was thought to make the victim a vampire, although this belief varied by culture; sometimes one bite was enough, other times it took several bites,[15] and sometimes the individual had to be completely drained of blood—more than a gallon for an average-sized person, and a lot for a vampire to drink![16] Someone might become a vampire because something happened to him or her that wasn't the person's fault at all. A child born out of wedlock, someone whose burial didn't follow all the rites and rituals correctly, or a person who was murdered could all rise from the grave and become vampires.[17]

In the 1800s, some villages in Europe and in early America fell into a kind of "vampire hysteria," blaming everything that went wrong on the undead creatures supposedly walking their streets. This problem was heightened by the spread of "consumption," now known as tuberculosis, which was the plague of that time. It was extremely contagious and could wipe out entire families.[18] The victims coughed up blood, became very pale and listless, and died of what seemed to be no reason.[19] People saw these symptoms as irrefutable proof that the sick person was gradually being drained of his or her blood by a vampire.

In addition, when a grave was opened to find out if the sick person buried there was really was a vampire, the appearance of the undecayed corpse confirmed it. The mouth had blood around it; its teeth, fingernails, and hair appeared to have grown after death; its body was bloated and swollen, even though the individual had been thin and wasted when death occurred; and when the heart was pierced by a stake, a gush of blood was released. Today, there are medical explanations for these symptoms: decay doesn't start as soon as an individual is dead or buried; it can be delayed for weeks or months by cold or other factors, including soil type, condition of the body at death, or humidity, giving the appearance that the body will not decay, because the individual has become a vampire. Intestinal decomposition can force blood up into and out of the mouth and nose, and can also create bloating, making the body look larger than it did when it was buried.[20] When a body is staked, intestinal gases are released, creating a horrible stench, said to be characteristic of destroying a vampire. Hair and fingernails look longer, as if they had kept on growing after death, but this is normal, as the flesh of the body retracts after death.[21] Teeth may appear to be longer because the gums have also receded.[22] The skin also changes color, becoming greenish and then purple-white, the skin color of vampires.[23] While all these things are normal and easily scientifically proved today, centuries ago, when little was known about illness or how our bodies work, it was far easier to blame symptoms on supernatural causes.

The Classic Aristocrat

Bram Stoker's *Dracula* is the best known vampire story, but it was not the first; six English novels about vampires were published before *Dracula*. The influence of Stoker's story is seen in the thousands of stories, novels, and movies that have been published in the years since it was written in 1897.[24] Three of the pre-*Dracula* novels contributed characteristics to the classic vampire template that Stoker used when creating his story.

Polidori's Vampire

The origin of the first Western vampire story is well known but also somewhat controversial. *The Vampyre* was written by Dr. John Polidori, based on a story fragment that George, Lord Byron wrote in the summer of 1816, at Villa Diodati, near Lake Geneva, where he and Polidori were staying. This was "the year without a summer," cold, damp, and gloomy. In Europe and America, there were snows and frosts in July and August, and crops died. While there are explanations for all of the weather problems, at the time it just seemed like the weather had gone crazy.[25] When Percy Bysshe Shelley; his wife, Mary Wollstonecraft Shelley; and her stepsister, Claire Clairmont, came to visit Byron and Polidori, it was too cold and wet and miserable to do anything outside, so Byron proposed that they tell ghost stories and then write their own, to see who could write the best one. During the following days, Mary Shelley wrote *Frankenstein; or, The Modern Prometheus*, Byron wrote a fragment of a novel about a vampire, and Polidori based a novel on that fragment, called *The Vampyre*.[26] There is also controversy about exactly when Polidori wrote the book, with several experts disagreeing on the time frame and whether it was written during the summer at Lake Geneva or later, after he and Byron had become estranged.[27]

Byron forgot about the fragment until he saw it expanded and published in the *New Monthly Magazine* in 1819, under his own name.[28] Polidori had replaced Byron's protagonist with a unmistakable and derogatory portrait of Byron as an attractive and evil vampire.[29] The mistake about crediting Byron with something he didn't write and the characterization of Byron as Count Dracula opened a rift between them, and although Polidori and Byron had been close prior to this, their conflict over which of them was more responsible for *The Vampyre* ended this friendship.[30]

However, there is no controversy or question about what Polidori did in writing *The Vampyre*. He created the prototype Western/classic vampire—"the Ruthven formula"—named after the suave, wealthy nobleman who is turned into a vampire after he is killed and left out all night when the moon was full.[31] Ruthven lived a normal life, but during the full moon, he turned into a blood-drinking vampire, attacking anyone he could, especially young ladies. He was cold, calculating, and intelligent, frequently killing those that he wanted or needed out of his own way. He was both immortal and immoral.[32]

Polidori's contributions to the classic vampire template included the following:

- Vampires are the dead who have reanimated themselves.
- Vampires live in the present and walk undetected among the living, passing as humans.
- Vampires are wealthy aristocrats who travel frequently, one of the necessities of immortality.
- Vampires are dark and moody, mysterious and seductive; humans are their food, and they have no compunction about killing them.
- Vampires are sexual creatures, and their bite is erotic and overwhelming. The sensual element is equally or more important than the feeding element.
- Vampires are able to hypnotize humans, and so they can be psychic vampires as well as blood vampires.
- Vampires are supernatural and have a strong connection with the moon.[33]

Varney—Rymer's Vampire

Varney the Vampire by James Malcolm Rymer was published in the 1840s as a newspaper serial novel that ran for two years. It was almost nine hundred pages and appeared in 220 installments. In 1847 it was republished as a book.[34] In *Varney*, Rymer took the Ruthven formula and tweaked it in several ways,[35] the same thing that Stoker did when starting to write *Dracula*. Varney was described much like a folkloric vampire, tall, gaunt, almost skeletal, with long fangs and fingernails and lustrous, compelling dark eyes. He lusted not only for blood but also for money, preying on the wealthy, using vampirism to satisfy both his hungers.[36] But when necessary, he was able to appear in polite society as Sir Francis Varney, his vampiric elements, especially his eyes, downplayed and humanized.[37]

This is also the first literary attempt to create sympathy and empathy for the vampire, something that would not be repeated for over 150 years, when Anne Rice began writing her *Vampire Chronicles*.[38] In the novel's ending, Varney had come to see himself more clearly, hated his condition, his needs, and his lack of humanity, which eventually drove him to commit suicide by jumping into the crater of Mount Vesuvius, ending his story.[39]

Carmilla, the Female Vampire

Carmilla, the story of the first female vampire, was published in 1871 by Sheridan Le Fanu. Carmilla was also the first vampire who had to sleep in her coffin, on her native soil; the first killed by a stake in her heart; and the first who rose from the dead rather than being a corpse possessed by evil spirits. Her bite didn't kill or turn her victims to vampires. It took time and several bleedings to change a human to a vampire. And, in a genre that focuses so much on the sexual and the sensual, it is interesting to note that Carmilla was also the first lesbian vampire.[40]

Stoker's Count Dracula

Stoker's genius in writing his most famous novel was in blending the old and the new characteristics of vampires. He included many of the elements from folklore and from the Ruthven model, but set those elements in his present day and combined them with that time's cutting-edge science—including shorthand, the phonograph, and blood transfusions, taking the vampire story into the twentieth century.[41] However, in spite of hundreds of years of rumors, there is little to suggest that there is a connection between the book and the historical figure of Vlad Tepes Dracula, beyond the name and a few elements that Stoker incorporated into the book, such as a fear of garlic and religious objects.[42] In fact, Stoker had almost finished the novel before the main character went from "Count Vampyre" to "Dracula." Stoker had never been to Transylvania and knew little about the country, the people, and their beliefs,[43] basing his descriptions and geography on books and maps.[44] He also interviewed Armeniur Vanbury, a professor from Budapest University, and they discussed at length Vanbury's theories on vampires, Vlad Tepes, and the history of Romania and Transylvania. It's not known how much Vanbury's stories influenced Stoker when he began to create the character of Dracula and the castle where he lived. The only link between fiction and reality is Stoker's description of Castle Bran, a castle built in 1382 to defend the Bran Pass in the Carpathian Mountains, which became Stoker's Castle Dracula. The similarities are too accurate to be just a coincidence.[45] However, there are no direct links between Vlad Tepes and Stoker's novel.[46] In fact, Stoker wrote much of the novel while he was in Whitby, England, and got his information on Tepes and Wallachia, Transylvania and the Borgo Pass from a book he found in the library there, William Wilkerson's *An Account of the Principalities of Wallachia and Moldavia*.[47] Stoker took from it and from Vanbury's stories his descriptions of the eerie countryside; surreal and dense forests; bogs that trap the unwary traveler; tall, majestic mountains that seem to reach the sky on sunny days and wrap themselves in thick mist when the days are less propitious. There is no doubt that it was a perfect setting for the reclusive count.[48] In addition, Stoker consulted about thirty other resources about the geography and history of Romania and the folklore about vampires of that area.[49] However, Stoker did little research on the real Dracula, Vlad Tepes, using only one six-page German essay, published in 1488, including semiaccurate biographical information and a list of some of the atrocities he committed.[50] Stoker used Dracula just because he liked the name—there was never anyone named Count Dracula.[51] And Stoker got his inspiration for Dracula's physical characteristics and some of his forbidding temperament from his good friend, Henry Irving.[52]

The historical Dracula—Vlad III Dracula—for whom Stoker's count was named, was the ruler of a small region of Transylvania called Wallachia. He called himself "Dracula" because his father had been called "Dracul," which could be translated "Devil" or "Dragon." With the final *a*, his father's name meant "Son of the Devil/Dragon," and Dracula was the name Vlad III preferred.[53] While there is no evidence that he ever drank blood or ate men's flesh, he was just as cruel and bloodthirsty and evil as the fictional Dracula. He was generally known as Vlad Tepes, or Vlad the Impaler, because he liked to impale his enemies on long stakes or spears and then watch them as they slipped farther and farther down the stake as they died. Vlad tortured and murdered thousands of his enemies and fellow countrymen alike,[54] but he wasn't a vampire. There is no evidence that Stoker knew anything about him other than his name and the general area where he lived, which he learned about from Wilkerson's book.[55] There is no Castle Dracula, although there have been several proposals for a Dracula Theme Park; none have been built, yet the rumors still abound.[56]

Dracula was published in 1897 to mixed reviews, and there is no indication that Stoker ever felt that he had done anything remarkable in writing it. Stoker died in 1912 and never knew that he had created one of the most widely read books of all time, nor that it would never be out of print from its first publication in 1897.[57] His wife, Florence, retained the copyright to all his books, and *Dracula* has been continually in print for over 114 years.

Dracula is perhaps the only book in which all aspects (historical, folkloric, and literary) of the "traditional" or "classic" vampire story are included,[58] which is one reason why it is the vampire story we remember even though stories of vampires had been around for six thousand years when *Dracula* was written. Why has this version of the story been so long lasting?

If it had not been adapted for stage and screen, two mass-market mediums that spread the image and story of Dracula much more quickly and widely than it could have been spread by print alone, there is little doubt that the story would have become as obscure as Stoker himself and the rest of his writings.[59] The visual images solidified the image and the character of the vampire, and cemented the wealthy, suave, sexy, and sophisticated count as the template of the Western vampire. Had it not been for Stoker's novel and Bela Lugosi's performance, the vampire as we know him today would never have existed.[60]

The first mass-market version of the book came after Stoker's death. The first movie based on the book, *Nosferatu*, was made in Germany in 1922, with Max Schreck as the vampire, Count Orlock. Names and settings had been changed, but the movie was obviously based on Stoker's novel, and the film company did not have permission for doing so. Florence Stoker sued immediately and won, ensuring that all copies of the film would be destroyed. But at least one copy existed and was reproduced widely—it has become a cult classic.[61]

Nosferatu went back to the image of the folkloric vampire, including the horrible appearance of the vampire—huge size, clawed hands, pointed teeth, terrifying ratlike features—and appears to be one of the last examples of the vampire as he had traditionally been depicted, before the Ruthven formula standardized the vampire's characteristics in *The Vampyre*.[62] Aside from being an excellent and truly creepy and frightening silent movie, it is also known as the first example of a vampire being destroyed by the sunlight of the dawn.[63]

In 1924, an extremely popular theater version of the novel was produced, and its popularity persuaded Universal Pictures to take the story to the big screen in 1931. Bela Lugosi had been the star of the stage production, and when Lon Chaney (who had been the director's first choice) died of throat cancer in 1930, Lugosi was cast as the count in the movie.[64] After that, he was typecast as a horror actor and the world's best known vampire,[65] something that he sometimes bitterly regretted.

Lugosi's portrayal of the count is the image that most people see when asked about Dracula, including the thick, rolling East European accent and extravagant wardrobe. When the film was made, Lugosi didn't speak English, and he had to learn his lines phonetically, based only on how they sounded, not what they meant, making his well-delivered and nuanced lines a major tribute to his acting ability, and even more amazing than if he'd memorized them. His portrayal of the vampire was so threatening and frightening, combining sophistication and menace, that during the premiere, several women fainted, overcome by fear.[66] But even though that film version has become the standard by which vampires are defined, it's important to remember that it followed the Ruthven formula created in the literature several years previously by Polidori.[67] The impact of this film is made even more dramatic when you look at it in context: almost 700 vampire films have been made, and Count Dracula has been in more than 130 of them, more than any other fictional character, except Sherlock Holmes.[68]

Only one characteristic has remained consistent over the years, in all the portrayals of vampires, regardless of the format they appear in: the two sides of the same coin—fear and desire; all humans in all times fear vampires and desire immortality. But they fear death far more than vampires and yearn for immortal life, making vampires as attractive as they are frightening.[69] This emotion is as strong today as it was thousands of years ago, when stories of vampires were first created, and as a result, vampires continue to be popular, both in print and in film. But it is also important to remember that the vampire adapts to his setting, and tomorrow's vampires may not resemble today's any more than today's are like those of the past.[70] Every society creates the vampires it wants or sometimes deserves.[71]

Today, with the popularity of vampires and other monsters, we can also see differences in the way they are portrayed in titles for children, for teens, and for adults. While titles for adults and teens have featured vampires that are more scary and dangerous, and sometimes erotic and sexy, titles for children include more friendly vamps, like the one in the easy reader called *Dick and Jane and Vampires*—a classic fanged, caped vampire with whom the children make friends.[72] And the *Bunnicula* series by James and Deborah Howe, about a vampire rabbit, has been popular ever since the first book came out in 1979.[73]

As mentioned earlier, in the history of the literary vampire, there have been two massive shifts that have changed the portrayal of the vampire, both in print and on the screen, in significant and dramatic ways. The first we have already discussed—the change from the zombielike revenant to the sophisticated and elegant count. Dracula has some of the characteristics of the revenant—he is undead and he drinks his victims' blood—but he rises from the dead as a complete humanlike form, without the rotting body and shuffling gait of the revenant. He has not risen from his grave for a specific reason, and he doesn't return to it when that act is finished. And a new set of characteristics has been added to the vampire template: pale skin, fangs, black cape, fear of garlic, inability to cross running water or a line of salt, can be burned or hurt by holy water or religious relics, no reflection in mirrors, needs to be invited to come into home, evil, frightening, mesmerizing/hypnotic, manipulative, biting victim's neck to feed, sleeping on native soil in a coffin, "dead" or "asleep" during the day, "awake" or "alive" during the night, supernatural power, ability to shift into a bat, wolf, or mist. This vamp was very dangerous, and stories about him weren't told from his point of view, but from the hunter's or the victim's. The setting was dark and creepy, very gothic, unfamiliar, and a long way away from the reader's real world, emphasizing the differences between vampire and human.[74] But 150 years after Stoker's novel was published, there was another major shift in the template of the vampire.

The Modern Aristocratic Vampire

The 1970s saw the second major shift in vampire literature with the publication of Anne Rice's *Vampire Chronicles*. She allowed the vampire to step into the spotlight as the protagonist and let the reader see how tortured and lonely his life truly was.[75] No longer were vampires required to emulate the cold and evil Count Dracula, sophisticated, wealthy, controlled, able to hypnotize anyone by staring into their eyes or change his shape into a bat or a wolf or a scrap of mist. When *Dracula* was written, and later when Bela Lugosi created the iconic film character, there was only one representation of the vampire, the Stoker-Lugosi one, based on the Ruthven formula, with several significant tweaks. Today, there is a proliferation of different vampire images, as authors and directors try to make their vampires unique. This proliferation has created a "new vampire" that stands in stark contrast to old one.[76]

But it is essential to remain aware of Rice's importance in this second major shift in vampire literature. She was the first to humanize the vampire without taking away our fear of and fascination with him. This new vamp walks a narrow line between monster and human—he must balance the new qualities or characteristics he has been given with the older ones he has had for centuries and that have made him continually fascinating and popular.

The new vampires are less powerful and more human, easier for humans to identify with. They tend to be more social and less isolated than the original Dracula. They live in groups and support each other. While they are still killers (at least some of the time), they can be tortured by their need to kill, and some try to get along on animal or synthetic blood.[77] Others drink human blood but limit the amount of blood they take from each victim, instead of drinking each one dry.

In addition, the new vampire is no longer the expression of pure evil opposing the pure goodness of God—the vampire is responsible for his or her own acts.[78] This disconnection from the battle between Good and Evil has allowed today's vampire to be seen as either good or evil, or a combination of both.

Many of the characteristics of the old vampire have fallen by the wayside. The new vampire may no longer be able to shapeshift, but may be impervious to garlic, sunlight, and religious items or symbols and may be reflected in mirrors. Their appearance is no longer in sharp contrast to a human's, and they tend to look more like your next door neighbor than a pale-skinned foreign count who shuns the sunlight. Their need to drink blood has been ascribed to a variety of causes, primary among them some kind of viral infection similar to AIDS[79] or the presence of tiny nanobots that live in the bloodstream and repair any damage to the vampire's body. In the latter case, it is the nanobots that need blood to feed on. But while modern vampires still need blood to survive, some of them also eat the same things humans do—increasing their resemblance to humans.

The new vampire has been secularized, socialized, and humanized. While Dracula felt only dark emotions—hunger, hate, bitterness—today's vampires relate to other vampires and to humans in a variety of ways, and can experience love, guilt, friendship, jealousy, regret, doubt, as well as the ability to question themselves and their motivations.[80] They are still attractive, intelligent, sophisticated, and many are wealthy, as a result of years of saving and/or investing.

Zanger compares today's vampires to the Mafia as it is portrayed in Puzo's book and in the three *Godfather* movies. We see the Mafiosi with their families and their friends, at home and at church, playing with their children, and we understand their joy, their pain, their love. But they are still killers, ruthless, nonemotional, bloody. It's their business, one they cannot escape or turn away from.[81] They are civilized killers, but only when it's essential and mostly when it's offstage. Is this not how many vampires are seen today? This is yet another example of their duality—the killer and the protector, the "family man," willing to do whatever is necessary to protect those he loves.

These vampires are not so much scary as noble, fighting against their inherent natures for the sake of love. "America has taken the vampire story and tied it to teen romance," says Ken Gelder, author of *Reading the Vampire*.[82] Rather than being attracted to the darkness of the vampire, the female leads love their fanged paramours for their essentially decent personalities—along with their bad-boy allure—and are able to get beyond the whole lust-for-blood thing. It is not the vampire's passion that is sexy, but his self-control. He is exactly the vampire we want right now: he's strong, he's handsome, he can fly, and his skin sparkles in sunlight, but more important, he knows exactly how the world works, so he's not going to go and do anything stupid.[83] But not all vamps are honorable—the hero has to have someone to fight and guard his girl from. In general, vampires are just as unpredictable as humans—part good, part evil, and no way to know for sure which part is in control at any one time.

There are specific psychological reasons why characteristics of the vampire make him a fascinating and appealing figure to adolescents. Based on research, adolescents identify four of the most appealing characteristics of the vampire as self-identity, power, sexuality, and marginality.[84]

According to Erikson, adolescents are going through the stage of life relating to self-identity development and definition.[85] This is the middle stage of the eight stages of life, and it's the most important one because during it, the adolescent can begin to resolve the problems encountered in the first three stages, and if this stage is not successfully completed, the rest of life will be affected. Many, many adults in therapy are (according to Erikson) still trying to resolve the problems they encountered during adolescence and were unable to find solutions for.[86]

Adolescents try on different roles to see how well or poorly they fit, discarding the ones that don't fit. They play different roles with different people and situations, which is why most parents have no idea how their child acts when out of their sight and influence. Parents recognize the person they see at home but not the completely different person their child becomes with their friends, when they are a part of the adolescent culture. Teens question who they are and what their life, their existence means, and they are struggling to create their own philosophy, their own belief system.[87]

The vampire stands in stark contrast to this. He knows who he is and why he exists. He is solidly set in his own timeline, able to remember his life, which may have lasted for thousands of years, and his actions, which have kept himself and his loved ones (if he isn't a solitary vampire) safe. He knows his place in his world and is comfortable and confident in it. He has a set of ethics, which he uses to define and defend his behavior. His certainty about his identity and purpose cannot help but be attractive to adolescents who are so uncertain about theirs. The vampire is also a figure of marginality, who exists at the borders of our lives, where reality meets the supernatural, at the boundary between safety and danger, and he is completely comfortable there, whether he is alone or not. He is at home in his own skin, living within human culture while still remaining separate from it, accepting and expressing both the acceptable and taboo elements of his life and himself. To adolescents who are also marginalized figures, outsiders struggling to become insiders or to become comfortable with their outsider status, the vampire's self-acceptance is something to aspire to. He is proof positive that their questions can be answered, the problems and mysteries they face can be resolved, letting them leave adolescence behind and enter the adult world. Identifying with the vampire also lets them explore the darker side of their personalities, to examine and perhaps take on some of the roles expressed by that less-acceptable, perhaps even taboo side.

Piaget also sees adolescence as a critical time in an individual's life. Formal operational skills are beginning to develop, and the individual is starting to think more abstractly and metaphorically, to evaluate evidence and make informed decisions, and to predict outcomes based on those decisions. But not everything fits into a predictable pattern. Formal operational thinking doesn't arrive all at once, and some of the adolescent's actions and decisions are based on earlier ways of thinking and processing information. Recent research suggests that formal operational thinking does not become consistent until sometime in the twenties.[88] The adolescent is caught between childhood and adulthood, demanding to be seen and treated as an adult, and yet unwilling to fully embrace adult responsibilities and act like a functional adult. Ready for adulthood, yet looking longingly at the security and innocence of childhood. Parents and other trusted adults, who used to be able to guide the adolescent into adulthood, are more absent than ever before, busy with their own lives, leaving them no time for the deep one-on-one conversations adolescents need and want to have.[89]

The vampire is on the other side of this quandary, having defined himself and his identity, retained his own power to control his life and his world, and used his sexual nature to draw others to him and to reproduce himself with sensuality rather than sexuality. All these characteristics make him overwhelmingly appealing to the adolescent, who is both intrigued by and fearful of sex, wanting the experience, yet fearful of failure due to inexperience and ignorance. There is no shortage of passion, of sexual tension, yet the experience ends short of sexual completion with the vampire's bite. It is more like the petting, necking, and "hickeys" that teens are familiar with prior to their first sexual encounter and continue to participate in afterward. And the vampire's emotions, like the adolescent's, are intense and powerful, but he isn't frightened by them, as the adolescent is. He uses them to draw humans to him and to enhance his incredible beauty—just as the adolescent would like to do.

Stoker changed the vampire from a frightening zombielike creature in the folktales of Eastern Europe, to the debonair count with his fortune, his castle, and his brides. No longer to be feared, Dracula was a powerful, sensuous, attractive man, who drew women to him with ease. His bite left them swooning in sexual ecstasy. He was the vampire that all subsequent vampires have been based on, but as times and societies have changed, so have vampires, because they reflect the cultures and societies that create them.[90] And Rice changed them yet again, as we and our vamps moved into a new century. Auerbach notes in her seminal work *Our Vampires, Ourselves*, that each generation gets the vampire it creates—or perhaps deserves.[91] Vampires are changing more rapidly today, as technology gives us a vamp for every taste: from cereal boxes to soap operas, from romantic fiction to terrifying film, and from computer games to Facebook and Twitter—vamps are everywhere.[92]

And then there's the romance, the allure, of the modern vampire, the ultimate "bad boy" that every girl is attracted to. Megan Tingley, an editor at Little, Brown, says that "teenagers are [drawn] to the forbidden . . . the dark side. That's always happened—they like the bad boy, the mysterious guy. That's something that's existed for a long time and will continue to exist."[93] Every teen girl wants a hero, a Prince Charming whose attraction to her overwhelms everything else in his life as soon as he sees her for the first time. He loves her beyond measure, is devoted and committed only to her, and wants to cherish and protect her for as long as they live. He's also brooding, aloof, and just a little bit dangerous, sexy, forbidden, and appealing because he seems to have everything, wealth and beauty and power, but at the same time, he's tortured by his need for human blood, and preferably the blood of the human female who draws him to her with a love, a passion, and an innocence meant for him alone. The dichotomy between these two sides of the vampire is what's fascinating—he appears to be perfect in every way but is actually flawed and required to commit monstrous acts in order to survive.[94] Tortured by their need for human blood, these twenty-first-century vampires, who are no longer evil or terrifying, fall in love with humans and refuse to feed on them, trying to survive on animal or synthetic blood rather than human blood—domesticated vampire vegetarians.[95]

But no matter how domesticated these vampires may become, they always retain that bad-boy edge of excitement, adventure, and danger. Life with them will always be more titillating, deliciously frightening, surprising, and never boring, touched with the sexiness of the forbidden. Vampires today are mirrored sunglasses, black leather, and motorcycles, courting danger, yet never giving in to it. But they are also tender, gentle, protective—they take their beloved to the edge of danger, yet never let her feel more than that seductive edge, protecting her from any real threat of harm. A hero and a bad boy, all wrapped up in one person; he opens doors for her and brings her flowers, and then dares her to step out of her everyday world and into the darker and more dangerous one he inhabits and trust him to take care of her in that world, just as he does in this one—what more could a teenage girl ever want?

But there are also other reasons why today's vampires are so pervasive. The 9/11 bombings—when the terrorists came onto our territory, our home soil—changed the way Americans see the world. Terrorism, we learned, doesn't happen only overseas, but also here at home. Terrorists are people who operate outside our own definitions of good and evil, who hate our way of life and what our country stands for. But they are also people who look like us, their monstrosity hidden behind their normal appearance—just like the vampires created for this new generation of this new century, some of whom can even walk in the sunlight and live average, normal lives—at least average or normal for immortal, intensely powerful, and sexually seductive beings who must drink blood to survive. People who look like us, who are natural predators and struggle with the ethical issues that result from that behavior—perhaps we are more like today's vampires than we've realized. Whitley Strieber seems to agree with this, although he says we have a different and perhaps even more dangerous prey—"Our prey is our planet." Today's fear is not the cold war or AIDS; it's the fate of Earth: "We sense that there is something wrong with the environment, that the planet itself may not be able to sustain us very long, and so we are beginning to romance death once again."[96] And we only have to turn on the nightly news to hear confirmation of that, as the aftereffects of the BP oil spill continue to contaminate our southern coastlands. Perhaps reaching out to monsters we can control on a screen or between the covers of a book will help us cope with, and perhaps understand, the monsters we must confront in real life.[97]

Vampires have come late to YA literature—Annette Curtis Klause's *The Silver Kiss*, the first YA vampire novel, wasn't published until 1990, followed in 1991 by the first volume of L. J. Smith's The Vampire Diaries series.[98] Janice Harrell's Vampire Twins series began in 1994, Vivian Vande Velde's *Companions of the Night* came out in 1995, and M. T. Anderson's *Thirsty* was published two years later.[99] This is especially surprising when you consider that the adult vampire titles by Anne Rice, starting with *Interview with a Vampire*, were extremely popular with teens when they came out in the 1970s and '80s, although they were written for the adult audience.[100] But the last five years have more than made up for that earlier lack—the Twilight effect. The teen market for books continues to grow, the only part of the publishing industry that has not been flattened by the recession, spearheaded by the demand for more and more supernatural titles, with vampires the most popular of the monster heroes. It seems as if there's a new title or series out every day. But what's behind the craze? Why are adolescents suddenly fascinated by all things vampire?

Part of it is the sudden popularity of all kinds of monsters, although vampires have always been the leading edge of paranormal fiction; part of it is the unique attraction that the vampire has for the adolescent. Vampires are classy, suave, sexy, attractive, romantic, and rich,[101] and of all the monsters, they are the most human. They even feel regret or shame for their need for blood and try to control their urges, as Stephenie Meyer's vampires did in the Twilight series. They are powerful, strong, handsome, and immortal. They can bring death or eternal life. The vampire is sure of himself, recognizes his past, and looks to the future with confidence[102]—something every teen would like to do.

Adolescents are unsure of themselves, confused by the number of choices they have, the questions they must answer about their identity and their place in the world.[103] It's a time of new, intense, and unexpected feelings, as sexual maturation begins, with increased hormonal activity and a roller coaster of inexplicable emotions. Teens frequently feel out of place or alone in a world where no one really knows what they are going through, as if they themselves have become monsters. Stories about creatures that are also out of place and marginalized yet overcome their problems, even eliminate them completely, can help teens believe that they can do the same thing.[104]

Teens can also act as if they believe they are immortal or indestructible, and that's another gift the vampire can give—eternal life. Who wouldn't want to be forever young and beautiful? In today's fast-paced society, when there's a new fad or flavor every month, the allure of the eternal is truly seductive,[105] even if it is fictional.

The number of YA vampire titles went from one in 1990 to six in 1991, and the numbers have increased steadily since 2001, with a huge increase in 2006, going from nine in 2005 to fifteen in 2006; these books increased by about ten titles per year in 2007, 2009, and 2010. Series are far more popular than stand-alone titles, as teens want to revisit characters and worlds they have enjoyed discovering. Several YA authors have written more than one series, and several writers of adult vampire romance series have begun series for teens.

Notes

1. Matthew Beresford, *From Demons to Dracula: The Creation of the Modern Vampire Myth* (London: Reaktion Blooks, 2008), 7.
2. Beresford, *Demons*, 19.
3. Beresford, *Demons*, 20.
4. Beresford, *Demons*, 22.
5. Eric Nuzum, *The Dead Travel Fast: Stalking Vampires from Nosferatu to Count Chocula* (New York: St. Martin's Press, 2008), 38–39.
6. Beresford, *Demons*, 8.
7. Beresford, *Demons*, 42.
8. Nina Auerbach, *Our Vampires, Ourselves* (Chicago: University of Chicago Press, 1995), 5–6.
9. William Patrick Day, *Vampire Legends in Contemporary American Culture: What Becomes a Legend Most* (Lexington: University Press of Kentucky, 2002), viii.
10. Beresford, *Demons*, 22.

11. Rosemary Ellen Guiley, *The Encyclopedia of Vampires, Werewolves and Other Monsters* (New York: Checkmark Books, 2004), 287.

12. Guiley, *Encyclopedia*, 265–266, 290.

13. Beresford, *Demons*, 6, 20, 37, 66; James B. Twitchell, *The Living Dead: A Study of the Vampire in Romantic Literature* (Durham, NC: Duke University Press, 1981), 11–12.

14. Nuzum, *Dead*, 12.

15. Nuzum, *Dead*, 129–130.

16. Nuzum, *Dead*, 23.

17. Beresford, *Demons*, 31–32.

18. Troy Taylor, "From *Beyond the Grave*: The Horror of the Grave & the Dark Side of Death," PrairieGhosts, 2001, http://www.prairieghosts.com/grave_horror.html.

19. Benjamin Radford, "The Real Science and History of Vampires," *Live Science*, November 30, 2009.

20. Nuzum, *Dead*, 20.

21. Beresford, *Demons*, 28–29.

22. Jennie Yabroff, "A Bit Long in the Tooth," *Newsweek* 152, no. 24 (December 15, 2008): 74.

23. Beresford, *Demons*, 28–29.

24. Nuzum, *Dead*, 129.

25. *Wikipedia*, s.v. "Year without a Summer," accessed June 16, 2011, http://en.wikipedia.org/wiki/ Year_Without_a_Summer.

26. *Wikipedia*, s.v. "The Vampyre," accessed June 16, 2011, http://en.wikipedia.org/wiki/The_Vampyre.

27. Mary Y. Hallab, *Vampire God: Allure of the Undead in Western Culture*, (Albany: State University of New York Press, 2009); Nuzum, *Dead*, 127; Beresford, *Demons*, 117–118; Day, *Vampire Legends*, 14.

28. Nuzum, *Dead*, 127–128; Hallab, *Vampire God*, 75.

29. Hallab, *Vampire God*, 75.

30. Beresford, *Demons*, 118.

31. Beresford, *Demons*, 119.

32. Nuzum, *Dead*, 128.

33. Guiley, *Encyclopedia*, 301.

34. Guiley, *Encyclopedia*, 305.

35. Beresford, *Demons*, 121.

36. Guiley, *Encyclopedia*, 305.

37. Beresford, *Demons*, 29.

38. Beresford, *Demons*, 123.

39. Beresford, *Demons*, 124.

40. Nuzum, *Dead*, 129–130.

41. Beresford, *Demons*, 135.

42. Beresford, *Demons*, 139.

43. Nuzum, *Dead*, 62.

44. Beresford, *Demons*, 71.

45. Guiley, *Encyclopedia*, 54–55.

46. Beresford, *Demons*, 133.

47. *Wikipedia*, s.v. "Vlad III the Impaler," accessed June 16, 2011, http://en.wikipedia.org/wiki/Vlad_III_the_Impaler.

48. Barb Karg, Arjean Spaite, and Rick Sutherland, *The Everything Vampire Book: From Vlad the Impaler to the Vampire Lestat—A History of Vampires in Literature, Film, and Legend* (Avon, MA: Adams Media, 2009), 72.

49. Guiley, *Encyclopedia*, 104.

50. Nuzum, *Dead*, 118; Peter Day, introduction to *Vampires: Myths and Metaphors of Enduring Evil*, ed. Peter Day (New York: Rodopi, 2006), ix.

51. Nuzum, *Dead*, 62–62, 78.

52. Karg, Spaite, and Sutherland, *Everything*, 37.

53. Guiley, *Encyclopedia*, 307–308.

54. Beresford, *Demons*, 77.

55. Guiley, *Encyclopedia*, 308.

56. Carlyluvsunited, "Dracula Theme Park," *A Look at Romania and Romanians* (blog), May 14, 2009, http://alookatromaniaandromanians.blogspot.com/2009/05/dracula-theme-park.html.

57. Karg, Spaite, and Sutherland, *Everything*, 47–48.

58. Beresford, *Demons*, 138.

59. Guiley, *Encyclopedia*, 107.

60. Beresford, *Demons*, 139.

61. *Wikipedia*, s.v. "Nosferatu," accessed June 16, 2011, http://en.wikipedia.org/wiki/Nosferatu.

62. Beresford, *Demons*, 142.

63. Guiley, *Encyclopedia*, 217.

64. Beresford, *Demons*, 144.

65. Guiley, *Encyclopedia*, 188.

66. Beresford, *Demons*, 144.

67. Beresford, *Demons*, 145.

68. Guiley, *Encyclopedia*, 15, 108.

69. Beresford, *Demons*, 195.

70. Joan Gordon and Veronica Hollinger, *Blood Read: The Vampire as Metaphor in Contemporary Culture* (Philadelphia: University of Pennsylvania Press, 1997), 3.

71. Auerbach, *Our Vampires*, 6; Carol A. Senf, "Auerbach & Vampires," review of *Our Vampires, Ourselves*, by Nina Auerbach, *English Literature in Translation, 1880–1920* 39, (1994): 491.

72. Laura Marchesani, *Dick and Jane and Vampires* (New York: Grosset & Dunlap, 2010).

73. Deborah Howe and James Howe, *Bunnicula: A Rabbit-Tale of Mystery* (New York: Atheneum, 1979).
74. Leonard G. Heldreth and Mary Pharr, eds., *Blood Is the Life: Vampires in Literature* (Madison, WI: Popular Press, 1999).
75. Day, *Vampire Legends*, 143.
76. Jules Zanger, "Metaphor into Metonymy: The Vampire Next Door," in *Blood Read: The Vampire as Metaphor in Contemporary Culture*, ed. Joan Gordon and Veronica Hollinger (Philadelphia: University of Pennsylvania Press, 1997),17–18.
77. Yabroff, "Bit Long," 74.
78. Zanger, "Metaphor," 18.
79. Zanger, "Metaphor," 19.
80. Zanger, "Metaphor," 22.
81. Zanger, "Metaphor," 24.
82. Ken Gelder, *Reading the Vampire: Popular Fictions Series* (New York: Routledge, 1994), quoted in Yabroff, "Bit Long," 74.
83. Yabroff, "Bit Long," 74.
84. Joseph De Marco, "Vampire Literature: Something Young Adults Can Really Sink Their Teeth Into," *Emergency Librarian* 24, no. 5 (May/June 1997): 26–27.
85. Erikson, quoted in De Marco, "Vampire Literature," 27.
86. De Marco, "Vampire Literature," 27.
87. Joni Richards Bodart, "Books That Help, Books That Heal," *Young Adult Library Services* 5, no. 1, (2006): 31–34.
88. *Frontline: Inside the Teenage Brain*, DVD, produced by Sarah Spinks (Boston: Public Broadcasting Service, 2002).
89. Joni Richards Bodart, "Young Adult Authors as Trusted Adults for Disconnected Teens," *ALAN Review* 37, no. 1 (Fall 2010): 16–22.
90. Day, *Vampire Legends*, 16–17.
91. Auerbach, *Our Vampires*, 1.
92. Guillermo Del Toro and Chuck Hogan, "Why Vampires Never Die," *New York Times*, July 30, 2009.
93. Megan Tingley, quoted in Doree Shafrir, "Zombies, Schmombies! Teen Girls Are Vamping It Up!" *New York Observer*, March 4, 2008, http://www.observer.com/2008/zombies-schmombies-teen-girls-are-vamping-it?page=1.
94. Shafrir, "Zombies, Schmombies!"
95. Rodney Clapp, "Vampires among Us," *Christian Century* 127, no. 3 (February 9, 2010): 45.
96. Whitley Strieber, quoted in "For Love of Do-Good Vampires: A Bloody Book List," narrated by Margot Adler, *All Things Considered*, NPR, February 18, 2010, http://www.npr.org/templates/story/story.php?storyId=123115545.

97. Clapp, "Vampires among Us," 45.
98. Annette Curtis Klause, *The Silver Kiss* (New York: Delacorte Press, 1990); L. J. Smith, *Vampire Diaries: The Awakening* (New York: HarperCollins, 1991).
99. Janice Harrell, *Bloodlines* (New York: HarperCollins, 1994); *Bloodlust*, 1994; *Bloodchoice*, 1994; *Blood Reunion*, 1995; Vivian Vande Velde, *Companions of the Night* (New York: Magic Carpet Books, 1995); M. T. Anderson, *Thirsty* (Somerville, MA: Candlewick Press, 1997).
100. Anne Rice, *Interview with a Vampire* (New York: Alfred A. Knopf, 2006).
101. De Marco, "Vampire Literature," 26–27.
102. De Marco, "Vampire Literature," 26.
103. De Marco, "Vampire Literature," 26.
104. Clapp, "Vampires among Us," 45.
105. Del Toro and Hogan, "Never Die."

Bibliography

Anderson, M. T. *Thirsty*. Somerville, MA: Candlewick, 1997.
Auerbach, Nina. *Our Vampires, Ourselves*. Chicago: University of Chicago Press, 1995.
Beresford, Matthew. *From Demons to Dracula: The Creation of the Modern Vampire Myth*. London: Reaktion Blooks, 2008.
Bodart, Joni Richards. "Books That Help, Books That Heal." *Young Adult Library Services* 5, no. 1, (2006): 31–34.
———. "Young Adult Authors as Trusted Adults for Disconnected Teens." *ALAN Review* 37, no. 1 (Fall 2010): 16–22.
Clapp, Rodney. "Vampires among Us." *Christian Century* 127, no. 3 (February 9, 2010): 45.
Day, Peter. Introduction to *Vampires: Myths and Metaphors of Enduring Evil*. Edited by Peter Day. New York: Rodopi, 2006.
Day, William Patrick. *Vampire Legends in Contemporary American Culture: What Becomes a Legend Most*. Lexington: University Press of Kentucky, 2002.
De Marco, Joseph. "Vampire Literature: Something Young Adults Can Really Sink Their Teeth Into." *Emergency Librarian* 24,no. 5 (May/June 1997): 26–28.
Frontline: Inside the Teenage Brain. Produced by Sarah Spinks. 2002. Boston, MA: Public Broadcasting Service, 2002. DVD.
Gordon, Joan, and Veronica Hollinger. *Blood Read: The Vampire as Metaphor in Contemporary Culture*. Philadelphia: University of Pennsylvania Press, 1997.

Guiley, Rosemary Ellen. *The Encyclopedia of Vampires, Werewolves and Other Monsters*. New York: Checkmark Books, 2004.

Hallab, Mary Y. *Vampire God: Allure of the Undead in Western Culture*. Albany: State University of New York Press, 2009.

Harrell, Janice. *Bloodlines*. New York: HarperCollins, 1994.

———. *Bloodlust*. New York: HarperCollins, 1994.

———. *Bloodchoice*. New York: HarperCollins, 1994.

———. *Blood Reunion*. New York: HarperCollins, 1995.

Heldreth, Leonard G., and Mary Pharr, eds. *Blood Is the Life: Vampires in Literature*. Madison, WI: Popular Press, 1999.

Howe, Deborah, and James Howe (1979). *Bunnicula: A Rabbit-Tale of Mystery*. New York: Atheneum, 1979.

Karg, Barb, Arjean Spaite, and Rick Sutherland. *The Everything Vampire Book: From Vlad the Impaler to the Vampire Lestat—A History of Vampires in Literature, Film, and Legend*. Avon, MA: Adams Media, 2009.

Klause, Annette Curtis. *The Silver Kiss*. New York: Delacorte Press, 1990.

Marchesani, Laura. *Dick and Jane and Vampires*. New York: Grosset & Dunlap, 2010.

Nuzum, Eric. *The Dead Travel Fast: Stalking Vampires from Nosferatu to Count Chocula*. New York: St. Martin's Press, 2008.

Radford, Benjamin. "The Real Science and History of Vampires."*Live Science*, November 30, 2009.

Rice, Anne. *Interview with a Vampire*. New York: Alfred A. Knopf, 2006.

Senf, Carol A. "Auerbach & Vampires." Review of *Our Vampires, Ourselves*, by Nina Auerbach, *English Literature in Translation, 1880–1920* 39, (1994): 491–494.

Shafrir, Doree. "Zombies, Schmombies! Teen Girls Are Vamping It Up!" *New York Observer*, March 4, 2008, http://www.observer.com/2008/zombies-schmombies-teen-girls-are-vamping-it?page=1.

Smith, L. J. *Vampire Diaries: The Awakening*. New York: HarperCollins, 1991.

Taylor, Troy. "From *Beyond the Grave*: The Horror of the Grave & the Dark Side of Death." PrairieGhosts. 2001. http://www.prairieghosts.com/grave_horror.html.

Twitchell, James B. *The Living Dead: A Study of the Vampire in Romantic Literature*. Durham, NC: Duke University Press, 1981.

Velde, Vivian Vande. *Companions of the Night*. New York: Magic Carpet Books, 1995.

Yabroff, Jennie. "A Bit Long in the Tooth." *Newsweek* 152, no. 24 (December 15, 2008): 74.

Zanger, Jules. "Metaphor into Metonymy: The Vampire Next Door." In *Blood Read: The Vampire as Metaphor in Contemporary Culture*, edited by Joan Gordon and Veronica Hollinger, 17–27. Philadelphia: University of Pennsylvania Press, 1997.

1

The Silver Kiss by Annette Curtis Klause

The Silver Kiss (1990), by Annette Curtis Klause, was the first vampire book written for teens and is a thriller as well as a romance, born of the author's lifelong fascination with vampires. Klause's vampires have many of the standard characteristics—fangs, pale skin, superhuman strength, agility and speed, intolerance of sunlight, the ability to dissolve into mist, the inability to enter a home without an invitation. They are repelled by crucifixes, must sleep on or stay near their native soil, and prefer dressing in black. But Simon, one of the two protagonists, refuses to feed from humans except when hunger overtakes him, although he usually sees humans as food, rather than as individuals. He is attracted to Zoe and wants to protect her, two traits of the modern vampire, who is dangerous yet "good."

Christopher, Simon's older brother, who turned Simon into a vampire, has no sympathy at all for humans and shows all the characteristics of an evil, twisted monster. Turned when he was only six years old, he is stunted in physical and emotional growth, killing brutally and greedily whenever he can, feeding on fear as well as blood, even though he could stop while his victims are still alive. In spite of his innocent appearance, Christopher is evil, a little boy who has stuffed his battered teddy bear with his native earth so he can have it with him all the time. Claiming to be lost, he lures his victims into the darkness, where he attacks and kills them, enjoying both the hunt and the kill. Simon has been stalking him for hundreds of years, describing him as "trapped forever in the body of a child, with a child's anger. His body whispers secrets to him that he will never know, because he can't quite hear them. I think that's why he kills so brutally."[1]

Simon and Zoe are drawn together by their loneliness, their need to connect with someone, somehow. Simon has been alone for three hundred years, unable to trust or connect with either humans or other vampires. Zoe's best friend is moving across the country, her mother is dying, and her father is fixated on his wife, abandoning his daughter. As Simon and Zoe grow closer, they share their stories with each other and realize that together they are not so alone, and are able to give each other strength to do the things that must be done: kill Christopher and face their mutual fear of death.

The book's good-versus-evil theme is clearly played out between Simon and his brother as well as between Simon and several neighborhood bullies, who jeer at him and attack him, first for fun and then for revenge, after he puts one of them in the hospital. The themes of death, and loss and the power of love to overcome both, are seen in the relationship between Simon and Zoe, and in Zoe's relationships with both her parents. While a minor character, Zoe's mother is one of the most powerful figures in the novel, because it is she who convinces both her husband and her daughter to believe that love is stronger than death, and that they must let her go, no matter how much they want her to stay. She is the one who pulls them all together, gives Zoe and her father the power to continue after her death, and convinces them that when life is filled with illness and pain, death is sometimes welcome. And it is her mother's strength that allows Zoe to support Simon until he fades into mist as the first rays of the sun touch his face.

Klause's style is simple, lyrical, and romantic, drawing the reader into the heartbreaking romance between Simon and Zoe. But it is also an impossible love, because in this world, vampires and humans can never live together. Yet it is pure, light, strong enough to support both Simon and Zoe through the trials they must both face, and it stands in stark contrast to the darker characters of Christopher and Kenny and his cruel and callous friends.

It is a novel of contrasts, good and evil, light and dark, life and death. For Zoe, letting go means embracing life and moving on. For

Simon, it means finding the peace that has eluded him for centuries. The story takes place within only a few days, using only a few characters, and encompassing fewer than two hundred pages, yet it addresses eternal issues that will echo in the reader's mind long after the last page has been read and the cover closed.

Recently, a new paperback edition of *The Silver Kiss* was published with a cover reminiscent of *Twilight*, including two new short stories, ensuring that the story's longevity will continue for years to come.[2] "Summer of Love" is set in 1967, decades before Simon meets Zoe, when he wanders the streets of San Francisco, drinking from one girl after another, unable to love, unable to feel any emotions, eternally sentenced to solitude. The only creature able to get close to him is a cat who shares his daylight hideaway. After she dies, he realizes she has opened him up to love like nothing had been able to do since he became a vampire. Now that he has remembered love and experienced it again, he will yearn for it and search for it, eternally, a search that will eventually, years later, lead him to Zoe.

"The Christmas Cat" is set a year and a half after *The Silver Kiss*. Zoe is studying at San Francisco State College, and she befriends a little cat, who mysteriously turns out to be the same one Simon had loved. She goes to bed on Christmas Eve but wakes up in the middle of the night to see Simon sitting on the foot of her bed with the cat in his lap. He tells her that many times he thought that love had abandoned him, but the love he felt for her and for this cat proved him wrong, because we never really lose the ones we love. Zoe remembers what Simon said when she wakes up and knows that one day, somehow, she will find all that she has lost, and that in the meantime, she will try not to be so lonely.

Klause wrote the two stories for the readers who wrote to her begging for more about Simon and Zoe. These tales, like the book, are about life and death and love. Simon's story explains how his heart was opened to love and helped him to conquer the demons and darkness inside him. It reveals why he was able to love Zoe when they reached out to each other. Zoe's story brings her a deeper sense of peace and recovery that she didn't have when *The Silver Kiss* ended. Simon's visit and his quiet words have helped her begin to move on and to reach out to others, where before she avoided them. And finally, there is a hint (maybe more than a hint) of another connection between Simon and Zoe in the stories. Simon remembers a girl he picked up at the Fillmore, wearing fringes and a swirly skirt, who told him about her three cats and said he was like Jim Morrison, beautiful and scary at the same time. He almost drank her dry, but then he thought of the three cats she had, and he left her in Golden Gate Park to wake up the next morning and wonder if someone had slipped her some acid the night before. And one of the reasons why Zoe decided to go to San Francisco was because of her mother's memories of the city, and the fringes and beads everyone wore, and the concerts in Golden Gate Park. Perhaps something in Simon recognized in Zoe some part of that long-ago girl.

The Silver Kiss opened the door, and others quickly followed: in 1991 L. J. Smith's four-volume The Vampire Diaries series was published.[3] It soon went out of print, but was republished in 2007. Smith has also written several other volumes in this and other series since then, including the popular Night World series, starting in 1996.[4] Caroline Cooney's The Vampire's Promise series was published between 1991 and 1993.[5] Janice Harrell's Vampire Twins series began in 1994;[6] Vivian Vande Velde's Companions of the Night came out in 1995,[7] and M. T. Anderson's Thirsty was published two years later.[8] Amelia Atwater-Rhodes's Den of Shadows series, the first books of which were published when she was a teen herself, began in 1999.[9]

In all, about 60 YA vampire novels, including series and stand-alone titles, were published between 1990 and 1999. In contrast, over 175 YA vampire novels have been published in the ten years since then, most of them in series with female protagonists. They vary widely in quality, and most are thinly clad romantic teen-angsty novels with boyfriends who just happen to be immortal bloodsuckers. While they are wildly popular, there is a sameness to them and they seem to blend together. And in 2005, Stephenie Meyer published the first volume of the Twilight series, and the number of vampire books and series exploded.[10] Meyer's series will not be discussed in this study because there has already been much published about it, writings both popular and scholarly, in which the series has been thoroughly analyzed and dissected. However, the huge impact of the series, both the books and movies about them, is undeniable.

And now even adult authors are beginning to get in on the demand for more and more vampire titles. Katie Maxwell wrote two YA vampire titles in 2005 and 2006, Got Fangs? and Circus of the Darned;[11] Julie Kenner wrote two in 2007, Good Ghouls Do and

Good Ghouls' Guide to Getting Even.[12] In 2010, Gena Showalter and Sherrilyn Kenyon, both of whom have long series of adult vampire novels, began YA series with male protagonists, and although neither is a vampire, they both interact with vampires; in Showalter's Intertwined series, Aden becomes the ruler of the vampires when he kills their king at the end of the first volume.[13] Kenyon's series, The Chronicles of Nick, is an offshoot of her adult Dark Hunters series and covers the adolescence of one of the human characters in that series, Nick Gautier.[14] However, the protagonists are not actually vampires, and the books include plotlines and characters from her adult series that are definitely not appropriate for young adults.

In light of the massive number of vampire series available, with more coming every day, this study will choose to focus on only series that have more complex worlds and backstories than vamp romance and bickering friends, and whose vamp heroes have an interesting assortment of vampire characteristics. These include the Tantalize series by Cynthia Leitich Smith,[15] the Blue Bloods series by Melissa de la Cruz,[16] the Drake Chronicles by Alyxandra Harvey,[17] the Chronicles of Vlad Tod by Heather Brewer,[18] and *Jessica's Guide to Dating on the Dark Side* by Beth Fantaskey.[19]

Notes

1. Annette Curtis Klause, *The Silver Kiss* (New York: Delacorte Press, 1990), 143.

2. Annette Curtis Klause, *The Silver Kiss* (New York: Delacorte Press, 2009).

3. L. J. Smith, *Vampire Diaries: The Awakening* (New York: HarperCollins, 1991); *Vampire Diaries: The Struggle*, 1991; *Vampire Diaries: The Fury*, 1991; *Vampire Diaries: Dark Reunion*, 1991.

4. L. J. Smith, *Night World: Secret Vampire* (New York: Simon & Schuster, 1996); *Night World: Daughters of Darkness*, 1996; *Night World: Spellbinder*, 1996; *Night World: Dark Angel*, 1996; *Night World: The Chosen*, 1997; *Night World: Soulmate*, 1997; *Night World: Huntress*, 1997; *Night World: Black Dawn*, 1998; *Night World: Witchlight*, 1998; *Night World: Strange Fate*, 1998.

5. Caroline B. Cooney, *The Cheerleader* (New York: Scholastic, 1991); *The Return of the Vampire*, 1992; *The Vampire's Promise*, 1993.

6. Janice Harrell, *Bloodlines* (New York: HarperCollins, 1994); *Bloodlust*, 1994; *Bloodchoice*, 1994; *Blood Reunion*, 1995.

7. Vivian Vande Velde, *Companions of the Night* (New York: Magic Carpet Books, 1995).

8. M. T. Anderson, *Thirsty* (Somerville, MA: Candlewick Press, 1997).

9. Amelia Atwater-Rhodes, *In the Forests of the Night* (New York: Laurel-Leaf, 1999); *Demon in My View*, 2000; *Shattered Mirror*, 2001; *Midnight Predator*, 2002.

10. Stephenie Meyer, *Twilight* (New York: Little, Brown, 2005); *New Moon*, 2006; *Eclipse*, 2007; *Breaking Dawn*, 2008.

11. Katie Maxwell, *Got Fangs? Confessions of a Vampire's Girlfriend* (New York: Smooch, 2005); *Circus of the Darned*, 2006.

12. Julie Kenner, *Good Ghouls Do* (New York: Berkley, 2007); *Good Ghouls' Guide to Getting Even*, 2007.

13. Gena Showalter, *Intertwined* (Ontario, Canada: Harlequin Teen, 2009).

14. Sherrilyn Kenyon, *Infinity: The Chronicles of Nick* (New York: St. Martin's Press, 2010); *Invincible: The Chronicles of Nick*, 2011.

15. Cynthia Leitich Smith, *Tantalize* (Somerville, MA: Candlewick Press, 2007); *Eternal*, 2009; *Blessed*, 2011.

16. Melissa de la Cruz, *Blue Bloods* (New York: Hyperion, 2006); *Masquerade*, 2007; *Revelations*, 2008; *The Van Alen Legacy*, 2009; *Misguided Angel*, 2010; *Bloody Valentine*, 2010; *Keys to the Repository*, 2010.

17. Alyxandra Harvey, *Hearts at Stake* (Fairfield, PA: Walker Books for Young Readers, 2009); *Blood Feud*, 2010; *Out for Blood*, 2010; *Bleeding Hearts*, 2011.

18. Heather Brewer, *Chronicles of Vladimir Tod: Eighth Grade Bites* (New York: Dutton Juvenile, 2007); *Ninth Grade Slays*, 2008; *Tenth Grade Bleeds*, 2009; *Eleventh Grade Burns*, 2010; *Twelfth Grade Kills*, 2010.

19. Beth Fantaskey, *Jessica's Guide to Dating on the Dark Side* (Boston: Harcourt Children's Books, 2009).

Bibliography

Anderson, M. T. *Thirsty*. Somerville, MA: Candlewick Press, 1997.

Atwater-Rhodes, Amelia. *In the Forests of the Night*. New York: Laurel-Leaf, 1999.

———. *Demon in My View*. New York: Laurel-Leaf, 2000.

———. *Shattered Mirror*. New York: Laurel-Leaf, 2001.

———. *Midnight Predator*. New York: Laurel-Leaf, 2002.

Brewer, Heather. *Chronicles of Vladimir Tod: Eighth Grade Bites*. New York: Dutton Juvenile, 2007.

———. *Chronicles of Vladimir Tod: Ninth Grade Slays*. New York: Dutton Juvenile, 2008.

———. *Chronicles of Vladimir Tod: Tenth Grade Bleeds.* New York: Dutton Juvenile, 2009.
———. *Chronicles of Vladimir Tod: Eleventh Grade Burns.* New York: Dutton Juvenile, 2010.
———. *Chronicles of Vladimir Tod: Twelfth Grade Kills.* New York: Dutton Juvenile, 2010.
Cooney, Caroline B. *The Cheerleader.* New York: Scholastic, 1991.
———. *The Return of the Vampire.* New York: Scholastic, 1992.
———. *The Vampire's Promise.* New York: Scholastic, 1993.
De la Cruz, Melissa. *Blue Bloods.* New York: Hyperion, 2006.
———. *Masquerade.* New York: Hyperion, 2007.
———. *Revelations.* New York: Hyperion, 2008.
———. *The Van Alen Legacy.* New York: Hyperion, 2009.
———. *Misguided Angel.* New York: Hyperion, 2010.
———. *Bloody Valentine.* New York: Hyperion, 2010.
———. *Keys to the Repository.* New York: Hyperion, 2010.
Fantaskey, Beth. *Jessica's Guide to Dating on the Dark Side.* Boston: Harcourt Children's Books, 2009.
Harrell, Janice. *Bloodlines.* New York: HarperCollins, 1994.
———. *Bloodlust.* New York: HarperCollins, 1994.
———. *Bloodchoice.* New York: HarperCollins, 1994.
———. *Blood Reunion.* New York: HarperCollins, 1995.
Harvey, Alyxandra. *Hearts at Stake.* Fairfield, PA: Walker Books for Young Readers, 2009.
———. *Blood Feud.* Fairfield, PA: Walker Books for Young Readers, 2010.
———. *Out for Blood.* Fairfield, PA: Walker Books for Young Readers, 2010.
———. *Bleeding Hearts.* New York: Walker Children's, 2011.
Klause, Annette Curtis. *The Silver Kiss.* New York: Delacorte Press, 1990.
———. *The Silver Kiss.* New York: Delacorte Press, 2009.
Maxwell, Katie. *Got Fangs? Confessions of a Vampire's Girlfriend.* New York: Smooch, 2005.
———. *Circus of the Darned.* New York: Smooch, 2006.
Meyer, Stephenie. *Twilight.* New York: Little, Brown, 2005.
———. *New Moon.* New York: Little, Brown, 2006.
———. *Eclipse.* New York: Little, Brown, 2007.
———. *Breaking Dawn.* New York: Little, Brown, 2008.
Smith, Cynthia Leitich. *Tantalize.* Somerville, MA: Candlewick Press, 2007.
———. *Eternal.* Somerville, MA: Candlewick Press, 2009
———. *Blessed.* Somerville, MA: Candlewick Press, 2011.
Smith, L. J. *Night World: Secret Vampire.* New York: Simon & Schuster, 1996.
———. *Night World: Daughters of Darkness.* New York: Simon & Schuster, 1996.
———. *Night World: Spellbinder.* New York: Simon & Schuster, 1996.

———. *Night World: Dark Angel*. New York: Simon & Schuster, 1996.

———. *Night World: The Chosen*. New York: Simon & Schuster, 1997.

———. *Night World: Soulmate*. New York: Simon & Schuster, 1997.

———. *Night World: Huntress*. New York: Simon & Schuster, 1997.

———. *Night World: Black Dawn*. New York: Simon & Schuster, 1998.

———. *Night World: Witchlight*. New York: Simon & Schuster, 1998.

———. *Night World: Strange Fate*. New York: Simon & Schuster, 1998.

———. *Vampire Diaries: The Awakening*. New York: HarperCollins, 1991.

———. *Vampire Diaries: The Struggle*. New York: HarperCollins, 1991.

———. *Vampire Diaries: The Fury*. New York: HarperCollins, 1991.

———. *Vampire Diaries: Dark Reunion*. New York: HarperCollins, 1991.

Velde, Vivian Vande. *Companions of the Night*. New York: Magic Carpet Books, 1995.

2

The Tantalize Series by Cynthia Leitich Smith

This series stars not only vampires but also fallen angels and a variety of shapeshifters, from the standard werewolves to a werearmadillo and a wereopossum, among others. Cynthia Leitich Smith has been fascinated by vampires since she was a child and used that fascination and the Austin, Texas, setting where she lives to create a unique world populated by equally unique characters. When she first read Bram Stoker's *Dracula*, Smith was intrigued by a character from Texas, one of the vampire hunters, Quincey P. Morris. When she began working on *Tantalize*, she decided to "bring the gothic tradition 'home' to Texas,"[1] and to name her protagonist Quincie P. Morris, a descendant of the hunter. Smith also included the world-famous bat colony under the Congress Avenue Bridge, 1.5 million strong,[2] and other actual places and events in Austin to create a strong sense of place. In fact, the settings of all three of the books are places she has lived and of which she has vivid memories.[3]

Preparing to write the first book in the series, *Tantalize*, Smith researched not only the standard vampire texts but also the myths and folklore about vampires and shapeshifters from around the world. She knew she had to understand where the monsters came from in order to create her own unique contribution to vampire and shapeshifter literature.[4] She also knew she had to discover why the archetypes of bloodsuckers and shapeshifters have been psychologically important, and perhaps even necessary, for centuries in order

33

to create realistic characters that both follow and break the rules of the genre.[5] Smith says, "Reading about violence and horror is a way for a person to not only clarify their stance on moral issues by exploring the alternatives (and in doing so give license to the anti-social creature within in a safe venue) but to exercise their responses to the terrible and be prepared for it in real life."[6] She is also not an advocate of protecting teens from the darker sides of life, since such experiences, especially from the safe perspective of a book, give teens information and preparation to deal with the unthinkable or unbelievable when it actually occurs in their lives.[7]

Smith based her vampires on Stoker's *Dracula*, but she tweaked their characteristics to make it easier for them to pass among humans. Her vampires (they call themselves "eternals") also have their own culture, wealth, and power. They are aristocrats, living in secret, drinking from willing victims. While they live apart from humans for the most part, the vampires are able to intermingle with humans undetected because they don't act like Stoker's Dracula— for example, these vampires can be in the sun and they are not sustained by blood alone. These "typical" vampire characteristics and others are portrayed as myths that Smith's vamps use to stay hidden not only from humans but also from the weres, who are their bitter enemies. Humans know that vampires exist, but they are assumed to be very rare, almost extinct, when actually there are great numbers of them spread all over the world, living in compounds and mostly associating only with their own kind.

Smith examines the society of the vampires in great detail, especially the aristocracy, many of whom live in a gated suburb of Chicago, although there are other compounds in this country and in Europe. Since they live so long, most vampires are extremely wealthy and have scores of humans who work for them in varying capacities, often several generations of families who bring up their children to follow in their parents' footsteps. It is a hierarchical society, with an aristocracy, a gentry, and lesser subjects and servants, ruled by a king or queen, who takes the title of The Dracula and holds the Mantle of the Dracul. They have no need to kill to survive and drink from willing victims, although deaths do occur. Vampires are stronger and faster than humans or shifters, although they prey only on humans. And just like shifters and humans, there are some good vampires and some not so good. They are also very careful about creating new vampires because they don't want to create a food shortage. While they live with their human servants and blood donors, vampires tend to socialize with each other and not with human society in general. The suburb of Chicago where The Dracula lives is populated almost entirely by vampires and their families. When they socialize, they socialize with each other.

Vampirism is a demonic infection that gradually rots the soul. Transformation takes about a month from the time the human first tastes vampire blood and is complete when the new vampire drinks blood from a live human for the first time, killing the victim because the thirst for blood is so overwhelming the new vampire cannot stop once he or she has started. Sunlight doesn't hurt them, although it does weaken their powers; they don't have to kill their victims, once the first bloodlust has been satisfied, and older vampires are able to transform into other creatures, including bats, or into mist, while young vampires, neophytes, can transform only into wolves. They can be killed by beheading, by fire, or by having their hearts destroyed or removed. Wooden stakes are optional.

Smith's werecreatures trace their heritage back to the Ice Age, when many species were much larger than they are today.[8] They are natural-born species, and several, such as the armadillo, are included because of the series' Southwestern setting. Werecreatures can mate with humans and produce hybrid children, like Kieren and his little sister, but the were community, especially werewolves, frowns on it.

Shapeshifters and humans have had a rather confrontational relationship with each other from the time, hundreds of years ago, that humans first learned that shifters existed when a werebear changed in the middle of a large social gathering. They are treated like minorities have been treated throughout human history—being outed as any kind of a were can mean losing one's job, being forced to leave one's neighborhood or town, or being subjected to a variety of other bullying and discriminatory practices. Humans hate and fear weres and are likely to kill or injure any they find, considering them to be just animals, so murder isn't involved. This is why Kieren's inability to control his shifting is so dangerous to him and his family, and why his mother is so determined that he find a pack as soon as possible. He and his sister are only half wolf—their father is a human. When his parents fell in love, his mother left her pack and werewolf culture to live as a human. Being revealed as a rogue wolf would put her in danger from the packs in the area, because they don't believe werewolves should live outside the pack or marry humans and have children with them.

But Kieren needs the protection of the pack to help him master shifting and to keep him away from more fragile humans when he's unable to control his emotions or his body. In addition, wolves mate for life, and Kieren's mother (who is definitely the alpha in their family) wants him to marry a shifter, even though she is well aware that Quincie is in love with her son, the boy-wolf that Quincie's known for her entire life. Kieren himself knows he needs to leave and find a pack—having injured Quincie once when they were much younger, he's terrified of doing it again, and the scars on her hand are a constant reminder. Kieren has spent his life studying vampires, and his mother hopes that his knowledge will help him overcome the stigma of being a half-wolf and living outside of pack society for his entire life, and allow him to be accepted by a pack.

Tantalize is both a love story and a gothic fantasy. Quincie and Kieren's love is impossible at the beginning because he's a werewolf and she's a human. They've avoided thinking about the reality of it, pretending to be best friends and no more for as long as they could. But life crashes in on them with Vaggio's murder and the subsequent plotting against Quincie. Trying to ignore their growing love for each other also creates problems because of miscommunications and assumptions. And as Kieren becomes more and more a person of interest to the police working on Vaggio's murder, his mother becomes increasingly insistent about his leaving town as soon as possible to join another pack, even though it means he won't be coming back to Austin. Joining a pack means he will stay with it for life, leaving his family and Quincie behind. This traumatizes Quincie, because she hadn't realized he wouldn't be back; she thought he would go to the pack, learn how to control his shift, and come home—sort of like going off to college and coming back home afterward. But she is determined to do the right thing, believing in herself and Kieren, and the strength of their love. Even after she's transformed into a vampire, she manages to do what is most important—overcome Bradley and her bloodlust and save Kieren, also saving herself in the process, although she doesn't know that until the end of the third book, titled *Blessed*.

One of the most interesting things about the first volume is the way Smith uses what seem to be actual documents to provide extra information about the plot, such as ads for a new chef, Bradley's curriculum vitae, announcements about Sanguini's opening, and reviews of the restaurant's food. But central to the volume are the two menus Bradley creates, one for predators and one for prey. The prey menus are vegetarian and feature dishes that might be found in any upscale restaurant. The predator menu, however, includes dishes that are decidedly carnivorous, like the tongue and blood sausages, or the dessert of chilled baby squirrels, simmered in orange brandy and bathed in honey cream sauce. This dish is the vehicle to help Bradley create his own private clan of vampires, with him as their king. If you eat the baby squirrels, you will transform into a vampire thirty days later.

Shifters of all varieties tend to hang together. Kieren's two best friends are Travis and Clyde, a werearmadillo and a wereopossum, respectively, who work at Sanguini's. Weres take on some of the characteristics of their animal, their "dark other," so when startled or frightened, Travis shifts to his armadillo and curls up in a ball to protect himself, and Clyde plays dead, which he can do as either an opossum or a human. But later, Clyde is not hesitant to defend Kieren when he thinks Quincie is threatening him. One of Smith's favorite characters, the sarcastic marsupial with a taste for crickets, has unplumbed depths that he doesn't show until the third volume of the series.

Smith also clearly defines the difference between shifting—what a wereanimal does—and changing—what a vampire does. Shifting is difficult and painful and results of lots of messy undefined body fluids and doesn't include clothing, which is shredded in the process, so the transformation back to human leaves the person naked. Changing, on the other hand, is instantaneous, magical, neat, and does include clothing. Changing is always deliberate, but shifting is sometimes accidental or unintentional, happening when a were is very angry, startled, or frightened.

Smith introduces a new creature in her second volume, titled *Eternal*: an angel. Zachary is a guardian angel who makes a mistake when he thinks the life of the teenage girl he guards is in danger and reveals himself to her in all his heavenly glory, something he is forbidden to do. As a result, she is captured by a vampire, Radford,

The Dracula, and turned into a vampire princess. Zachary is given a chance to redeem himself by saving her soul, and in doing so, sets up part of the plot of the third volume, *Blessed*.

In that book, Smith adds a new twist to her vampires, changing them in unforeseen ways that add to the complexity of the series and create new problems for Quincie and her friends. It seems that there are two kinds of vampires—the ones everyone knows about, and the Carpathians, who were created by Stoker's original Count Dracula himself, have very different threats and abilities, and are infinitely more powerful than the current vampires. The Carpathians had all been hunted down and destroyed centuries ago, after the count's death at the hands of the vampire hunters.

Count Dracula was so powerful that he was able to send his essence and his power into the weapon that killed him, so that with the right incantation, he would be able to release himself from the weapon and go into a new body. But when he was killed with two knives at the same time, that essence and power were split between the knives and rendered inert. As long as one person did not have both weapons and conjure the vampire's power into his own body, Dracula would be "dead." However, if one person were able to get both knives, Dracula's powers and his essence, his evil personality, would possess the owner of the knives, and Dracula would live, undead, once more. The neophytes he would then create as Dracula Prime would rise as Carpathians, completely soulless, completely demonic. But if the body Dracula possessed was killed before its own personality had been taken over, Dracula's victims would also have the characteristics of the victims of the original Dracula—that is, they would return to normal, completely human, their souls safe. Using this backstory allows Smith not only to return to the original characterization of Dracula, but also to create a being even more powerful and evil than any that she has created before. If the person Dracula has possessed can be killed while only partially Dracula, all will be well. If Dracula Prime takes over completely, chaos will reign.

This title has the most information about the culture and characteristics of both vampires and Carpathians because of the research Quincie must do about them, but there is also a wealth of information about werewolf culture and how Kieren and his family are seen by the worldwide wolf pack network. Centuries ago wolves may have accidently created the vampires of their world through sorcery when they were trying "to cull the human threat," although that is not confirmed. But whether or not they were the source of the problem, the wolves have studied vampires for generations and killed as many as they could. At one time, there were many wolves who studied vampires all the way back to Dracula Prime and the Carpathians he created, but because of several "long-ago mishaps," most of them now specialize in the healing arts, like Kieren's mother does, rather than explore the ancient demonic magic. But that ancient knowledge is what is now needed to conquer the new Dracula.

The Tantalize story can also be seen from Kieren's perspective in the graphic novel (GN) *Tantalize: Kieren's Story*. Smith grew up reading comics and feels that she is coming back to her mother tongue in this rendition of the story.[9] Because it's a collaborative process, it's very different from turning over a manuscript to an illustrator and hoping for the best.[10] She was so pleased with the final product that she has decided to do GN versions of the other books. The next one will be *Eternal: Zachary's Story*.[11]

The key to this outstanding series is the amount of research the author did on the rules of the supernatural beings, so she could choose which ones she wanted to bend or break. These are densely written books in that they convey large amounts of information and backstory on each of the characters, while still remaining exciting and enthralling reading. They are books to be tasted, retasted, and savored, much as the dishes on Sanguini's menu were savored. Blood and tongue sausages, anyone? Or perhaps the chilled baby squirrels?

Notes

1. David Gill, "A Lawyer She Was, an Author She Is: An Interview with Cynthia Leitich Smith," *Teacher Librarian* 35, no. 5 (June 2008): 64–65.

2. Cynthia Leitich Smith, "Author Cynthia Leitich Smith" (Elluminate presentation, San José State University, San Jose, CA, April 5, 2011).

3. Smith, "Author Cynthia Leitich Smith."

4. Cynthia Leitich Smith, e-mail message to author, January 9, 2011.

5. Smith, "Author Cynthia Leitich Smith."

6. Smith, e-mail to author.

7. Smith, "Author Cynthia Leitich Smith."
8. Smith, "Author Cynthia Leitich Smith."
9. Cynthia Leitich Smith, "Cynthia Leitich Smith Book Chat Transcript," *ALAN Online*, July 31, 2008, http://www.alan-ya.org/wordpress/wp-content/uploads/2008/07/clschat.pdf.
10. Smith, "Author Cynthia Leitich Smith."
11. Cynthia Leitich Smith, "Forthcoming," Cynthia Leitich Smith: Official Author Site and Home of Children's & YA Lit Resources, http://www.cynthialeitichsmith.com/cls/cyn_books.html.

Bibliography

Smith, Cynthia Leitich. "Author Cynthia Leitich Smith." Elluminate presentation, San José State University, San Jose, California, April 5, 2011.
———. *Tantalize*. New York: Candlewick Press, 2007.
———. *Eternal*. New York: Candlewick Press, 2009.
———. *Blessed*. New York: Candlewick Press, 2011.

3

The Blue Bloods Series by Melissa de la Cruz

When given the chance to write a paranormal novel, Melissa de la Cruz decided she wanted to write a huge epic fantasy about vampires. In order to give her vamps a backstory and to organize them throughout history, she created her vampires as fallen angels, expelled from Heaven for siding with Lucifer in his attempt to rule Heaven, made immortal and forced to live on the blood of humans to survive.[1] Two of the archangels, Gabrielle and Michael, volunteered to go with them when they fell, and became the Uncorrupted, vampires by choice, not sin. They existed in Europe and the Mediterranean for centuries, but left there because of the increasing religious persecution, and sailed for North America on the *Mayflower*. They called themselves the Blue Bloods.

Gabrielle and Michael created the Code of the Vampires, the set of rules vampires lived by that would help them someday return to their heavenly home. But Lucifer and the fallen angels closest to him refused to obey the Code, preying on vampires instead of humans, draining them completely and taking their essence into their own bodies, until they were beings of chaos, angry and insane. Their blood turned silver, and they became the enemies of the Blue Bloods, glorying in doing the wrong thing. The Blue Bloods and the Silver Bloods, or Croatan, clashed in a huge battle in ancient Rome, when Michael locked Lucifer himself in the fires of Hell. The Blue Bloods believed that the Silver Bloods had been wiped out during that battle. Michael has since refused to believe anything else, and he has been the ruler of the Manhattan Coven since then.

However, the Blue Bloods who came to America on the *Mayflower* soon discovered that there was a Silver Blood among them. There were mysterious disappearances at Plymouth, and the entire settlement at Roanoke disappeared, leaving only the single clue "Croatan" nailed to a tree. (De la Cruz includes many historical details in her books, blending her world of the series into the reality of our world. The actual unsolved mystery of the lost colony of Roanoke and the meaning of the word "Croatan" are only two of those details. She says that when she ran across the story of the lost colony, it was like a lightbulb went on in her head, and suddenly, she couldn't write fast enough![2]) Little was heard of the Silver Bloods after that, and Michael was able to convince the Blue Bloods that all the Silver Bloods had been hunted down and killed, although rebels in the coven, especially the Van Alen family, never believed him and remained vigilant. However, four hundred years later, in the first volume of the series, the Silver Bloods reappear, attacking and draining adolescent Blue Bloods who have not yet come into their full power. Some on the Conclave of the Elders (the most powerful Blue Bloods, who rule the vampire world, with representatives from each of the seven main houses) believe not only that the Silver Bloods have reappeared, but also that one of the oldest families has been corrupted by an extremely powerful Silver Blood, who is part of the Conclave itself. This danger is threatening to tear all the families apart and to destroy everything they have struggled to build over the years.

This is the world in which de la Cruz sets her series, as a group of young Blue Bloods and humans struggle to bring peace and healing to their immortal community. That will mean not only drawing together the various quarreling factions of the Blue Bloods but also defeating the Silver Bloods, this time destroying them altogether. The series is ongoing, and currently there are five novels, one short story collection, and one "nonfiction" title that goes into detail about the background of the series, revealing information about the characters and the action that inform and support the rest of the titles.

The series revolves around three Blue Blood girls (Schuyler, Mimi, and Bliss) and three boys—Jack, who is Mimi's twin; Dylan, who is a Blue Blood, but lives outside the Blue Blood community;

and Oliver, who is Schuyler's bonded human familiar and conduit, whom she loves and relies on. But the saga includes a huge cast of characters that is almost impossible to keep track of. It also includes hundreds of details about the history, culture, language, and activities of the vampires and the humans they interact with, from the time they first fell from Heaven to the present day. De la Cruz has created an entire universe going thousands and thousands of years back in time, requiring a monumental backstory. Like Smith's Tantalize series, this series is incredibly densely written, requiring the reader to remember large amounts of information to understand precisely what is going on and why it's important. Fortunately, it is also intriguingly well written, and the mystery and suspense it includes makes it easy for the reader to keep going.

The fifth volume of the series, *Keys to the Repository*, allegedly nonfiction, provides some of that background information. The Repository is the library of the Blue Blood universe, and it includes all known and even some top secret or forbidden information. This volume contains some excerpts from its immense collection, selected and organized by conduits whose vampires have passed on, and others who have chosen to work there, supervised by Conduit Renfield, the longest lived of the Repository staff. It should be noted that while the Repository is said to contain all of the extant information on the Blue Bloods, there are some places where there are gaps in that information.

Keys to the Repository includes an brief overview of the series as well as backgrounds, biographies, and present locations of several members in the Van Alen, Force, and Llewellyn families; one member of the Martin family, one member of the Ward family, and several of the Fallen Brethren from the House of Morningstar, including Lucifer. Several stories are included that were not included in the books but that give extra insight into them. There is also an explanation of the Gates of Hell, of the seven ruling houses of the Conclave, and of the Committee, a network of charitable causes, foundations, and educational institutions that allow the vampires to fulfill their goal of bringing beauty, peace, and harmony to the human world. Three appendices include a list of secondary characters, a partial list of canine familiars, and a dictionary of terms. While this information isn't necessary to enjoy the series, it does give the reader a richer and fuller experience and understanding of the Blue Bloods universe.

However, it also includes a variety of spoilers for the first books in the series, and readers might want to postpone reading it until they've read those four titles. All of the books also contain snippets from the Repository files, separated from the rest of the text by formatting, showing that they are outside the story but contribute to it.

De la Cruz uses few of the "standard" characteristics of vampires, instead making them myths created to keep humans, Red Bloods, from learning of the existence of the Blue Bloods. While the vampires and humans are not enemies, the vampires prefer to remain in the background, and the Code forbids them from entering too fully into the human world. The myths about sunlight, garlic, crosses, and all the rest, were just that—myths. The truth is that vampires are immortal, just as they were before the Fall. They go through life cycles much like humans, called the Cycle of Expression. They are "alive" for about a hundred years, which is called Expression, and when the physical shell dies, in a process called Expulsion, one drop of blue blood is saved, in which all the DNA is present; when it is time to call up the spirit of that person for another cycle, it is implanted in a vampire woman, the child is born, and the process of Expression begins. In between "lifetimes" the spirit rests, and experiences Evolution, preparing for the next Expression. Some spirits choose to remain at rest, without expressing another life, which is their right. This has resulted in some of the families being very loosely knit because there are no real blood ties. When the child is born, it has no vampire characteristics; the blue blood does not begin to take over the human blood until adolescence, a process called Transformation or Blood Manifest. At that time, their blue veins become visible, their bodies begin to require blood instead of human food, and memories of past Expressions begin to return. The years from about fifteen to twenty-one are known as the Sunset Years, during which the young vampires are vulnerable since they have not come into their full powers, and the transformation process can make them sick, weak, dizzy, and confused at unpredictable times. They also gradually gain access to their memories of prior lifetimes, although they are not as complete nor as organized as they will be when they reach adulthood. This is why the Silver Bloods choose to attack them during those years. When fully adult, vampires have access to all the memories and wisdom from all of their lifetimes. They have perfect photographic memory, able to remember anything they have seen or experienced—huge libraries of information. Adult vampires are also able to show the *illuminata* and glow in the dark, which is useful to identify themselves to each other. Other powers include telepathy or mind reading, suppressing or overcoming the will of another, suggesting or putting an idea in someone's mind, issuing a direct order to someone's mind, and *Consummo Alienari*, which is the complete takeover of another's mind and is very dangerous. Vampires are also able to exhibit *mutatio*, which allows them to change into the elements of fire, water, or air, including mist or fog. Some can also change their physical shell to that of another human or animal. All vampires can move at superhuman speed, which makes the Red Bloods believe they have the ability to be invisible, and have superhuman strength. Human blood is necessary for their life and strength, and so they do have fangs, called wisdom teeth, which can be extended and retracted—not the front canines, but further back on the sides.

There are also a limited number of vampires experiencing Expression at one time. The Code states that only four hundred members of a coven or community can express at one time. There are a number of covens all over the world, in Europe, Asia, China, and both North and South America, but the total number of Blue Bloods that exist in all of the cycles of Expression in all of the covens is difficult to calculate. The Manhattan Coven is the most powerful because Michael and Gabrielle are members of that coven, and so it is the one that de la Cruz focuses on, although different volumes include glimpses of others.

It is possible to kill a Blue Blood, and a number have died. They can be attacked by a Silver Blood and totally drained of their blood and their spirit. This is the final death, since there is no blood left to save for the next cycle. It is annihilation. Their human bodies can be so old or damaged that they are unable to recover and regenerate, but if there is blood left in them, it can be saved, and their spirit will return in their next cycle. This is, perhaps, a paradox that makes de la Cruz's vampires so intriguing to teens—they have overcome death. Dying is merely an illusion to simplify their relations with humans. But they can also be killed, finally and absolutely. This means that an individual's spirit or personality, that which makes him or her unique and recognizable, is gone, and the community mourns the vampire's final death, just as we mourn death today.

Blue Bloods are beyond death, yet they are not. In addition, de la Cruz kills off characters only to bring them back in some way, or hints that there is a chance for their return in future volumes.

Many, although not all, of the Blue Blood families are fabulously wealthy because they have been able to grow their fortunes for centuries, and the Manhattan Coven has been prominent in society since the late nineteenth century. Through the Committee, the Blue Bloods try to influence humans to create Paradise on earth. They are not the dark or evil creatures humans believe vampires to be (although the Silver Bloods are both), but strive to do good for humans, helping to stop disease and spread beauty and peace and light in the world. They abide by the Code, hoping that someday they will be allowed back in Paradise. De la Cruz's vampires are unique, driven to make the earth a better place and treat the humans who live there with respect and dignity, rather than seeing them merely as food, living outside human culture, and feeding on fear as well as blood. These vampires are not to use their superhuman powers to dominate or control humans. The Code even lays out regulations for how vampires feed from humans. Humans are never to be killed or injured during feeding and may not be used more than once every four days. Draining a human is the most serious infraction of the Code. Human familiars may not be abused in any way and are to be treated with courtesy and affection because of the essential services they provide to an individual or to a family.

However, that doesn't mean that all Blue Bloods are saintly or without flaw. Mimi Force, daughter of the most powerful man in New York, Charles Force (Michael), is arrogant, self-absorbed, selfish, and constantly pushes the regulations of the Code, feeding too much from one human and taking the person far too close to being drained. She also feeds from many different humans, creating human familiars who are then bound to her for life. She believes that the Code is far too restrictive and doesn't see any reason to refrain from using her powers on humans to control them. She thinks Blue Bloods should flaunt their superiority, not try to blend in. She also enjoys others' discomfort or pain or torment and is very possessive of her twin, Jack, objecting vehemently when he is attracted to Schuyler Van Alen. Mimi and Jack are Azrael, the Angel of Death, and Abbadon, the Angel of Destruction, respectively—the most powerful vampires after the Uncorrupted. They are Lucifer's former lieutenants, who turned from him before the Fall and fought on the side of the Heavenly Host but were still ejected from Heaven. They were among the Blue Bloods who hunted Silver Bloods after the fall of Rome, believing that they were wiping them off the face of the earth. They are the reason the Blue Bloods exist today.

Several of the older Blue Bloods are also somewhat unlikeable. Bliss's stepmother, BobiAnne Llewellyn, is a superficial social climber, furnishing their home in an ostentatious way designed to impress other Blue Bloods, who are much less showy about their wealth and turn up their noses at BobiAnne's coarse and unrefined style, appearance, and mannerisms. Forsyth Llewellyn, her husband, has just been elected a New York senator, which is against the Code, although that part has not always been strictly enforced. More important, however, is that he betrayed Charles Force and, had it not been prevented, would have loosed Lucifer himself, the Abomination, on the world.

Cordelia Van Alen is Schuyler's grandmother; she is cold, distant, intolerant, and snobbish. She takes care of her granddaughter but doesn't show her any affection. However, Cordelia does protect her granddaughter, and she sends Schuyler to her grandfather when Cordelia's own cycle ends. She also has closed off most of the Van Alen mansion, saying they couldn't afford to keep it open or have more than one servant. She told Schuyler they were almost penniless, their entire fortune gone, forcing Schuyler to shop at thrift stores, use public transportation, and put up with teasing and bullying from her wealthy schoolmates. In truth, as her grandfather Lawrence Van Alen reveals when he returns to New York, they are not as wealthy as some families, but they are far from being as close to penniless as Cordelia told Schuyler they were.

Blue Bloods is more than just a vampire series. It is a multigenerational family saga, with all the twists, turns, mysteries, plots, and conspiracies that the term implies. Just when readers decide that they know what the author is up to, de la Cruz turns the tables on them and reveals a fact or an interaction she had carefully kept hidden, and sends them off in a new direction. *The Keys to the Repository* gives some of the answers, but not all of them, and it is primarily limited to the secrets in the first four books. In addition, there are many false leads and red herrings. Characters that seem known suddenly turn into someone, or some*thing*, else. All this means that fans can read the books more than once, discovering new facts and new clues with every reading.

Romantic connections and misconnections abound, growing more and more complex with each new volume. At first, it's Mimi and Jack, Schuyler and Oliver, Bliss and Dylan. But then Jack and Schuyler are mysteriously attracted to each other. Dylan disappears, and Schuyler realizes Oliver suddenly seems more like a boyfriend than the best friend he's always been. And with that, the game is on—will she, won't she; will he, won't he; it's decided, but it's not; it's forever, it's never; it's in the past and over, then in the present and on again. The reader never knows quite what to expect—with one exception. Oliver's love for Schuyler never sways or strays. It is rock solid.

Schuyler is one of the pivotal characters, because as a new soul, born of Gabrielle and a human father, she has not been through all the cycles, and her appearance in the vampire world changes relationships in unpredictable ways. Vampires and humans are not able to have children, so her very existence is a mystery, perhaps related to the fact that her mother was the archangel Gabrielle, one of the Uncorrupted, rather than a fallen angel. Some of the Blue Bloods and the Silver Bloods want to kill her because she is neither human nor vampire, and they believe the prophesies about her bringing death and destruction to the vampire world.

Mimi and Jack Force are also pivotal characters as the most powerful vampires after the Uncorrupted. They are bound together, mated for eternity, and must seek each other out during each cycle. Schuyler's appearance changes that, when she and Jack are mysteriously attracted to each other, and Mimi seethes with jealousy and anger, willing to do anything at all to keep Jack by her side, as he has been throughout the centuries. That anger provides motive for several of the plot twists, and drives one of the later novels almost completely. De la Cruz has done a magnificent job of comparing and contrasting the relationships between the various couples in the books, showing how possessiveness can backfire and how love can grow when it's given its freedom. Love cannot be demanded or coerced, and attempting to do that results in negativity and sorrow.

Bliss is another mystery, holding a secret that even she doesn't know about. She's a transplant from Texas and doesn't fit in with the urbane and sophisticated vampire teens at school. She seems to be alone through most of the books, not really connecting with anyone other than Dylan and Schuyler, and unaware of her dark heritage, until the knowledge is forced upon her, and she must decide what her destiny will be. Her one positive connection is to her younger sister, Jordan, but finally even that one is taken from her.

Oliver is the only one of the six main characters who is a Red Blood. His family has been tied to the Van Alen family for centuries, and he was bound to Schuyler as her conduit at birth. They share a special friendship, and she loves and depends on him much more than she realizes. He wants what is best for her, even when it isn't what is best for him. It is the antithesis of Mimi's selfish love for Jack.

Dylan is one of the six protagonists, but a minor character, making brief, but significant, appearances. He and Bliss are not a couple for long, and he doesn't seem to connect in a significant way with anyone else. He is manipulated by several of the other characters to create plot twists and seems to serve no other purpose except as a love interest for Bliss.

De la Cruz uses several stylistic elements in all of her books to set parts of the story apart, including diary entries, newspaper clippings, transcripts of conversations, excerpts of reports of various kinds, and other sources that introduce information not known to the core characters or pertinent to the main story line, but that inform the reader about some of the plot twists that are ongoing or approaching. The different formats and typefaces alert readers, letting them know that this is important information, even if it doesn't fit with what is currently happening in the novel. In several of the volumes these elements can be read separately, and they create their own story within the larger story. For instance, in *Blue Bloods*, the first volume, Catherine's diary tells the story of the Blue Bloods' arrival in the New World, the hardships they endured, the loss of the colony at Roanoke, and the discovery that the Silver Bloods they had battled for so long had followed them to the New World.

De la Cruz has nine titles planned for the series, in three three-book story arcs, although her editor has hopes of getting past volume 19! She completed all the outlines, mythology, and characters sketches before she started to work on the first book and is looking forward to staying in the Blue Bloods world for a while.[3] *Witches of East End*, the first book in her new adult fantasy series, which takes place in the Blue Bloods world, was published in 2011, as was the next volume in the Blue Bloods series, *Lost in Time*. She is also working on a Blue Blood spinoff series starring Bliss, and the first volume of it will be *Wolf Pact*, which is tentatively scheduled for 2012.[4]

Notes

1. Cynthia Leitich Smith, "Author Interview: Melissa de la Cruz on *Blue Bloods*," *Cynsations* (blog), September 25, 2007, http://cynthialeitichsmith .blogspot.com/2007/09/author-interview-melissa-de-la-cruz-on.html.
2. Smith, "Author Interview."
3. Smith, "Author Interview."
4. Melissa de la Cruz, "Publication Dates and Award News," Official Website of Melissa de la Cruz," http://www.melissa-delacruz.com/.

Bibliography

De la Cruz, Melissa. *Blue Bloods*. New York: Hyperion, 2006.
——. *Masquerade*. New York: Hyperion, 2007.
——. *Revelations*. New York: Hyperion, 2008.
——. *The Van Alen Legacy*. New York: Hyperion, 2009.
——. *Misguided Angel*. New York: Hyperion, 2010.
——. *Bloody Valentine*. New York: Hyperion, 2010.
——. *Keys to the Repository*. New York: Hyperion, 2010.

4

The Drake Chronicles
by Alyxandra Harvey

The Drake Chronicles series, by Alyxandra Harvey, features a shy
vampire princess with seven overprotective older brothers and a
fearless, snarky best friend. Solange Drake is the first female blood-
born vampire in over nine hundred years, and the current ruler of
the vampires is determined to destroy her. It's all because of an old
prophecy about all the different tribes of vampires being united by
a daughter born to an ancient family, and the current ruler, Lady
Natasha, isn't from an ancient family, so the moment Solange was
born, the Drake family was exiled from the courts.

The family is one of three ancient families that form the Raktapa
Council (the Drakes, the Amritas, and the Joiiks), which was created
hundreds of years ago when they realized they were not like other
vampires—their change to vampire is not because of a bite, but
because of genetics, passing the vampire gene down through the
male line. They transform into vampires on their sixteenth birthday,
after being mortal for the first fifteen years of their lives. For several
weeks just before the transformation, they become very weak and
tired and are very vulnerable. The transformation itself is somewhat
dangerous, requiring close supervision and both vampire and human blood to survive.

Most vampires, however, are made rather than born. When the
transformation is monitored, and the genetic changes go smoothly,
made vampires are very similar to born vampires. New vampires,

both born and made, are particularly vulnerable to sunlight and to bloodlust when they wake up, vulnerabilities that take several years to wear off. Most bedrooms of new vampires have a small refrigerator stocked with bags of blood, so they can feed as soon as they wake up with a terrible and uncontrollable blood thirst. It can be dangerous for humans to be around young vampires at this time because the young human blood smells so good, but those who live and work with the Drake family know they are safe. The Drakes are vegetarian vampires, who drink only animal blood, except for emergency situations, such as a severe injury, when they drink only from willing humans.

There are several groups of vampires. "Normal" vampires, either blood born or made, live under the rule of a queen (unless they've been exiled, as the Drake family has), and many of them choose to live on animal blood rather than human blood, unless they are ill and require more powerful blood. However, Lady Natasha does feed from humans and is not particularly circumspect about it, which has resulted in some criticism and controversy. As a result, some vampires do not support her and are quietly counting on Solange to make the prophecy come true, something she is not enthusiastic about. Most of these vampires do not kill unless they are forced to do so; they live peacefully with the humans around them, for the most part. Most humans do not know that vampires exist.

Lord Montmartre is feared by all the vampires, because he is an ancient, twisted vampire who has been turning humans for years. He has been so violent when he does it that he has created three other types of vampires. He leaves the humans half-turned and usually buried in the ground, so they have to complete the transformation on their own, without any help. The process is so difficult that it changes them, giving them two sets of fangs instead of one. Those that survive and remain loyal to Montmartre are under his control and are called the Host.

The ones that survive the transformation and turn from Montmartre call themselves the Cwn Manau, or the Hounds of the Mothers. They were either strong enough to survive on their own, or they were rescued by other Hounds and remain loyal to that clan. They are determined to kill Montmartre and his Host and find as many of his victims as possible and rescue them. Reclusive cave dwellers, they are ruled by a *shamanka*, a female shaman or witch, and are able to create and use magic. They are all warriors and hunters, both men and women, and their society is matriarchal. They are seen as primitive because they live in caves and wear bones in their hair; they are disdained by other vampires, even while they are feared as Montmartre's creations. However, a visitor to one of their caves would be surprised at the level of luxury they have managed to achieve. These caves aren't dank and damp, but warm and inviting.

The Hounds are also a very canine-oriented culture and are especially known for their wolfhounds, who bond with an individual Hound for companionship, protection, tracking, and hunting. Hounds are always accompanied by at least one dog, and usually more. In addition to their close connections with their own dogs, Hounds also have power over other dogs belonging to either vampires or humans and are acknowledged as alphas by them.

The most dangerous of Montmartre's creations are the Hel-Blar, who are the most damaged in the transformation process. Their skin is blue from the bruising and the bloodlust during their transformation, and all of their teeth are sharply pointed fangs that cannot be retracted, as can those of all the other types of vampires. Their bite or their saliva can turn both humans and vampires into Hel-Blar. They are uncontrollable, vicious, and live to kill. Even Montmartre is afraid of them, because they want to kill him and his Host even more than the Hounds do. They don't seem to have any real society or culture. They are just killing machines.

In this universe, vampires are accepted by some humans and hunted by others. Many vampires marry and have children because they are not undead but possess a genetic mutation that they can pass on to their children, if they marry a human, and can pass on to a human by biting him or her. Most vampires turn their human spouses into vampires when both consider the time to be right, so they can live their long lives together. Other humans work with and serve as guards for the vampires, who are unconscious during daylight and so must be protected. Very old vampires are less affected by the sun, but still must be careful. The Drakes live in a home with specially treated glass that blocks the dangerous UV rays, so if they are awake during the daytime, they are able to enjoy the sun inside. However, vampires can burn to death in the sun if left in it long enough. They can also be burned by "holy water"—something used by the Helios-Ra (vampire hunters; see later explanation) as a weapon. This holy water is charged with UV rays and vitamin D, two substances to which vampires have a deadly allergy when encountered in a concentrated form.

Vampires have superhuman strength, speed, and senses, and disappear in a puff of ashes when staked in the heart. This latter quality may have been a strategy evolved over time to prevent their bodies from being discovered by humans. Another safety measure are the pheromones that vampires emit that keep humans confused and attracted to them at the same time and allow vampires to feed from them without humans remembering it. Some vampires have stronger pheromones than others, and because Solange is close to transformation, hers are attracting many male vampires who are determined to be with her. Bouquets of flowers and gifts litter the foyer of Solange's home. Even Montmartre is sending gifts, because he believes in the prophecy and wants to be king to her queen. But not all of the vampires smell good—the pheromones of the Hel-Blar smell as horrible as the vampires look.

Some humans live peacefully with the vampires, but others see them as monsters who prey on humans. Some of the latter have formed the Helios-Ra, a paramilitary organization devoted to hunting and killing vampires. Members of the Helios-Ra can be identified by the stylized sun tattoo they all get when they join. Liam Drake, father of Solange and her brothers, made a treaty with Hart, the Helios-Ra leader, before any of his children were born. The family would not feed from humans, and the Helios-Ra would leave the family alone. But now the treaty has been broken, or at least the Helios-Ra believe it has, and they are once again going after the Drakes as well as any other vampires they can find. In addition to the stakes and holy water mentioned earlier, they also have Hypnos powder that gives them the power to paralyze humans or vampires, forcing them to do whatever the vampire hunter tells them to do. It contains several zombie herbs and also small amounts of ancient vampire blood, old enough to be from Enheduanna, the oldest vampire in existence. Her blood has a hypnotic effect that takes away the willpower of the individual it touches. Even Hel-Blar can be controlled by it. How the Helios-Ra got it is unknown, but some theorize that their scientists actually created it.

The first character we meet in the Drake Chronicles is Lucy, who is Solange's best friend, a human who has grown up with the Drake family because their parents have been friends for years. Her parents are hippies, who value peace, light, meditation, and tofu. They make Lucy crazy, but she loves them, and they love her. They don't really approve of Lucy's getting the same kind of fighting training that all of the Drake children have, nor of her inclination to jump into situations feetfirst without evaluating them. Her mother is particularly concerned about Lucy's temper, which is getting worse. In a fight-or-flight scenario, Lucy will always choose to fight, creating bad chi and karma for herself. Her parents go to a variety of hippie events and conferences, and Lucy stays with the Drakes while they are gone.

Lucy speaks her mind—something that Harvey says made her great fun to write—and is always up to mischief and mayhem.[1] She is fierce about defending Solange and other vampires from those who speak against them, saying that vampires are just as human as she is, but with a disease that makes them "differently abled." She believes that calling them monsters is racism, pure and simple. She adores Liam and Helena Drake, seeing them as secondary parents, and the brothers all treat her like a second sister. Lucy is smart, fearless, sarcastic, and snarky, and she provides much of the humor in the books. She has style and loves beaded scarves, silver and turquoise jewelry, and slinky skirts. Her relationship with Nicholas, Solange's youngest brother, has always been confrontational, until suddenly it's not, and they move from irritating friends to a committed couple. Their story is told in *Hearts at Stake*, the first book in the series.

Solange contrasts sharply with Lucy's ferocity and fire because she's quiet and shy, and is almost painfully apart from the world of humans. She has been protected as a vampire princess all her life and has always been homeschooled because of it. But she received the same training in fighting as her brothers and knows how to protect herself. As a result, Solange hates that everyone around her tries to take care of her, and she chafes under the obligation to stay safe. She loves to make pots and prefers comfortable rather than stylish clothes—cargo pants and a T-shirt, frequently stained by clay. Not only has she learned all the standard school subjects, but she's also a skilled fighter, and her many-times-great aunt, Hyacinth, who lives with the family, has taught her as many of the skills of an old-fashioned lady as she can—how to curtsy, make a proper pot of tea, and hold a polite conversation. Solange however, didn't take to embroidery, fashion, or music.

When Kieran Black, a Helios-Ra, comes to the Drake home as a bounty hunter, Solange is strangely attracted to him, as he is to her. Everyone around her is deeply concerned about her upcoming transformation. Drake males have been transforming for centuries, so everyone knew what to expect when her older brothers transformed. But no one knows exactly how the process will affect Solange, as a female. Kieran and Solange's story is also told in *Hearts at Stake*. The brothers Drake all watch over their sister and fight for their family, and according to Harvey, are all fated to find their mates by the time the series ends, sometime in the future.

Logan, who is next to Nicholas in age, is a fighter with style. He prefers the velvet frock coats and lace-cuffed shirts of the 1700s to a T-shirt and jeans but can hold his own in a fight nevertheless. He is a match for shy Isabeau, one of the Hounds, who was turned to a vampire just after the French Revolution but was buried underground for two hundred years until she was found and unearthed by Hounds sent to England to dig her up and bring her to the United States. It has only been a year and a half since then, and she is more comfortable with Logan's manners and style, which remind her of the boys she knew when she was human. She is also very powerful when using magic and is apprenticed to the leader of the Hounds. The second volume of the series, *Blood Feud*, includes Isabeau and Logan's story.

Quinn and Connor are twins, born a year before Logan. In *Out for Blood*, Quinn falls for Hunter Wild, a member of the Helios-Ra and Kieran's close friend. An inveterate flirt until he meets Hunter, Quinn has been called crazy more than once because of the delight he takes in fighting. He's always happy to get into a good fight, especially if it's with several opponents.

Connor is a computer genius who makes sure that the family's technology works, but Quinn's phone has so many girls' numbers in it, that sometimes even Connor can't fix it. In *Bleeding Hearts*, the fourth volume, Connor falls for Christabel, Lucy's cousin who comes to live in the same town. He says he's the smarter twin, but Quinn maintains he is the cuter. Like many twins, they are very close, sometimes almost able to read each other's minds. Although she has planned for a fifth volume, and perhaps more,[2] author

Alyxandra Harvey has not yet revealed her plans for the three older brothers, Sebastian, Marcus, and Duncan.

Harvey's inspiration for the series was Snow White and the Seven Dwarves,[3] but she wanted to create a vampire family with alpha males and warrior females.[4] She also wanted to create families that were close even when they rubbed each other the wrong way, with strong parents whose bonds are unbreakable, even when they disagree. Her female characters are able to stand up to the men in their lives and believe they can take care of themselves, even when maybe they can't. Helena Drake is a warrior, always ready for battle and furious when her sons or her husband try to protect her. Liam is the peacemaker, interested in creating alliances with the Helios-Ra and Hounds and uniting the vampire tribes and families under his wife's rule. But Liam is still just as much of an alpha male as his sons are, and while he isn't usually able to control his wife, he is always able to persuade her and to compromise with her.

By creating several different kinds of vampires, Harvey is able to allow some of them to be appealing and others frightening, setting up a good-versus-evil battle. Locating some of her characters outside the vampire culture gives them a chance to change their perspectives when they come in contact with different kinds of vampires and learn that there are some you fight and some you love.

Harvey also uses multiple perspectives in her books to increase the complexity of the plot and allow the same situation to be seen from two points of view. *Hearts at Stake* is narrated by Lucy and Solange, and *Blood Feud* is narrated by Logan and Isabeau. *Out for Blood* is narrated by Hunter and Quinn, and *Bleeding Hearts* is narrated by Lucy; her cousin, Christabel; and Connor. Harvey says using multiple perspectives also gave her a chance to examine the human and the vampire parts of the stories separately, giving her more flexibility in how she was able to move around in the world of the series.[5]

Harvey's interest in period dress, the Middle Ages, sword fighting, and archery is also reflected in the series.[6] She uses these and other things to create separate cultures for the vampires, the Helios-Ra, and the Hounds. The Hounds use magic of various kinds to create charms and spells and to tell the future. Their culture is strongly matriarchal, and they are determined to wipe out Montmartre and his Host, and so are skilled trackers and fighters.

The Helios-Ra have a military culture that encourages young volunteers to combat the monsters they believe vampires to be. Their culture seems to be more male dominated than the other two. Young hunters train at the Helios-Ra Academy, a four-year school that involves classroom subjects and also a wide variety of fighting techniques. The students in the different years are frequently set off against each other for training purposes. The teachers are well known for their hunting skills, and getting through the academy successfully is not easy, to say the least.

Notes

1. SciFiGuy, "Guest Author—Alyxandra Harvey," *SciFiGuy.ca* (blog), December 15, 2009, http://www.scifiguy.ca/2009/12/guest-author-alyx andra-harvey.html.
2. SciFiGuy, "Guest Author."
3. SciFiGuy, "Guest Author."
4. Hagelrat, "Alyxandra Harvey—Interview," *Un:Bound* (blog), December 11, 2009, http://hagelrat.blogspot.com/2009/12/alyxandra-harvey -interview.html.
5. Hagelrat, "Alyxandra Harvey."
6. Hagelrat, "Alyxandra Harvey."

Bibliography

Harvey, Alyxandra. *Hearts at Stake*. Fairfield, PA: Walker Books for Young Readers, 2009.
———. *Blood Feud*. Fairfield, PA: Walker Books for Young Readers, 2010.
———. *Out for Blood*. Fairfield, PA: Walker Books for Young Readers, 2010.
———. *Bleeding Hearts*. New York: Walker Children's, 2011.

5

The Chronicles of Vlad Tod by Heather Brewer

Heather Brewer was an outcast when she was a teenager, bullied, picked on, and the most unpopular kid in her small town of about eight hundred.[1] She was also drawn to the darker side of life, so it's no surprise that when she started to write, she chose to write about an outcast half-vampire. She sets her story in Bathory, a nod to the famous Erzebet (Elizabeth) Bathory, the Countess of Blood, who lived in the 1500s and bathed daily in the blood of young virgins.[2] The closest town is Stokerton, and when Vlad graduates from high school, he is heading to Stokerton University—or Stoker U. Sly humor runs through the series and gives it a lightness that is in sharp contrast to the somewhat dark world that Vlad lives in, especially in the later volumes.

The vampire world of Elysia (the "Elysian Fields" in Greek mythology is the place where the blessed and the virtuous go after death) is overlaid on the human world, with entrances or tunnels that connect them. There are nine councils of vampires, and they are spread all over the world. They are bound by vampire laws, and the punishment for breaking many of them is death. There is also a prophecy that many vampires believe—that one day a boy will be born of a vampire and a human, who will be the Pravus and who cannot be killed. He will rule vampiredom and enslave all the humans. There is only one person who has been born of a human and a vampire—Vladimir Tod. Some dismiss the prophecy as a fairy tale, others believe in it passionately, and its presence drives the series in many ways.

Brewer's vampires eat food just for appearances, but it doesn't really nourish them like blood does. They do not have to kill a human to feed, although most of the time they do, depending on the level of hunger and the strength of their will. They have fangs, can read and control minds, fly, and vanish from sight. Vlad can rise, descend, and hover in midair, and when he's older, he also develops superhuman strength and speed. He has a reflection, and neither silver nor crosses bother him at all, but he can't eat Italian food, because garlic is a deadly poison for vampires. Going outside means Vlad always has to wear sunblock—he'd burn without it, although he isn't as allergic to sun as some vampires, who burst into flames if they go out in the sunlight. He also has trouble sleeping at night; his vampire genes keep him awake, so he's tired a lot of the time during the day. Thin and pale and geeky, Vlad is a perfect target for bullies, and Bill and Tom have picked on him for years. He has only one friend, Henry, whom he's known all his life. They are very close throughout the series, and Henry is the only human who knows that Vlad is a half-vampire. They have been "blood brothers" since they were eight, when Vlad accidentally revealed to Henry that he was a vampire, and Henry asked Vlad to bite him. However, they don't realize until much later that their exchange of blood has made Henry Vlad's drudge, a blood slave who must obey Vlad's every command.

Vladimir Tod is in eighth grade when the series begins, and it ends with his high school graduation. He is a half-vampire—his mother was human, and his vampire father deserted Elysia because he loved her. They both loved Vlad very much, and he remembers them as gentle, caring parents. But they were killed when he was only ten, and he's always blamed himself for their deaths and continues to mourn their loss. He now lives with Nelly, who was his mother's closest friend and helped Mellina deliver him. Vlad's vampire half requires blood, so it's handy that Nelly is a nurse, and she steals blood from the hospital just before the date on the bag expires. (She must be very good at it, since she's never caught, and at one point in the series, Vlad is drinking numerous bags a day.) She also makes him peanut butter and jelly sandwiches for lunch every day, with capsules of blood in them, to make sure he doesn't get hungry at school. And, of course, he has blood for breakfast, dinner, and the occasional snack, often with the chocolate chip cookies Nelly makes, the only thing she cooks well. Vlad is thin, pale, and weak, because his father taught him to never feed directly from humans, but his hunger is growing, and soon he may not be able to resist.

Brewer had to create an enemy for Vlad and did so in Joss, one of Henry's cousins, who has been a member of Slayer Society since he was a very young child. Slayers are very secretive, and while there are over a hundred slayer families, there's only one slayer per generation and only a slayer can recognize the others. They are carefully trained and even brainwashed to believe that vampires are human-killing monsters, although Brewer only hints at the lengths to which those in charge will go to ensure instant and unquestioning obedience. Each slayer carries a tool kit of weapons—a stake tipped with silver, garlic serum, a crucifix, a rosary, and other things to use when slaying a vampire. By the time the reader meets Joss, he has killed twenty-five vampires and has never failed on a mission. He saw his little sister killed by a vampire when she was only five and decided to become a slayer. Every time Joss kills a vampire, he whispers, "For you, Cecile" just before he stakes them. When Joss finds out Vlad is the vampire he must kill, their friendship ceases to matter. He knows Vlad, but still believes he is a monster who deserves to die.

While the first two books (*Eighth Grade Bites, Ninth Grade Slays*) are shorter and involve less violence, which is appropriate for Vlad's age in those volumes, the last three (*Tenth Grade Bleeds, Eleventh Grade Burns, Twelfth Grade Kills*) are significantly longer and increasingly dark and violent, especially the final volume when Vlad comes into the full power of his Pravus nature. Particularly disturbing is the scene in which he controls all the beings in Bathory with just a single word and bends them to his will. There are also several other disturbing scenes, as a number of the major characters are killed off for various reasons. The latter volumes include layers of lies, betrayals, and treachery that make the plots complex and characters' reactions sometimes difficult to read. There are losses and deaths that must be mourned, secrets told and untold, mysteries revealed and not revealed, relationships that tear apart and mend together, people who are not what they seem or what they say. Readers will frequently be moved to tears, while they are unable to stop reading.

But these layers work in the context of the series, since Vlad and his friends are getting older and must deal with much more complex issues involving questions of ethics, philosophy, bigotry, self-identity, and the existence of evil.

Vlad also has to deal with his relationships with Meredith and Snow, his two loves. They are polar opposites—Meredith, a pretty and popular girl who is frightened by the darkness she sees in Vlad, and Snow, a broken girl who finds the strength to overcome her background. Vlad must decide what love is, and who is able to love him, before he's able to make the choice between them. He is able to release Meredith when he realizes that Snow is far more important to him and far better for him, because she accepts and loves him unconditionally just as he is. Meredith is unable to cope with the darker side of Vlad's life, while Snow, with her abusive background that is *her* darker side, is able to; there are no lies between Vlad and Snow. She loves with her whole heart, while Meredith always held back some of herself.

In the last two volumes, Vlad's special vampiric powers continue to increase every time he is threatened and has to fight back. There is no doubt that Vlad is no longer a normal vampire. He is the vampire Pravus, and he is a human. He straddles two worlds, the world of humans and the world of vampires. Finally accepting that he is both a unique human and a unique vampire, Vlad decides to bring those two conflicting worlds together and introduces Joss to his father. Introduces a slayer to a vampire. Mortal enemies. Both people he loves. When Henry questions him about it, Vlad says, "I stand between mortal enemies. I needed to know, just for one moment, that peace is possible."[3] He is suddenly aware of how the different parts of his life are tearing him apart and how much he wants the conflict to be over. He needs what passes for normalcy in his life.

Yet he is still the Pravus and must cope with the visions he begins to have about his power and how it tempts him to go over to the dark side, something he is determined not to do. Resisting the dark side becomes easier once he learns that the visions are no more than a snapshot of reality, a picture of what *might* happen, rather than what *will* happen, and they must be interpreted to be understood. But when Snow is staked and Vlad is unable to transform her, that dark side takes over, resulting in a difficult scene in which Vlad demonstrates just how much power he has—more than any other vampire, slayer, or human has ever had or will ever have.

Vlad is forced to face the dark side of his nature, as well as his increasing and threatening powers that allow him to kill a man with just the force of his will and control both humans and vampires with just a word. Throughout the series, Vlad is betrayed by people he trusts, and he must uncover this network of lies and treachery and learn to trust others again. He is forced to break bridges and then rebuild them. And he must look inside himself and face the monster he fears he has become. Vlad must also face his fear of intimacy, of loving and of connecting with someone he's loved almost from the first moment he saw her. He must not only learn to trust others around him but also learn to trust himself. Vlad loses great chunks of his being and must learn how to live without them. He has, however, at the end of the series, come to peace with who he is, anticipating his destiny and what lies ahead.

The last volume is one that readers will want to read again as soon as they've finished it, because seeing all the lies and implications and betrayals as they are built up through the book, knowing when lies are being told, gives an extra insight into the author's structuring of the book. Heather Brewer is adamant that this is the end of the series, but the first volume of a spinoff series, The Slayer Chronicles, titled *First Kill*, was published in 2011. It begins about a year after this series ends, and while Vlad's series focuses mostly on the school year, with only glimpses of the summers between them, Joss's series focuses on the summers, when he is part of the Slayer Society, and shows readers what he had to go through to be trained as a slayer. Brewer promises that some of the characters whom readers have grown to know and love will make appearances in the new series as well.[4] Perhaps Brewer's not as eager to leave Bathory and Stokerton—and Vlad—as she says she is.

The popularity of this series seems to be due to the realism of the characters and the situations and settings in which they find themselves. Teens and tweens are going to recognize them from their own lives and immediately identify with them. I also think it is due to the duality of Vlad's character, his being both a vampire and a human. It has to do with his being thin and weak and pale in eighth grade, and powerful enough to do anything by the time he's a senior. He moves from hating himself and his life, through learning about himself, to understanding that he can become the person he wants to be. He is an outcast who turns into a hero. Over and over, things are taken away from him, and one way or another, he manages to bounce back. As he does, he learns, and changes, and grows. And if *he* can do it, then maybe someone else can too.

In addition, Vlad, in spite of being a vampire, is a deeply good and ethical person. He feels guilt for his parents' death, he refuses to drink directly from humans for fear of harming them, and he pushes both Meredith and Snow away from him because he doesn't want to hurt them. He even believes that the evil and insane D'Ablo might have been saved had he not been killed before Vlad could convince him to change his ways. Even though Joss tries to kill him several times, Vlad refuses to give up on their friendship and forgives him unconditionally each time. He struggles to believe in the good in people but doesn't always see the good in himself. He is a purely good soul, able to resist the dark lure of the absolute power of the Pravus.

Vlad is not the only character who develops throughout the series; the other teens in the stories grow and change too. Snow goes from a girl who allows her stepfather to abuse her to one who finds the strength to fight back and to win. She goes from hanging on the edges of the goth group, to being her own person, understanding herself, being sure of herself, and being able to take care of herself. She is able to keep herself from being abused and open herself to love and to happiness, a difficult process she could not have accomplished without great inner strength. And all without losing her sense of style! This is a powerful message for teens who come from similar situations.

Snow's attracted to Vlad first because he protects her, and then because when he gets to know her, he also understands her, her scars and fears, and is ready to help her overcome them. But while she has grown stronger, Snow sometimes still doubts her worth. When she and Meredith are at Vlad's Thanksgiving dinner in the final volume, Vlad is careful to pay close attention to Snow, knowing without having to ask that she is afraid of Meredith because not only is she Vlad's ex-girlfriend, but she is also beautiful, and while Snow has begun to believe in herself, because of her background she still isn't always able to see her own beauty or that she is worthy of

Vlad. But Vlad does and is ready to stand by her until she sees how good and how beautiful she is, inside and out.

Henry also grows and changes in some ways, while always staying constant in others. His loyalty to Vlad is unswerving, and even when he wants to be released from being Vlad's drudge, he doesn't pull very far away from him. From the time he finds out that Vlad is a vampire, Henry is fascinated rather than repulsed or afraid. He doesn't desert Vlad when he himself becomes a part of the popular crowd, and he listens to Vlad's insight and advice. The two of them are a pair, whether it's because of the blood bond or not. And by the end of the series, Henry has come to understand that Vlad needs him, relies on him in ways that he relies on no one else. They learn from each other because of their closeness and their trust. Henry teaches Vlad humility and how to use his power wisely, and Vlad teaches Henry the pain of treating others like things rather than like people. Their friendship, their connection, is no less a marriage than Vlad's connection with Snow, and it will be there for them as long as Henry lives.

Joss is something of an enigma, which is perhaps the reason Brewer decided to write a series about him—so she could find out more about him. When we meet Joss, he has obviously been manipulated by adults wanting to use his talent for staking to their own advantage. He doesn't seem to have had much of a childhood since by the time he's a freshman in high school, he's traveled all over the world at the bidding of the Slayer Society, staked twenty-five vampires, and has never missed. Henry is Joss's cousin, but Vlad becomes his only friend, someone who likes him and enjoys being with him without the obligation of a family member. This seems to be something he's never experienced before, and the strength of that connection comes into sharp conflict with his years of slayer experience when he finds out that Vlad is the vampire he's been sent to kill. Joss is stuck in his life, always reliving the pain of his sister's death and the guilt he feels for not trying to save her, in spite of how young he was when it happened. He doesn't seem to make much progress during the series because he is unable to let go of the pain in his past. Joss makes friends with Vlad and regrets staking him, yet after he is retrained, his resolve returns, only to weaken again when Vlad refuses to see him as an enemy. Joss is unable to see that by not missing when he staked Vlad the first time, he actually helped Vlad prove that he is the Pravus—since Vlad should have died because Joss never misses. When he finally realizes that vampires are people too and repairs his relationship with Vlad yet again, he finally begins to distrust the slayers and their fanatical doctrines. But he still doesn't seem able to get over his past. Even on graduation day, he cringes from Vlad, apologizing yet again, as Vlad tells him once more that everything's okay, he forgave him months ago, and he needs to move on. It will be interesting to see how Joss develops in the new series.

The author has also chosen teen characters from several stereotypes—goth, jock, popular crowd, outcast—and shown that under the skin they are more alike than not. It doesn't matter what people look like on the outside; it's who they are and how they live their lives that's important. Certainly this is a vital message for teens today. Brewer has salted the mixture with teens that are more twisted, mean, or just broken, who regress instead of progressing. Eddie is a particularly good example of this. When he's first introduced, Joss feels sorry for him, but Eddie has already been too bullied for too long and isn't willing to trust anyone. And once he decides that Vlad is different, he is unwilling to accept Vlad's or Henry's denials, always wanting to know what's going on, no matter the cost. There is no doubt that Eddie is broken from the beginning, and as he gets more and more invasive, twisted, angry, and vengeful, Vlad's original sympathy turns sour. In the end, Eddie gets what he wants—to be a vampire—only to find that he will have a huge price to pay for it. He ends up in Elysia, as Em's "annoying pet."

The goth group is the most interesting group of all. They are outcasts, shunned by the rest of the school, yet they are also the most accepting of the teen characters. They are the only ones who accept Vlad for what he is from the very beginning, trust him unconditionally, and offer him genuine friendship and love. They keep to themselves, knowing what the others think of them, but when Vlad rescues Sprat, they have the courage to thank him publicly and offer their friendship. Kristoff is the only one who doesn't accept Vlad, but that's just because Vlad is a real vampire, something Kristoff would like to be—although when vampire Eddie wants to bite him, Kristoff changes his mind and runs. The goths are Vlad's true friends—always there when he needs them.

The series is also enhanced by Brewer's website, particularly her blog. She loves to connect with her "Minion Horde" and spends a great deal of time responding to readers. As a former outcast, she empathizes with teens who feel alienated and ostracized, and shares her wisdom with them through her blog.[5]

While some authors are less willing to share with their readers, Brewer talks about her appearances, with lots of pictures of fans; about how to write a novel; about herself and her life—including the coffin couch in her office, of which she is inordinately proud. She shares herself and her feelings with them, offering both support and advice, and has been doing so for years.[6]

This is one author who seriously cares about her readers and knows that sometimes they need the encouragement and escape that they find in her books and her characters, and in herself. I have no doubt that while Vlad and his friends have changed the lives of the teens and tweens who have met them, Brewer has changed many more with the online connections she has made with her readers.

Notes

1. PenguinYoungReaders, *Heather Brewer Discusses the Chronicles of Vladimir Tod*, video, YouTube, July 27, 2009, http://www.youtube.com/watch?v=cgvvRfAreJg.

2. Barb Karg, Arjean Spaite, and Rick Sutherland, *The Everything Vampire Book: From Vlad the Impaler to the Vampire Lestat—A History of Vampires in Literature, Film, and Legend* (Avon, MA: Adams Media, 2009), 134.

3. Heather Brewer, *Twelfth Grade Kills* (New York: Dutton Juvenile, 2010), 156.

4. Heather Brewer, The Slayer Chronicles, "Heather's Books," Heather Brewer.com, http://heatherbrewer.com/books/index.php#slayer.

5. Heather Brewer, *Heather's Blog*, HeatherBrewer.com, http://heather brewer.com/blog/.

6. Brewer, *Heather's Blog*.

Bibliography

Brewer, Heather. *Chronicles of Vladimir Tod: Eighth Grade Bites*. New York: Dutton Juvenile, 2007.

———. *Chronicles of Vladimir Tod: Ninth Grade Slays*. New York: Dutton Juvenile, 2008.

———. *Chronicles of Vladimir Tod: Tenth Grade Bleeds*. New York: Dutton Juvenile, 2009.

———. *Chronicles of Vladimir Tod: Eleventh Grade Burns*. New York: Dutton Juvenile, 2010.

———. *Chronicles of Vladimir Tod: Twelfth Grade Kills*. New York: Dutton Juvenile, 2010.

Karg, Barb, Arjean Spaite, and Rick Sutherland. *The Everything Vampire Book: From Vlad the Impaler to the Vampire Lestat—A History of Vampires in Literature, Film, and Legend*. Avon, MA: Adams Media, 2009.

PenguinYoungReaders, *Heather Brewer Discusses the Chronicles of Vladimir Tod*. Video. YouTube, July 27, 2009. http://www.youtube.com/watch?v=cgvvRfAreJg.

6

Jessica's Guide to Dating on the Dark Side by Beth Fantaskey

When Beth Fantaskey started thinking about writing a novel, she didn't know that it would be a YA novel,[1] and she didn't know that she would become an author of the supernatural. She had a summer free to write and had been thinking about her two adopted daughters and what their birth parents might have been like and how finding out about those parents might change her daughters.[2] When she decided to take that idea to the extreme and make Jessica's parents vampires, she embraced the supernatural world. And she loves it—YA readers are interactive, and she enjoys communicating with them on her website. Some of her readers have also become good friends.[3] When those readers demanded to know more about Jessica and Lucius, she wrote a twenty-three chapter novella about their wedding and had her fans choose the wedding gown, the music for the wedding, and even whether there would be a kiss, a bite, or both at the end of the ceremony.[4]

But Fantaskey has a great deal of respect for her readers and doesn't underestimate their intelligence or the depths of their emotions. She thinks they feel just as profoundly as, maybe more profoundly than, adults, and she knew that as long as she got the emotions right, teens would connect with her books.[5] She also wanted to create a strong female lead, a character who embraces her own strength and her dark side and takes charge of her own destiny.[6] She deliberately made Jessica a normal-sized teen, with curves and frizzy hair, and enjoys letters from readers who comment on it, saying that finally a girl who's their size gets the guy—without having to get skinny first.[7] Lucius loves her just as she is, size, hair, and all—even her being an American teenager, free of the darker influences he had to grow up with.

Fantaskey didn't have to create the characters of Jessica and Lucius piece by piece, planning out character traits; they just sprang to life in her mind, with clear and distinct voices. When she was writing Lucius's letters to his uncle, she was literally able to hear his voice in her mind as she wrote, and his sarcasm and turns of phrase allowed her to inject some humor into the story. But because she wanted it to be Jessica's story and Lucius was such a strong character, she had to be very aware of how much she let him speak. In addition to giving Jessica more time onstage, limiting Lucius's voice also kept him at a distance, letting some things about him stay a mystery until the end.[8]

Fantaskey did do research on Romania when she was writing the novel but didn't do any research on vampires—in fact, she says she just tossed out all the classic characteristics and started from scratch. She had to be practical, since Lucius had to move within the human world Jessica lived in. So her vampires don't care about the sunlight (and *don't* sparkle); they aren't repulsed by garlic; they have reflections (Lucius wonders how he could comb his hair or tie his tie without a mirror); they can be hurt and recover quickly, although not instantaneously; and they can be killed only with a stake through the heart—although that would kill just about anyone. They don't transform into animals or mist, or sleep in coffins. They rule the dark side of nature, and Lucius's upbringing has certainly given him a dark side as well. And they do have fangs and drink blood, although they don't have to kill to do it. (Lucius carries around a giant-size "Strawberry Julius" for most of the book.) Males get their fangs at puberty, but females have to be bitten to make them come in—some reviews have commented negatively on this plot detail. Because Jessica seems so clueless about his kind, Lucius gives her a book about being a vampire: *Growing Up Undead: A Teen Vampire's Guide to Dating, Health, and Emotions.*

When Jessica learns about her heritage and destiny as Antanasia Dragomir, a Romanian vampire princess, her life goes through a complete upheaval, several times, as she begins to discern and experience her vampiric nature, as she realizes how deeply she has fallen in love with Lucius, and when she begins to understand just how dark and dangerous he is because of his upbringing. Fantaskey decided to make Lucius and Jessica betrothed from birth to give Jessica a reason to pay attention to him and recognize the link between them—she is a very rational girl who might otherwise have just brushed off this totally irrational person.[9]

This hilarious, snarky, and sarcastic novel turns upon the idea of identity—who am I, and what makes me, me? Do I control myself, or am I controlled by others or by the experiences I have had? Do I have a destiny, and how can I find it? What is weakness, what is strength, what is power? What is love? What is duty? Who am I? These are questions all teens ask, and they will be able to see themselves in Jessica and Lucius. The relationship between Lucius and Jessica has a "come here, come here, go away, go away" aspect to it, as do many teen relationships. They must both get to know themselves before they can get close enough to know each other.

Jessica may be eighteen, but she's never had a boyfriend and has been sheltered all her life, living on a nonproductive organic farm just outside a small rural town. She's a geeky mathlete and doesn't have a lot of friends. Lucius scares her, with his sophistication and wealth. She always thought she'd fall in love and get married, but Lucius doesn't even pretend to be in love with her or care about her. He wants to marry her to fulfill a pact and prevent a war. He wants to own her. Lucius is correct when he tells his uncle she could never be a princess or a queen—she doesn't believe in herself enough to rule. Not even finding out she is a Romanian princess and that Lucius is telling the truth about their betrothal makes any difference in her self-esteem. It's only when she discovers Lucius's lies and goes to confront him that she finally realizes her own power.

Lucius is arrogant, demanding, and rigid. But that exterior hides a boy who had a terrible childhood, brought up by his cold, harsh uncles, with cruel punishments for breaking the rules, and major duties and responsibilities that weigh heavily upon his shoulders. But he is also charming, courteous, intelligent, honorable, gallant, charismatic, powerful, friendly, and protective of women, especially Jessica and her mother. He believes that vampires are far superior to humans, and because he is a prince and has been given all that wealth and power can give him—private education, tailor-made clothes, and the best of everything—he is also demanding and arrogant and more than sure of himself. But he hasn't ever felt the comfort of someone who loved him or the freedom to do what he wants to do rather than what he's supposed to do. And sadly, until he comes to the United States and meets Jess and her parents, Lucius doesn't even know what he's missing. He must realize that gentleness and caring don't indicate weakness, and that real love is a true indicator of great strength. He knows what his duty is, but he neither believes in nor likes himself. He doesn't enjoy life—he endures it. And while Lucius doesn't think Jessica could be his princess, he is nevertheless hurt by her rejection and covers it up with arrogance. When he kisses her after she comes home from her Halloween date with Jake, he is beginning to see Antanasia in her, beginning to care about her. But she rejects him yet again, wounding him deeply.

Lucius's accident and injury change everything. Jessica realizes she really is a vampire, because when she sees Lucius drink blood, she feels its call to her, her vampiric nature asserting itself. But she also realizes how important he is to her, how she has connected with him, and how deeply the thought of losing him hurts her. "But the one thing I couldn't explain away was what I'd felt when I'd actually believed Lucius was dead. Grief. The deepest grief I could imagine. Like a jagged hole ripped in my soul."[10]

But Lucius sees her tears as a sign of weakness, making her even more unsuitable for him. She is too soft, too weak to survive in the cold harsh world of vampires, with its blood, violence, and endless struggle for domination. He is sure that his uncles mean to kill her after they are married and rule through him, as a puppet on the throne. He decides to break the pact and suffer the consequences.

The dance shifts, as Lucius begins to pull away from Jessica, seeing his own dark nature ever more clearly in sharp contrast to her love and purity, just as she begins to move toward him, finally attracted to the goodness she sees in him and the undeniable pull of their joined destiny. Faith serves as a tool, making Jessica aware that she has begun to think of Lucius as hers and the two of them as a couple. Unfortunately, Faith also reinforces Lucius's negative view of himself, and makes it easier for him to pull away from Jessica.

He falters only twice, and both times Jessica is able to get closer to him, able to show him how she is changing, beginning to believe in herself and believe in him and in them. But while Lucius sees that strength and admires it, he is still unable to see the goodness in himself and struggles with his attraction to Jessica, wanting to protect her from himself. By Jessica's birthday, he is able to recognize her new strength and beauty, but refuses to relent from his decision to stay away from her.

It is only when Jessica travels to his home in Romania and challenges him to kill her and prove that he is wholly evil that Lucius realizes he is unable to hurt her. He is finally able to accept her love and her trust in his goodness, even after all he has done. He begins to see himself as not completely broken, as he once believed he was, but someone who can love and be loved in return. In the end, he is finally able to see Jessica's true power, the power of her love and her faith, and let it bring him back to life and to wholeness. He will always have a dark side, but with Jessica he will have a light side as well.

The story of their wedding day, posted on Fantaskey's website, allows a glimpse of the people they are becoming and will be. They have been together in Romania for four months now, growing closer than ever, getting to know each other better, recognizing that they are, as Jessica puts it, "two flawed individuals who brought not only deep love but also old wounds to our marriage. Places inside of one another that we would always have to be careful with. I would always need to remember Lucius's awful childhood, and understand those times when he grew quiet and retreated into himself. And Lucius would always need to reassure me that the dark side of himself would never be unleashed on me."[11] After all the turmoil they have been through, they are marrying for love, and there is little doubt that their love and their connection will last a lifetime, however long that lifetime might be.

Fantaskey has promised that in the second volume, *Jessica Rules the Dark Side*, Jessica will have to learn to be a ruler, first with her husband, and then without him, as he is accused of murder and imprisoned. Jessica is completely out of her depth in this book, just as Lucius was in the first volume. But more is at stake this time—Lucius's life is at risk unless Jessica can find the murderer and have Lucius released. She will have to believe in herself and in her own power more than ever before—the Vladescus have not stopped plotting, and brand-new rulers are easy to overthrow. Jessica will have to achieve her full power as a princess and as a vampire if she and her husband are to survive.[12]

Notes

1. Julie, "Interview with Beth Fantaskey—Author of *Jekel Loves Hyde*," *Manga Maniac Café* (blog), February 14, 2010, http://www.mangamani accafe.com/?p=3761.
2. Kmont, "A Chat with Author Beth Fantaskey," *LurvViews* (blog), January 13, 2009, http://www.lurvalamode.com/2009/01/13/lurvviews -a-chat-with-author-beth-fantaskey/.
3. Chrissy, "Interview with Beth Fantaskey," *The Fictionistas* (blog), August 22, 2009, http://fictionistas.blogspot.com/2009/08/interview-with -beth-fantaskey.html.
4. Julie, "Interview."
5. Kmont, "Chat."
6. Adele, "Interview—Beth Fantaskey," *Persnickety Snark* (blog), February 19, 2009, http://www.persnicketysnark.com/2009/02/interview-beth -fantaskey.html.
7. Alex Bennet, "Author Interview: Beth Fantaskey," *Electrifying Reviews* (blog), April 25, 2010, http://www.electrifyingreviews.com/2010/04/ author-interview-beth-fantaskey.html.
8. Kmont, "Chat."
9. Adele, "Interview."
10. Beth Fantaskey, *Jessica's Guide to Dating on the Dark Side* (Boston: Harcourt Children's Books, 2009), 142.
11. Beth Fantaskey, *The Wedding of Antanasia Jessica Packwood and Lucius Valeriu Vladescu*, online book, 2009, bethfantaskey.com/wedding/wedding -chapt1.html.
12. Beth Fantaskey, "*Jessica Rules the Dark Side*: The Highly Anticipated Sequel to Jessica's Guide to Dating on the Dark Side," BethFantaskey.com, http://www.bethfantaskey.com/jessica-rules.html.

Bibliography

Fantaskey, Beth. *Jessica's Guide to Dating on the Dark Side*. Boston: Harcourt Children's Books, 2009.
——. *The Wedding of Antanasia Jessica Packwood and Lucius Valeriu Vladescu*. Online book, 2009. http://bethfantaskey.com/wedding/wedding -chapt1.html.

II

SHAPESHIFTERS: THE TRANSFORMING MONSTER

Werewolves are much more common animals than you might think.

—Daniel Pinkwater

Even a man who is pure in heart
and says his prayers by night,
may become a wolf when the wolfbane blooms
and the Autumn moon is bright.

—Curt Siodmak, in *The Wolf Man* (1941)

Werewolf stories have been told for centuries, and date back to the time of the earliest humans. The word "werewolf," or "man-wolf," was first recorded in Old English in the eleventh century,[1] but the word "shapeshifter" was not used until 1887;[2] and the word "lycanthropy," meaning to have the ability to change to the shape of a wolf, comes from Ancient Greece.[3]

While Ice Age hunters went after the same prey as wolves, there was no shortage of game, and the two species existed peacefully. Early humans might even have viewed wolves as fellow hunters from whom much could be learned.[4] Wolves were better equipped to hunt and kill—they had four legs, more speed and agility, and better teeth to attack prey. They were also more adaptable to harsh seasons like winter, and better at tracking, hunting, and working in a pack to find and kill much larger animals.[5] It may also be that early humans saw social and cultural commonalities between themselves and wolves—wolves mated for life, lived in extended family groups, shared food rather than competed for it, and participated in group ceremonies. Humans and wolves were both social animals, worked together in hierarchal groups, and both sexes helped care for and raise their young.[6] These similarities created a connection between them in the minds of early humans,[7] and helped establish strong bonds with wolves. But as humans became more sedentary, adopting an agricultural way of life to which wolves did not adapt, attitudes toward wolves changed. Instead of being admired for their hunting skills, they were seen as predators that were a danger to the new agricultural culture, feeding on farm animals and on the game humans hunted for food.[8] Wolves were seen as hostile, dangerous, unable to be civilized or tamed, and by the Middle Ages, they had also become associated with the devil.[9] They had been exterminated across Great Britain and Scandinavia by the thirteenth century, and virtually wiped out elsewhere in the world, particularly in the United States. The first U.S. bounty on wolves was enacted in 1630, and millions of dollars in bounty money was paid over the next three hundred years, resulting in the near eradication of the wolf by the 1970s, when there were only a few hundred animals left. The wolf was declared an endangered species in 1974, one of the first species to be so designated.[10] Perhaps this drive toward annihilation reflects our hatred of the more animalistic part of our own nature and an attempt to eliminate it.[11]

Many humans thought that wearing the skins of wolves would give humans wolflike powers, and some of the earliest religions had gods and goddesses with animal attributes.[12] Anubis, an Egyptian god, had the head of a jackal and was sometimes seen in full canine form;[13] Horus had the head of a falcon; and the famous giant Sphinx, one of the pyramids at Giza, had the head of a woman and the body of a lion.[14] Gods could also be shapeshifters who could turn into a variety of animals, and who could also turn humans into animals.

Many Greek and Roman myths include incidents of shapeshifting, and it is a prominent part of Scandinavian and Teutonic mythology.[15] Wolf packs roamed the forests of Norway and Denmark, and wolf spirits were worshipped in villages across Scandinavia, not only as predators, but also as protective and beneficial guardians. Some people believed that in the depths of winter, as the year ended, these spirits rewarded people who had worshipped them faithfully all year. Wolves were beginning to be seen as a symbol of protection as well as for power, cunning, and strength.[16] In 400 BC, a werewolf won medals at the Olympics, and in AD 77, the Roman philosopher Pliny wrote about the characteristics and lifestyles of the werewolf in his *Natural History*.[17] In *The Odyssey*, written near the end of the eighth century BC,[18] Homer included the story of Circe, a goddess that transformed men into animals, including lions and wolves. These wereanimals had the bodies of animals and the minds of men, but they had no way to communicate with humans. When a group of Odysseus's men went to investigate the smoke they'd seen in the forest, they were captured and turned into animals. Only one escaped to tell Odysseus what happened. After he visited the god Hermes, who was able to give him a cure for Circe's potion, Odysseus was able to rescue his men.[19]

By the late 1100s the idea of a man being able to transform into a wolf and back again had become solidified as part of the psyche of the human consciousness. In Britain and in France, books had been written by respected philosophers that confirmed that werewolves did indeed exist. Stories and poems were written about men who had become wild beasts, and the idea has come down to the present day—the ancient, savage beast lurking just below the surface of what we believe to be our civilized society. It embodies some of our oldest fears—separation from nature, fear of the wild places, fear of cannibalism, and even fear of ourselves, the primitive part of ourselves that reacts with wild, fierce emotion, rather than from behind the reasoned, civilized face with which we face daily life. Even the sound of the wolf howl, long and lonely, calling for its pack or its mate, could be the eerie echo of our worst and most primitive nightmares.[20]

Native Americans saw the wolf quite differently from Europeans. To them, it was a hunter and predator they admired, similar to the way Ice Age hunters saw the animals. Wolves had the cunning, speed, endurance, and fierceness when hunting prey and protecting the pack that made them the perfect guardian and protector for the tribe. This protection was particularly extended to the members of the tribe less able to take care of themselves—the youngest and the oldest—and to young men going through the rites of passage ritual, as they moved from childhood to manhood.[21] Even today, many individuals and tribes have the wolf as their totem.[22]

There are also stories of dogs who became men,[23] men who became dogs,[24] and saints or races of men who had the heads of dogs. These stories came from all over the world—Britain, Europe, Greece, Rome, Turkey, North Africa, Egypt, Crete, India, China, and Japan.[25] In the Scandinavian countries, berserkers were men who wore the pelts of bears or wolves and used psychological or psychotropic means to induce a "killing frenzy," making them fight more like the animal whose skin they wore, with greatly enhanced strength, speed, and ferocity. There is little doubt that these stories are all part of the heritage of the modern werewolf.[26]

Werewolves and shapeshifters have also been a part of folk and fairy tales from around the world. Sorcerers and witches can curse people into other shapes. A prince is turned into a beast or a frog because he unknowingly offends a witch. Little Red Riding Hood meets a talking wolf in the woods, who eats both her and her grandmother. A mermaid is transformed into a human, selkies change from human to seals when they put on their sealskins, and six princes are changed into six swans by their evil stepmother, and only their sisters can save them. *Aesop's Fables* also includes a number of stories of wolves who sometimes use disguises to go after both animals and people.[27] There have been animal husband folktales from countries and cultures around the world,[28] and *Beauty and the Beast* is probably the best known of the transformation fairy tales that developed from them. In *Beastly*, Alix Flinn focuses her story on two teens abandoned by their parents, left virtually alone to find their way in the world, deserted by the adults who were supposed to take care of them, and struggling to find someone to connect with.[29] This rendition offers today's teen much to identify with, as adolescent culture has grown increasingly disconnected from adult culture, forcing teens to learn how to grow up alone or with only their peers for company and advice.[30]

In the distant past, the boundary between humans and animals was not so clearly drawn as it is today. Humans and animals lived and hunted side by side, close to nature. Humans may have learned much from animals, especially canines, who were closest to them, taking on some of their characteristics and becoming aware of their own animalistic natures. And there was also the fear and fascination of the unknown, first what lies beyond the light of the campfire, and then beyond that, in strange lands never seen before. As humans spread further and further around the globe, exploring, seeing new sights, they brought home with them stories that tried to explain what they had seen—new lands, new animals, new peoples. It's not surprising that some of these stories involved man-beasts of various kinds, feral men who lived beyond the outskirts of civilization—the idea of a human who can also be a beast is a powerful one that addresses our fear of the unknown, both in the world and in ourselves. And what beast could engage the imagination more than our old friend and earliest enemy, the wolf?[31]

The animal that a shifter became varied by the location—generally the shifter became an animal that was feared in the area.[32] Werewolf stories and legends were particularly prevalent in Europe, where there were many wolves, and danger to humans was high. In contrast to this, there were fewer stories in England because in 1281, King Edgar I ordered that wolves be exterminated, although small pockets of wolves could be found in remote areas until about 1760, when the extermination was complete.[33] However, shifters could become many other predators, including bears, snakes, crocodiles, lions, leopards, and other dangerous creatures that would seem to outshine the wolf, except for its widespread reputation.[34] Modern authors have also created wereanimals that are less predatory and dangerous, including swans, other varieties of wildcats, foxes, opossums, birds, rats, dogs, hyenas, armadillos, and dragons.

Shapeshifters have always varied widely in their abilities and characteristics, depending on who wrote about them and the world they live in. A shapeshifter—or a therianthrope, a wereanimal—is defined as a human being who turns into an animal and later turns into a human being again.[35] The person has all the characteristics of that animal when in its form, so a werewolf could be a fierce hunter, attacking and killing both animals and humans, where a wereanimal of a less predatory species, say a rat or a fox, would be far less dangerous. The memories from the animal form may or may not be available to the person after returning to human form, and the human knowledge may or may not be available to the animal. The human part of the shifter may or may not be able to control or temper the actions or emotions of the animal.

Other variables include whether or not wounds to the animal carry over to the human shape or are healed by the shift. Most were-animals also heal supernaturally quickly, even if their injuries are not healed by their shifting. However, in some cases, wereanimals heal quickly only when wounded by a nonsupernatural creature. Wounds inflicted by another were or other supernatural creature may heal just as slowly as humans heal. There are also wide variations about how weres can be killed, and whether or not they are immortal or just live abnormally long lives. They share with vampires the need to move to prevent humans from discovering that they either don't age or age extremely slowly.

The transformation may be either voluntary or involuntary, depending on whether it is under the individual's control or forced upon him or her from the outside, such as shifting during the full moon or shifting as the result of a curse or the temperature/time of year.[36] There can also be a combination of causes for the shift, and it may be controlled by the individual to some extent until it is forced upon him or her. The shift may be instantaneous or prolonged, painless or difficult and painful, and may involve some sorts of bodily fluids as the human body shifts into an animal's form, changing from a bipedal humanoid to a quadrupedal or winged form. The level of pain the individual experiences also varies, and for some, it is connected with whether the shift was voluntary or forced. Some wereanimals are also able to half-shift and become a combination of human and animal. Generally, magical transformations are fast and smooth and may include clothing, while nonmagical ones are more lengthy and difficult and don't involve clothing, so that the shift from animal to human results in a naked human. There can also be differences based on whether the were is a hereditary were or a made one.

Some wereanimals who can control their shift—voluntary weres—are humans who transform themselves magically into their animal form whenever they choose to do so. They may go through some kind of ritual to do it, including putting on the pelt of an animal or chanting ritual words.[37] Others are true wereanimals, and their bodies actually change from human to animal form and back again by the force of their will and the power of their inner beast. Their change is under their control, but it may be triggered by intense emotion, such as fear or anger, that causes the shift to go out of control and occur even when the human half doesn't want it to.

For the were trying to live a human life, everything is overshadowed by the knowledge that the transformation will take place, and it may or may not be under the individual's control. There is also always the danger someone might be accidentally hurt or killed. If the were lives in a society where weres are not accepted, it's necessary to hide during the process of transformation and figure out how to change back somewhere near clothing, if it has to be removed prior to the transformation or is shredded during it.

There is also the question of whether or not the were has a human brain and can think when in animal form, or whether the animalistic brain of the were is in control of the animal body. If the predator's brain is in control there may be no way to prevent them from hunting and killing, other than caging the animal until the transformation back to human is complete. However, it's also important to remember that wereanimals are not always predators, and while in animal form, they may exhibit the gentler characteristics of their species as well.

The wereanimal infection is generally passed to humans through a bite, but in some cases, even a small amount of blood or saliva in an open wound can suffice. There are also hereditary weres, who are born as wereanimals and have never been human, although there are differences about when the first transformation takes place—some weres are able to transform from early infancy, others remain in human form until puberty. In some worlds/stories, hereditary weres can be born either male or female, but in others, the gene is passed down through one gender only, and members of the other gender must be bitten to become weres.

The connection between the moon and shapeshifting has been recorded since the seventeenth and eighteenth centuries, and grew even stronger in the nineteenth and twentieth centuries. The moon has always been connected with the idea of mental instability or mental illness. Our words "lunatic" and "lunacy" come from the French word for the moon, *la lune*. Greek physicians believed that since the body and brain were made up mainly of water, and the moon's gravitational pull had an effect on tides in the ocean, the moon could also have an effect on the water in men's bodies and brains, making them "off balance" and leading to strange and hysterical behavior around the time of the full moon, perhaps bringing out their "inner beast." It was thought that this beastlike behavior could be relieved by reducing the amount of water in the body and the brain, either by "trepanning" the brain (drilling a hole in the skull to let the excess water out) or by bleeding the individual, again to reduce the amount of water in the body.[38] This idea of the moon influencing human behavior has persisted until the present time, although we no longer use such inhumane and primitive methods to treat lunatics. But many police and fire officers swear that the number of strange crimes and other occurrences that are reported goes up at the time of the full moon, something that is anecdotally confirmed by others in public service professions, including librarians.

The werewolf is the most commonly seen shapeshifter or were-animal, perhaps because the idea of the wolf as a dangerous creature is prominent in the human psyche. Many languages include phrases or sayings that mention wolves. "The wolf at the door" implies impending danger that will soon arrive; "a wolf in sheep's clothing" refers to a person who is dangerous without appearing to be so, disguising his or her own nefarious schemes or violent purposes.[39] When someone is "thrown to the wolves," the person is abandoned to his or her own ruin; a "wolf" is someone who pursues women for his own benefit without caring about them; when someone is very hungry and eats very fast without much regard for manners or mess, he or she is said to be "wolfing down" food; and a "wolf pack" is a term used for a gang or a group of predators who are "on the prowl."[40] And in Christian terms, when speaking of Jesus as the shepherd and the church as his flock, the wolf who attacks the flock is representative of the devil.[41]

But the wolf is also a useful example to humans in many ways. The wolf (and other animals) lives in the constant present, without worrying about what is coming or has gone before, something that can seem refreshing to overstressed humans. The wolf is also assertive, standing up for what he believes to be important and right. He is quick to protect his mate, his children, and his pack. Even as a "lone wolf" he is not afraid, and is quick to defend himself. Self-assertiveness, when done in a nonaggressive way, is an effective way to problem solve, especially when confronted with a bully.[42] And the superhuman strength of werewolves may also be available to humans, since we have chemistry that makes us stronger in times of battle and aggression. Adrenaline is triggered by our fight-or-flight instinct and can give strength and endurance that can far outstrip what we can do without it, even without transforming into a wolf.[43] Stories (or urban legends) about mothers who lift cars to save their children caught under them are just one example of how werewolf superstrength can help us.

Werewolves must be constantly at war with themselves, straining to keep the savage beast half under the control of the civilized human half. In some novels, this conflict becomes more and more intense as the moon gets closer to the full moon; in others the struggle centers only on the night of the full moon. This duality is played out in other monsters as well, including other wereanimals, vampires, and even human split personality stories, such as *Dr. Jekyll and Mr. Hyde,* and is one of the sources of interest for teens, who are straddling the boundary between childhood and adulthood.

There are ways to prevent the transformation or make it less lethal, but there seems to be no cure. Professor Remus, from the Harry Potter series by J. K. Rowling, who was made a werewolf as a young child, must drink a daily potion in the week leading up to the full moon to ensure that his transformation is into a natural wolf rather than a deadly werewolf.[44] He was damaged mentally and physically when he was turned, and as an adult, he must still cope with that damage, as well as the monthly transformations he has to make. He is a brilliant intellectual and a deeply good and ethical man, a perfect example of how a curse can be evil, while the person cursed can still be a good and worthy human being.[45]

This more humane view of the werewolf is becoming more popular in today's literature and movies. Being a werewolf is just like having any other disastrous disease that people have to cope with, while trying to live a normal life. And the individual's struggle to control and contain both halves of his or her persona can teach those around him or her a new level of tolerance and compassion.[46] Teens are struggling with controlling themselves, as they learn to cope with the new sexual and emotional drives that are coming alive inside them. Their brains have not matured enough to allow them rational, logical decision making, and are instead controlled by a more primitive part, the amygdala, which responds to a perceived threat quickly, with violence and emotion and without "thinking through" the situation. The "inner beast" breaks out to overcome the "human side" of the individual.[47] It is all too easy for teens to respond as "beasts" with high levels of emotion triggered by the amygdala, even when they don't actually feel all that emotional. "Why am I acting like this? I don't really feel that intense."[48] The werewolf, snarling at danger, may also feel an emotional disconnect between its animal and human sides.

The appeal of the werewolf is in its ability to run free of civilized rules of society. It can let its beast out to play, whether it is the ravaging hunter or the more peaceful pack member and protector. As a wolf (or another animal), senses are keener, muscles are stronger, and power is greater. And the human side of the male werewolf is often the classic "bad boy," who can be so sexy, seductive, and attractive. The werewolf, in either form, is a rule breaker, a rebel who refuses to knuckle under to the strictures of civilized society. And at the same time, it is a member of a pack, a family that travels together and protects its members from outsiders who threaten them. Pack members have a history and a life together. They know where they belong and who they can count on. Life as a werewolf may involve fighting and violence, but it also involves safety and security.

These are some of the reasons why werewolves are so appealing to teens. Adolescents, the majority of them more or less alienated from their parents and other adults, are looking for family, protection, and information about how to live their lives today and in the future. They can find in werewolf novels today the kind of society that they would like to be a part of. The duality of the shapeshifter also appeals to teens, since they are doing shapeshifting in many ways themselves—their bodies, their emotions, and their ideas and assumptions are changing and shifting. From one day, hour, minute to the next, they are different people in the same body. Shapeshifter stories give them the chance to experience that duality and learn how to move from one world into the next.

In selecting titles to include in this book, both scary shapeshifters and those who aren't so scary have been included. Steve Feasey describes his Changeling series as horror-thriller-adventure, but Jennifer Barnes's Raised by Wolves series and the Wolves of Mercy Falls series by Maggie Stiefvater are more romance-adventure. The Nightshade series by Andrea Cremer is set in a world of witches and werewolves who are magical and powerful, but live in a society that is rigid and unyielding and secretive. The Firelight series, by Sophie Jordan, reveals another culture that is also rigid and unyielding, as the draki, descendants of dragon, must fight the humans who stalk, hunt, and kill them for their beautiful skin, their powerful blood, and the hordes of gems they have collected. And, of course, there's the seminal shapeshifter title *Blood and Chocolate*, by Annette Curtis Klause, who got the whole thing started back in 1997. In each of these series, teens must confront their own dual natures and learn to understand them so they can succeed. It's not always an easy task. These titles have been chosen for their variety, their quality, the unique ways that the authors have used and changed the shapeshifter folklore and mythology, and the detailed backstories and worlds that they have created.

Notes

1. Rosemary Ellen Guiley and Jeanne Keyes Youngston, *The Encyclopedia of Vampires, Werewolves, and Other Monsters* (New York: Checkmark Books, 2004), 316.
2. *Merriam-Webster Online*, s.v. "Shape-shifter," accessed May 14, 2011, http://www.merriam-webster.com/dictionary/shapeshifter.
3. *Wikipedia*, s.v. "Shapeshifting," accessed May 14, 2011, http://en.wikipedia.org/wiki/Shapeshifter.
4. Elizabeth A. Lawrence, "Werewolves in Psyche and Cinema: Manbeast Transformation and Paradox," *Journal of American Culture* 19, no. 3 (Fall 1996): 103–112.
5. Bob Curran, *Werewolves: A Field Guide to Shapeshifters, Lycanthropes, and Man-Beasts* (Franklin Lakes, NJ: New Page Books, 2009), 18.
6. Lawrence, "Werewolves."
7. Curran, *Werewolves*, 19.
8. Lawrence, "Werewolves"; *Wikipedia*, s.v. "Werewolf," accessed May 14, 2011, http://en.wikipedia.org/wiki/Werewolf#Origins_of_werewolf _beliefs.
9. Lawrence, "Werewolves."
10. Alliance for the Wild Rockies, "The Eradication of the Wolf," Wild Rockies Alliance, http://www.wildrockiesalliance.org/issues/wolves/ar ticles/history_of_bounty_hunting.pdf.
11. Lawrence, "Werewolves."
12. Guiley and Youngston, *Encyclopedia*, 316.
13. Curran, *Werewolves*, 29.

14. Jon Izzard, *Werewolves* (London: Spruce, 2009), 32.

15. Guiley and Youngston, *Encyclopedia*, 257.

16. Curran, *Werewolves*, 32.

17. William Hopper, "A Werewolf of Our Own," *Macleans* 115, no. 43 (October 8, 2002), http://heathensguide.com/Pages/Werewolf_files/story view(1).htm?content=75502.

18. *Wikipedia*, s.v. "Odyssey," accessed May 13, 2011, http://en.wikipedia.org/wiki/Odyssey.

19. Izzard, *Werewolves*, 128.

20. Curran, *Werewolves*, 13–15.

21. Curran, *Werewolves*, 33.

22. Curran, *Werewolves*, 32.

23. Curran, *Werewolves*, 35.

24. Curran, *Werewolves*, 34.

25. Curran, *Werewolves*, 36–50.

26. Curran, *Werewolves*, 59–61.

27. Izzard, *Werewolves*, 130–133.

28. Alix Flinn, *Beastly* (New York: HarperTeen, 2007), 301.

29. Flinn, *Beastly*, 303.

30. Joni Richards Bodart, "Young Adult Authors as Trusted Adults for Disconnected Teens," *ALAN Review* 37, no. 1 (Fall 2010): 16–22.

31. Curran, *Werewolves*, 90–91.

32. Guiley and Youngston, *Encyclopedia*, 258.

33. Guiley and Youngston, *Encyclopedia*, 316; Izzard, *Werewolves*, 126.

34. Guiley and Youngston, *Encyclopedia*, 258.

35. Izzard, *Werewolves*, 32.

36. Guiley and Youngston, *Encyclopedia*, 317.

37. Guiley and Youngston, *Encyclopedia*, 318.

38. Curran, *Werewolves*, 170–173.

39. Izzard, *Werewolves*, 27–29.

40. Izzard, *Werewolves*, 30.

41. Izzard, *Werewolves*, 34.

42. Izzard, *Werewolves*, 30–31.

43. Izzard, *Werewolves*, 48.

44. Izzard, *Werewolves*, 81.

45. Izzard, *Werewolves*, 80.

46. Izzard, *Werewolves*, 87.

47. Shannon Brownlee, "Inside the Teen Brain: Behavior Can Be Baffling When Young Minds Take Shape," *US News and World Report*, August 1, 1999, http://www.usnews.com/usnews/culture/articles/990809/archive_001644.htm.

48. Brownlee, "Inside."

Bibliography

Alliance for the Wild Rockies. "The Eradication of the Wolf." Wild Rockies Alliance. http://www.wildrockiesalliance.org/issues/wolves/articles/history_of_bounty_hunting.pdf.

Bodart, Joni Richards. "Young Adult Authors as Trusted Adults for Disconnected Teens." *ALAN Review* 37, no. 1 (Fall 2010): 16–22.

Brownlee, Shannon. "Inside the Teen Brain: Behavior Can Be Baffling When Young Minds Take Shape." *US News and World Report*, August 1, 1999. http://www.usnews.com/usnews/culture/articles/990809/archive_001644.htm.

Curran, Bob. *Werewolves: A Field Guide to Shapeshifters, Lycanthropes, and Man-Beasts.* Franklin Lakes, NJ: New Page Books, 2009.

Flinn, Alix. *Beastly.* New York: HarperTeen, 2007.

Guiley, Rosemary Ellen, and Jeanne Keyes Youngston. *The Encyclopedia of Vampires, Werewolves, and Other Monsters.* New York: Checkmark Books, 2004.

Hopper, William. "A Werewolf of Our Own." *Macleans* 115, no. 43 (October 8, 2002). http://heathensguide.com/Pages/Werewolf_files/story view(1).htm?content=75502.

Izzard, Jon. *Werewolves.* London: Spruce, 2009.

Lawrence, Elizabeth A. "Werewolves in Psyche and Cinema: Man-Beast Transformation and Paradox." *Journal of American Culture* 19, no. 3 (Fall 1996): 103–112.

7

Blood and Chocolate
by Annette Curtis Klause

Annette Curtis Klause led the way with YA shapeshifter fiction, just as she did with vampires, publishing *Blood and Chocolate* in 1997 and introducing Vivian Gandillion, a beautiful and sensuous werewolf who relishes her animal side and loves to run in the woods near her suburban Maryland home. Vivian is a powerful character with a fatal flaw—she has fallen in love with Aiden, a meat-boy, a human who writes haunting poetry about werewolves. She is sure that Aiden will be able to understand and love her wolf just as much as he does her girl. Klause's writing style is very different from the lyrical prose she used in *The Silver Kiss*; it is lush, sensual, and sexy. Vivian reveals just how physical werewolves are—the way they kiss, have sex, fight, and enjoy the heightened senses of their wolf bodies.[1]

Klause's wolves follow the classic form, leaving their clothes behind when they shift, but they are able to shift at will, although the full moon still calls to them and forces them to shift every month, when the pack runs together and celebrates members' dual nature. The urge to shift gets stronger as the moon gets fuller and is harder to control. Wolves may start to shift as a result of strong or intense emotions as well. Shifting is not magical and does involve some effort, but it happens quickly and with little pain, as long as it's a controlled shift. It's also possible for wolves to shift partway, changing their teeth or talons while in their human bodies.

Wolves are not immortal and can be poisoned or killed by silver if it gets into even the most minor wound—they are unable to heal themselves from it. They can also be killed by fire or if they break their spines.

Klause's wolves run in packs, and Vivian's pack has just recently relocated to Maryland after it was burned out of the compound in West Virginia where it had lived since the 1600s. The pack alpha, Vivian's father, was killed in the fire, and now the pack is in conflict about who will become the new alpha. In addition, several of the younger males about Vivian's age are starting to indicate their interest in her as a mate, although she doesn't return it, not trusting them because they were involved in the murders in West Virginia. Some of the adult members want to stay in the suburbs, rather than looking for a rural piece of land where they will have more privacy and room to run free. And two of the women are pursuing Gabriel, who's expected to become the new alpha, and have come to blows over him more than once. All of these conflicts make for a tense situation as the book opens, and Klause skillfully keeps the threads taut as the plot develops. When Vivian reveals she is dating a human, the relationship meets with immediate censure from the entire pack, further heightening the tension.

While the pack lives among humans, wolves are traditionally not supposed to mingle or become friends with humans and certainly never have an intimate relationship with them. While sex between wolves and humans is possible, they cannot reproduce, and since even in human form, the wolves are so much stronger, it's very dangerous for the human. Hurting or killing a human has been expressly forbidden from the earliest times of the werewolves, even if it is accidental.

Killing a human for pleasure, or for the taste of human flesh and blood, is punishable by immediate death, execution by the pack leader. There are no longer miles of forests to run in, no wilderness areas where travelers aren't missed for months, and modern police forensic science can learn far too much from violent murders to allow wolves who kill to remain secret. Those who endanger the pack in any way must be destroyed, no matter what rank they hold.

Pack rules state the way a new alpha must be chosen, if the pack is unable to agree on who should lead. The males must fight in their wolf form until only one is left standing—the Ordeal. The females must also fight each other for the right to mate with the new alpha—only the strongest and smartest will help ensure the pack's survival. Once the decision to have the Ordeal has been made, there is a waiting period of thirty days before it can be held, so that males from other packs will have time to find out about it and travel to where the Ordeal will take place.

Packs need different kinds of leaders at different times. Vivian's father was chosen by the pack and didn't have to fight, which was fine in a time of peace. But this is a time of conflict within the pack and conflict with the humans the pack lives among, and a leader is required that can fight both with brains and with teeth—a warrior. The Ordeal is the only way to choose such a leader.

During the Ordeal, adult males (over twenty-one years, or 252 months, old) who choose to be a part of it will fight all at once, each one dropping out when he has been blooded, or wounded. Wounded wolves are disqualified. The last two may fight to the death, if they choose to do so. After the alpha has been chosen, the females fight for the right to be his mate.

Unlike some werewolves, Klause's do not necessarily mate for life, although some do. Any unattached female can challenge another female to a fight for her mate. As the widowed queen, Vivian's mother is in a place of power in the pack because of that. She can have the male of her choice—as long as she can beat any other female who wants him.

Vivian's romance creates a conflict within her, as she enjoys Aiden's soft kisses and gentle touches, but yearns for something more like the fiery passion she's felt with pack members she's connected with. Within the pack, sex is something that's discussed openly and desire isn't covert, the way it is with human teens, who hide how they feel, pretending that they don't want sex so badly. Vivian's dual nature becomes more of a problem, as her two sides fight against each other. She may look human, but her inner attitudes and instincts remain wolflike—the physical nature of rough-and-tumble play; the wildness and thrill of overt sensuality; the honesty of direct speech and action, without hiding behind human evasiveness and excuses.[2] She has to learn the rules of the human world, and especially the cultural rules of her suburban high school, where she has trouble fitting in, while also living with the rules and customs of her pack, her animal world, where she is perceived very differently. She's always had the pack and doesn't understand how to make friends with human teens. She's tall and beautiful and understands that some of the girls might be jealous of her appearance, but not even the bolder of the boys approach her—she moves through the hallways alone—an outsider, something that teen readers will connect with immediately. Vivian craves a relationship where both sides of her nature will be accepted, but doesn't know how to find it. Even when she and Aiden start dating, she isn't completely accepted by his "pack," his group of friends, and has to step carefully, learning how to be with them. But when she finally shows Aiden her wolf half, he is terrified and puts Vivian, himself, and the entire pack in danger with his reaction. While Aiden doesn't tell anyone about what she changed into, he does reject her, kicking her out of his group at school, leaving her alone again, and finally, trying to kill her, seeing her as a unnatural and evil creature that must be destroyed.

What Vivian doesn't realize is that she is almost as ignorant of pack rules and customs as she is of the humans. She is becoming an adult member of the pack and must learn new rules she's previously been unaware of. When she fights Astrid after the Ordeal, she is defending her mother, rather than fighting for the right to be Gabriel's mate, and is horrified when all of the females acknowledge her superiority. She has become the female alpha of the pack, whether she wants it or not. Still in love with Aiden, she pushes Gabriel away, denying the wolf part of her that is attracted to him in spite of herself.

She is stuck between her two worlds, unable to make a choice between them, to move fully into one—is she child or adult, girl or woman, human or wolf? Where does she truly belong? It is therefore fitting that in the final section of the book, after Aiden shoots her, she is literally stuck between her two forms, half human and half wolf, unable to shift fully to either one, even during the full moon. It's not until Gabriel shares his own story of his human lover and how he accidentally killed her, then lived as a wolf for months afterward, too ashamed of what he'd done to take his human shape, that she begins to accept herself. His acknowledgment of the beast that exists in all of us—buried so deeply in humans that they aren't able to change, so sometimes it breaks out in angry or evil ways they can't understand—helps her see that being able to shift and to let the beast inside run free to exorcise the demons inside is both a blessing and a curse. Gabe also tells her that the ability to shift is her choice— she is choosing for her own reasons to stay half-shifted, out of fear, or guilt, or shame, and she is also able to choose to move from one body to another as she's always been able to. Suddenly, Vivian finds herself fully a wolf, and then fully human again. She has finally found her destiny, her choice, her balance, and in acknowledging that, has left the borderlands behind forever.

Notes

1. Kirkus' Review, review of *Blood and Chocolate*, Kirkus Reviews, June 1, 1997, http://www.kirkusreviews.com/book-reviews/childrens-books/annette-curtis-klause/blood-and-chocolate/?spdy=1997#review.
2. Kirkus' Review, review of *Blood and Chocolate*.

Bibliography

Klause, Annette Curtis. *The Silver Kiss*. New York: Delacorte Press, 1990.
———. *Blood and Chocolate*. New York: Delacorte Press, 1997.

8

The Wereling/Changeling Series by Steve Feasey

Author's note: The series includes five volumes, the first four of which I discuss here. For the first two volumes, I reference the American editions; for the next two, I reference the British editions, which, as of 2011, have not yet been published in the United States.

Steve Feasey was inspired to write his own adventure/horror series for boys by a BBC 4 program about how adventure series for boys flourished during the 1940s, '50s, and '60s, and then died away in the '70s, leaving a huge gap in the literature until the 1990s, when J. K. Rowling, Charlie Higson, and Anthony Horowitz began writing titles with modern, up-to-date protagonists that children (especially boys) wanted to read about and began to fill that gap. Feasey immediately began to plan a series of his own.[1]

He'd been a voluminous reader as a child, using books as a way to escape from his unhappy childhood, and discover worlds and people that existed only in those books;[2] he remembers clearly the lack of titles he was interested in as a teen.[3] He was twelve years old when he discovered horror fiction by reading *Carrie*, by Stephen King. It scared him so badly he had to sleep with the light on. But he loved it at the same time and is convinced that teens read horror books because they like to be scared,[4] especially when the fear comes from a book or a movie, where it's safe.

Feasey is also fascinated with the role imagination plays in horror and the way a few well-crafted sentences can make the reader feel excited or apprehensive or uneasy—or afraid to turn out the light. The mind has the tendency to imagine the worst possible thing that could happen, to increase the tension, and it can be triggered by the simplest things—a moving shadow, a creaky floorboard. The mind fills in the gaps, and anxiety instantly goes off the charts![5]

Horror also produces a heightened emotional state, a rush of adrenaline that can feel extremely pleasurable. Feasey compares it to a wild roller coaster ride, where you think you know what's coming, you're sure you're prepared, and then suddenly, the ground drops out from under you, and you can't do anything but scream—control suddenly yanked away from you, forcing you to face your fear. Tension in horror builds slowly to a release that spins the reader off in a new direction, uncontrollable, unstoppable, until the ride is over. Writing is supposed to produce emotions in the reader, and for horror writers, those emotions are apprehension, anxiety, and fear.[6]

But horror is about more than emotions. While some authors see it as purely plot driven, Feasey believes that characters are just as important, especially when writing for teens. Readers need realistic, three-dimensional characters in realistic settings, who have horrific things happen to them and who must react to extraordinary situations.[7] The way characters react to these situations allows readers to put themselves in the part of the character and imagine how they would react in the same setting—their school, their home, the town where they live.[8] The bigger the danger, the more dire the situation, the greater impact it will have on the character, either positively or negatively.[9] When readers identify with and empathize with the characters, they are pulled into the story and learn from the actions of the characters in it.[10] Teens also experience horror differently from adults, perhaps because they are going through such a confusing time of life, when it seems like they are all alone and everyone's against them—a common scenario in horror.[11]

When Feasey began the first book of the Changeling series (called the Wereling series in the United States), all he had was a character, Trey, a fourteen-year-old boy who's just learned he's a werewolf; a terrifying first scene; and a scene later in the book in which Trey's forced to confront who he is and what he's capable of.[12] Since the boy has no idea how to survive as a werewolf, Feasey gave him a friend and mentor: Lucien, a wise vampire who had his fangs and talons removed years before, and who has overcome the bloodlust and founded a large organization to help protect humans from the supernatural denizens of the Netherworld, many of whom are trying to wipe out humanity. Lucien is thousands of years old and one of the most powerful vampires in the world. The others in Trey's new "family" are Lucien's beautiful half-vampire daughter, Alexa, who is a powerful young sorceress and also a dhampir, or half-vampire; and Tom O'Callahan, a human warrior who is Lucien's right-hand man and knows all there is to know about battles, strategies, and weaponry.

Feasey did extensive research into the many myths of werewolves and vampires, not to mention the myriad of other creatures the series features, in order to decide how his characters would look and act. He wanted to create two kinds of werewolves: a ferocious man-eating beast that travels on all fours like a real wolf, which he called Wolfan, and man-beasts like Trey who can walk erect on two legs.[13] While some werewolves are the results of being bitten, others, like Trey, are born werewolves, and transform for the first time when they are about fourteen or fifteen. Up to that time, they seem to be completely human. Without any way to control their change, they become the Wolfan, huge, fierce wild beasts with an unstoppable need to kill and eat anything that moves. Shifting is extremely painful, and it is forced by the full moon, and the moon frenzy and bloodlust are overwhelming and uncontrollable, until they shift back after the full moon wanes. In the bodies of their wolves, there is no part of their humanity available to them—they are animals. They live and hunt in packs and are hunted by humans. Werewolves who choose not to hunt and kill must be locked in heavily reinforced cages for the duration of the full moon. These hereditary werewolves are always male. The genetic tag, or "curse," is passed down from father to son. Trey is the last of these hereditary wolves. The only female werewolves are bitten wolves, changed by the bite of a transformed werewolf. Bitten females are able to mate with the hereditary wolves and bear male children.

The only thing that can allow a werewolf to control his transformation is an amulet containing wolfsbane. When Lucien meets Trey, he gives him a silver necklace (vampires and werewolves are not affected by silver) with a pendant of a raised clenched fist, and tells him never to take it off. It allows a hereditary werewolf to shift halfway, into a bimorphic, half human and half wolf, able to control his wolf and maintain his human emotions and actions. The amulet also means that Trey is able to control his transformation. He still has to transform during the full moon, but he is also able to transform other times as well, whenever he wants or needs to. It also makes the shift very fast and very easy, almost without pain. However, if he takes it off, he has no control, and at the full moon, shifts all the way to a Wolfan.

When Trey shifts, he changes from a tall, slender, somewhat awkward teenage boy to a huge seven-foot wolf who is able to walk on two legs. His body is massive, fur covered, barrel chested, with solid, powerful, massive muscles. He has long talons or claws on his hands and his feet that are strong enough to rip through anything. His arms and legs are heavily muscled, yet he is able to move, jump, and spring with amazing speed and vanquish any creature that dares to challenge him, whether it's from the human world or the supernatural Netherworld. His head is large and shaped like a wolf's, his teeth and fangs long and needle sharp. Even his friends are a little nervous around Trey's wolf—he is incredibly intimidating and dangerous looking. Because his head and throat are a wolf's, he is unable to talk; he can only snarl and growl, which also helps the intimidation factor. However, he is able to use his human mind to think with, to control the intense emotions, especially anger, that come with the transformation, and to transfer his thoughts to someone else's mind, so he can communicate with those around him when he is in wolf form.

Feasey thought carefully about teens and werewolves and the things they might have in common when creating Trey. He liked the idea of a teen wolf, but didn't want him to be controlled by the cycles of the moon, so he created the amulet Trey wears that allows him to control his shift.[14] He's an outsider and an orphan, physically and socially awkward, with a deep-seated need to fit in and to be loved and accepted. However, he's brave and willing to trust people who care about him. And as he grows and changes over the course of the series, Trey learns that he can also trust himself. He has enemies to battle, but he must also learn to overcome his inner demons and turn his weaknesses into strengths.[15]

Feasey sees Trey's wolf as a metaphor for being a teenager. The hereditary werewolf changes from a human to a wolf for the first time as an adolescent, when he also has to deal with the changes involved in going from a boy to a man.[16]

And this is precisely what happens to Trey over the five books of the series—he learns to accept himself as he is, to value and use his wolf impulses and characteristics when it's appropriate and control them when it's not. His refusal to back down in the face of overwhelming odds against him teaches him how to think out of the box, examining the situation carefully for the smallest chance of victory and using that chance to its very best advantage. He becomes more insightful, able to recognize a friend from an enemy who merely appears to be a friend, see the lie and see the truth. Trey learns to take advice or counsel and profit from it, and he learns from his and others' mistakes. And he realizes, gradually, just how very valuable love and friendship are and how to protect and cherish those he cares about. But above all, he learns that victory does not come without a price, nor does it always come at all. Important lessons for a young werewolf and for the teens who read about his adventures.

When asked why he prefers werewolves to vampires and made Trey a werewolf, Feasey admits that he likes the brutal animal nature of the werewolf, which makes it the only predator that could take down a vampire in a straight-up, one-on-one fight.[17] And another reason why he's on Team Werewolf is that, after all, vamps are dead. Living under a curse and being dead are two different things, and Feasey votes for staying alive.[18]

He gave his vampires an assortment of classic and modern vampire characteristics and abilities. Vampires have lived among humans since time began—dependent on humans for survival. They usually appear pale and wan, with unusual hypnotic eyes. Vampires are extremely sensitive to sunlight and burn immediately and severely when they are exposed to it. Some can mitigate this with sunblock, heavy clothing, veils, and umbrellas. While they are not immortal, they can live thousands of years and maintain a youthful appearance. Male vampires are very attractive to women, in spite of their long fangs and talons on their hands, which some vampires, like Lucien, have had surgically removed. However, Lucien, like all vampires, still needs human blood to survive. He gets his from blood banks and uses an IV to drain the bags, rather than drinking it.

Vampires can be killed only four ways—burning to ashes, beheading, drowning, and staking, but only if the instrument actually pierces the heart. Myths about vampires include not having a reflection, sleeping in a coffin, and the ability to shift into the shape of another creature. However, vampires can move very fast, to human eyes seeming to disappear from view and appear somewhere else. It is called misting, but it doesn't involve actually changing to mist or fog.

The world of the series is divided into two parts: the human world and the Netherworld, which is home to the demons, djinn, and other creatures that seek out the darker side of magic and of life. The two worlds have existed side by side for millennia, and many demons and djinn choose to live and work in the human world, where they are safe from the dark magic and dangerous creatures of the Netherworld. They wear disguises, fake bodies that can be discerned only by magic, and most humans have no idea that their friends or coworkers are not all human. Most of those who live in the Netherworld are dangerous, cunning, and evil, but not all are, as Trey finds out when he gets to know some of them. He relies on several nether-creatures to help him accomplish the tasks he must complete during his journeys.

The demon lords have ruled the Netherworld and the portals between it and the human world for most of known history, making complex treaties and contracts with the humans, yet they have rarely been openly aggressive against humans. But as the series begins, all that has begun to change. Caliban, Lucien's evil older brother, who changed Lucien to a vampire, has lived in the Netherworld for years and has now decided he wants to rule both worlds, and crush humanity forever. He is obsessed with the Prophecy of Theiss and wants Trey dead, because he fears Trey is its fulfillment. The prophecy says that a nether-creature will arise in the Netherworld and become so powerful that it can launch deadly attacks on the human world that reduce humans to no more than slaves or cattle for the Netherworld creatures to feed on. But there will also be a werewolf, a hereditary wolf, who will fight the creature and vanquish it.

The demons of the Netherworld are ruled by a vast hierarchy, based on which of them are the most powerful, physically and magically. They are organized into four levels, with the different species separated into rigid categories that determine their roles and status in the Netherworld. Level-four demons have traditionally ruled the Netherworld, and level-three demons include some who are powerful fighters and killing machines, such as the Shadow Demons or Bone Grells, as well as less threatening creatures, like the shapeshifting Ashnon. Level-two demons are the largest group and many are quite dangerous, including the parasitic Necrotrophe and the Maug guards. Level-one demons are the lowest level of demon society, scorned by all above them, and most are servants who do the work the other demons consider beneath them. They are frequently tortured and beaten, and live wretched, miserable lives. Shentob, the demons' servant in *Demon Games* who helps Trey win the games, is a level-one demon.

Notes

1. YA Book Reads, "Interview with Steve Feasey," *YA Book Reads* (blog), January 16, 2011, http://yabookreads.com/blog/2011/01/16/interview -with-steve-feasey/; Tracy, "Interview with a Debut Author: Steve Feasey," *Tall Tales and Short Stories* (blog), March 9, 2009, http://talltalesandshortsto ries.blogspot.com/2009/03/interview-with-debut-author-4-steve_09.html.

2. National Literacy Trust, "Steve Feasey: Author Reading Champions Profile Author," National Literacy Trust, http://www.literacytrust.org.uk/ assets/0000/6540/Steve_Feasey1.pdf.

3. Write Away, "An Interview with Steve Feasey," Just Imagine, http://www.writeaway.org.uk/content/steve-feasey.

4. Bookzone, "Interview with Steve Feasey," *The Book Zone* (blog), April 21, 2010, http://bookzone4boys.blogspot.com/2010/04/interview-with -steve-feasey-author-of.html.

5. Groupthing, "Q&A with Horror Author Steve Feasey," *Groupthing* (blog), May 19, 2009, http://www.groupthing.org/blog/q-a-with-horror -author-steve-feasey.

6. Steve Feasey, "The Fear," Guest Author: Steve Feasey, Dark Faerie Tales, July 14, 2010, http://darkfaerietales.com/guest-author-steve-feasey -guest-post-giveaway.html.

7. Groupthing, "Q&A."

8. Write Away, "Interview."

9. Bookzone, "Interview."

10. Groupthing, "Q&A."

11. Write Away, "Interview."

12. Write Away, "Interview."
13. Write Away, "Interview."
14. Write Away, "Interview."
15. YA Book Reads, "Interview."
16. YA Book Reads, "Interview."
17. Bookzone, "Interview."
18. YA Book Reads, "Interview."

Bibliography

Feasey, Steve. *Changeling*. New York: Feiwel and Friends (Macmillan), 2010.
———. *Dark Moon*. New York: Feiwel and Friends, 2011.
———. *Blood Wolf*. London: Macmillan, 2010.
———. *Demon Games*. London: Macmillan, 2010.
———. *Zombie Dawn*. London: Macmillan, 2011.

9

The Raised by Wolves Series by Jennifer Lynn Barnes

Jennifer Lynn Barnes published her first book when she was only nineteen and had thought for years that she'd like to write a werewolf book; she had even started four or five, but none of them really seemed to fit. Then one day the opening scene in *Raised by Wolves* just came to her—a human girl interacting with the alpha of a werewolf pack that she's grown up in—and Barnes knew immediately that it would work for her, because it was a family story that brought up many issues and questions: If you are a human raised in a pack of werewolves, how human are you? How much of you is wolf? She wanted the story to be about family, the one you're born into, the one you create, the people who raise you, and the people you'd die for who would die for you as well.[1]

Barnes enjoys taking something fantastical or paranormal and combining it with something real in the lives of teens.[2] In this series, she combines the idea of werewolves with the reality of growing up in a family and rites of passage, when the pull of family and the pull of independence are equally strong.[3] She knew from the beginning that this series would be set in a very adult world, have major characters that were adults, and that their interactions with the teen characters would drive the plot, character development, and themes.[4]

She also enjoys creating different kinds of characters—girls with strength and determination and quirky characters who combine two

103

things that generally don't fit together, like Devon's being a werewolf and into all things metrosexual.[5] She used her own childhood and adolescence to help her create Bryn, because she remembers what it was like to be overprotected and underestimated because she was a girl. Bryn is also an outsider and always the underdog, weaker and more fragile than the rest of the pack, even though she is intelligent and quick witted, and has a strong personality.[6] She has always had to fight for herself, to stand up to the other members of the pack.

Barnes's pack structure and hierarchy was taken from her research on monkeys living in the wild, because like wolves, monkeys mate for life, live in large social groups with strict hierarchies within and between the groups, and use nonverbal communication to convey dominance and family relationships.[7] She spent years studying animal cognition and behavior, and once was one of the few researchers allowed on an island filled with thousands of monkeys allowed to run free.[8]

Raised by Wolves centers on the changes in Bryn's life when Chase, a bitten wolf, shows up in pack territory, and she realizes they share a special bond—they were terrorized by the same rabid wolf and responded by surviving when they should not have—and now they are determined to find and destroy him. Two other young packmates join them in their search, during which Bryn discovers that she is unique in the werewolf world in two ways: she has the ability to remake pack bonds, and she is the only human, female alpha leader of her own pack of survivors.

Trial by Fire continues the story of Bryn's pack, as it continues to face opposition from other packs and from a coven of humans with supernatural powers. But this time, Bryn's pack must act on its own, because Bryn's mentor and father figure isn't allowed to help her—she must work out her destiny and destiny of her pack on her own. The ending of this volume sets up a third volume, and Barnes plans a fourth as well, taking Bryn from fifteen to eighteen, roughly the same length of time that teens spend in high school.[9]

Barnes's wolves are either natural wolves, born as werewolves and able to shift from birth, easily and quickly, without pain, or bitten wolves, humans who became wolves after being bitten by a werewolf in wolf form. Their transformations are slower and more difficult than natural wolves. After birth, natural wolves who prefer their wolf to their human form tend to mature more rapidly than those who stay in human form more of the time. Because almost all of the natural werewolves are male, natural female werewolves are rare and valued. Most male wolves marry human females, but many of them don't survive pregnancy, even if their sons do. Human bodies were not meant for the kind of changes a werewolf pregnancy brings. The only females born are half of a set of twins, with a brother to protect them in the womb.

When the wolves mate, it is for life for the males. Even if the female rejects them later and takes another mate, the males are permanently tied to their first mate. The female, however, does not feel the tug of that bond, and can go on with her life, apart from her former mate.

The wolves live in packs that are scattered all over North America. Stone River Pack in Colorado is led by Callum, a centuries-old werewolf with the uncanny ability to see into the future, examine the possibilities, and take action to ensure that the future he wants to happen becomes reality. He is the oldest, most powerful, wisest, and least violent of the North American Pack alphas, and his pack is the largest. He is the central figure in Bryn's life, a mentor and advisor who has coached and trained her over the years, so that at fifteen, when Callum knows she must begin to face the future he's already seen, she is ready for it. Not that he has told her what that future is or even that he has seen it. Callum plays his cards close to his chest and chooses very carefully when and with whom to share his secrets.

Pack life is hierarchical, and as alpha, Callum is the final authority. His word is absolute and cannot be resisted by any of the wolves in the pack, whether members want to obey or not. There are many pack rules for pack members and for the alpha of the pack. All must be obeyed, and failing to do so means severe punishment, up to and including death. One of the most important rules prevents wolves from harming humans, because the wolves live secretly among them.

Eleven years ago, Callum and his pack rescued Bryn, a terrified four-year-old girl who had just seen a Rabid murder her parents. (A Rabid is a wolf who kills without guilt or regret—the equivalent of a human sociopath.) He Marked her to place her under the protection of the pack and make her part of the pack-bond that allows wolves to communicate telepathically.

Callum asked Alison Clare, a twenty-one-year-old human who had come to the pack looking for her sister, to be Bryn's foster mother, and she has always protected Bryn and stood up for her against every wolf in the pack, including Callum. Ali also keeps her secrets, just as Callum does, until it's necessary or unavoidable to reveal them. If she believes Bryn is better off not knowing about something, she does all she can to keep Bryn from finding out. Her loyalty is first to Bryn, then to Callum, and last to the pack.

Ali is one of the most powerful characters in the series—strong and determined when it begins, she grows more so as the story unfolds and her secrets are revealed. It was no coincidence that she was with the pack when Bryn was found, nor that Callum asked her to be a mother to Bryn. She is able to provide first discipline, support, and a sense of family, and later her wisdom gives Bryn the information she needs to succeed and survive, but Ali is unable to forgive anyone who hurts Bryn. This rigidity leads Ali to leave her husband and the pack to protect Bryn.

Bryn is definitely part Ali and part Callum, but she is mostly herself—determined, strong, and unwilling to let anyone control her. While the pack considers Bryn submissive to the group, she doesn't make it easy. She's found that annoying werewolves who can't hurt her is a great way to deal with frustration! Bryn is her own independent person—an essential when growing up in the midst of a pack of male wolves, all dominant to her, all testosterone loaded, and some despising her as a human, ready to kill her and Ali if not for their Marks and Callum's protection. As a human, Bryn is far more fragile than the wolves, and even the weakest of them could kill her easily, but she knows how to defend herself. While her senses and speed are not even close to that of the wolves, she is much faster, stronger, and more aware than other humans. Bryn is also assertive, stands up for herself, and is fearless, with a smart mouth and in-your-face attitude—all necessary to hold her own in the pack. She has a dual nature—born human, brought up by wolves—and feels the nature-nurture conflict within herself.

Callum has trained Bryn for years, teaching her not only how to defend herself physically, but also to defend herself mentally, so that her mind is as tough as her body. She knows how to think for herself, to consider the angles before acting, to look for the motives behind someone's words, and how to think several steps down the road, figuring out what the reactions to her actions might be. Two of Bryn's greatest assets are also her greatest weaknesses: first, she absolutely refuses to do what she is told she *must* do. In fact, the best way to get her to do something is to forbid her to do it. Second, she hates secrets of any kind and is driven to find out what is being hidden from her. If she can't find out by addressing the problem directly, she becomes more devious, willing to lie or cheat to get to her goal. She must figure out the secret, the puzzle, and meaning—she is categorically unable to let it go and ignore it. These are, perhaps, less-likable parts of Bryn, but they are parts of her that allow her to be strong when it is necessary, for herself and for her friends and pack-mates.

Bryn is also able to survive the most dangerous and deadly situations because when she is threatened and backed into a corner, her survival instinct—her power to survive—surges, overcoming anything she faces. When faced with the impossible, she figures it out, if not with her intelligence, then by the Resilience, a red haze of determination and power that overcomes her and forces her to do whatever's necessary to survive. When the haze passes and she returns to the present, it is always to find those opposing her flat on the ground. This Resilient part of her also recognizes Resilience in others and is the reason why she and Chase have felt connected since they met for the first time; it is also the reason why the Rabid kidnapped certain children and not others. A Resilient himself, he could tell which ones were Resilient and could survive the Change to become werewolves.

This series is partly about relationships and the changes to and redefinitions of those relationships that must happen over time.[10] Bryn has to realign her relationships over and over, as events occur and she learns new information. Her relationship with Callum is redefined over and over, because she is growing up, reaching for adulthood, and the closeness she has with him at the beginning of the series must ease, if he is to allow her room to grow. He must pull away, withdraw so she can begin to figure out how to become her own person.

Other relationships grow stronger and more important rather than weaker, as when Bryn and Chase reach out to each other, recognizing that they are alike and can connect in a way that they can't with anyone else. It started when they recognized each other as Resilient, and increased when they discovered they could mind-speak clearly and easily. They are deeply honest with each other, each allowing the other space when necessary and closeness when possible. Together they are able to find the peace they both need so badly.

And yet other relationships change, but stay strong, like the ones Bryn has with Devon and Lake. They have always been close, but when Bryn becomes alpha, the other two have to accept her power over them, even though she rarely uses it. Chase's presence also makes a difference in Bryn's relationship with Devon, who has to accept that there is someone closer to her than he is. It is to Devon's credit, and to his understanding of pack law and hierarchies, that this change comes with few fireworks.

The series also explores the question of nature versus nurture. How much of us is determined by our genetic structure and how much is determined by how we are brought up and the environment in which we live.[11] Bryn is at the center of this question, fully human, yet raised by animals (with the exception of Ali) since she was four. She feels the constant tug between wanting to be human and wanting to be a wolf. She runs with the pack as a human, feeling the wolves' fur as they circle around her, wondering what it would be like to be able to Change and run with the pack as an animal. This tension continues to develop throughout both books of the series, and while the question of whether or not Bryn will ever be Changed is touched on at the end of *Trial by Fire*, Barnes has not yet made that choice explicit.

Other characters also have to balance their upbringing with their nature, as Chase does. The reader sees only glimpses of his life before he was bitten. The reader knows that he lived in foster homes, and after he turned eighteen, got a job and was on his way home from work when he was attacked. But are his physical grace, movements that flow from one to another, a part of the wolf he has become or part of who he was before? Even Devon has two sides, his preferences, his hobbies making him different from the others in the pack. Maddy was under the control of the Rabid for many years, and bears the physical and mental scars of her ordeal. Will her own innate strength be able to overcome them? The answer is unknown, since she leaves the pack after Lucas's death. Teens will identify with these identity struggles, since most are likely to be dealing with the same kind of issues—who am I, and what makes me, me?

Devon Macalister is one of the most powerful wolves in the pack, and a natural werewolf, and he and Bryn bonded the first time they saw each other. He knew immediately that Bryn was his. His to love, his to protect, his to take care of. His. They have been best friends ever since that day. Their connection is special, unique, and obvious to everyone.

Devon is able to accept Bryn as she is, including the connection that she makes with Chase, which is completely different from the one he has with her. That he is able to accept that connection, when wolves are innately and intensely territorial about the females close to them, says a great deal about Devon. He will always be standing beside her, supporting her, whatever she decides to do—her fights are his fights, period. For both of them, losing the other would mean a chunk ripped out of their soul.

Lake Mitchell is Bryn's other best friend. She is a natural werewolf and lives with her father, Mitch, near the northern border of the pack's territory. They are "peripherals," pack members who choose, with the alpha's permission, to live apart from the main part of the pack. Mitch wants to remove the pressure on Lake as the pack's only eligible female as much as possible. He has brought her up in a rural, isolated environment in order to do that. He has also taught her to stand up for herself and to fight for her rights. She is ready and willing and even eager to kick the ass of anyone who tries to mess with her. Lake is an expert shot, good with knives, and an excellent archer.

Lake is as loyal to Bryn, and as willing to fight for her, as Dev is. She is fearless, outspoken to a fault, and doesn't do secrets. Bryn doesn't ever need to ask Lake for her support—Lake gives it before Bryn can ask for it, and like Devon, she's ready for fight for Bryn, no matter who the opponent is.

Chase is the other wolf who is special to Bryn, in a way that is at first confusing, then threatening, and finally, as essential as breathing. He is a bitten werewolf, one of the very few who survived, and was found after the attack in the pack's territory. When she sees Chase for the first time, Bryn feels an immediate, instinctive connection with him. They are alike, they fit together somehow. Later, when they are able to explore the depth and importance of this connection, they discover that Chase was bitten by the same Rabid that killed Bryn's parents and that they are both Resilient. They are able to mind-speak effortlessly, even over long distances, and are always aware of each other. Wolves mate for life, and it soon becomes obvious that Chase and Bryn are mates. With Bryn, he has found his home, just as being in his arms makes Bryn feel at home in a way she has never felt before.

This series centers on Bryn and her rites of passage from teen to adult, from pack member to alpha, and ultimately, from human to wolf. She is required to pass tests of her intelligence, her survival skills, her political skills, and her battle skills. She must fight on a variety of fronts, with a variety of opponents. She has to go through things all teens do—parents who hassle and control them, feelings and needs that are unfamiliar and hard to figure out, challenges that cannot be ignored, bad and evil people who enjoy hurting all that they touch, and, thankfully, friends who stand with them no matter what happens and love them just as hard as they can.

Bryn is easy to identify with, a real three-dimensional person, who draws the reader into her world on page 1 and never lets her go. As she fights for her independence, her right to decide her own life, teens will learn how to do the same. Teens seeing no way out of the box they feel trapped in will be able to examine how Bryn thinks her way out when escape is an impossibility and finds the solution, even when it isn't obvious. Bryn faces the monsters in her life, refusing to let them see her fear, and conquers them using whatever tools she has or can find. She learns from her mistakes and the mistakes of others. She looks for the truth, even when it is unpleasant or unacceptable, and makes it right for her. Bryn knows who she is, what she is, and why she is.

But if Bryn succeeds, she also fails. Members of her pack die. Events interfere in the closeness and connection she's felt with those most important to her. Change happens, and she must live with the consequences of her actions, both considered and unconsidered. Her life is complex and stressful rather than simple, obvious, or easy, and she has to figure out how to deal with it and get a little peace when she can. She is peeling back the layers of her life one at a time, learning more about herself as she goes. Bryn is a worthy example of an outsider that created her own inside group for herself and those close to her.

And those closest to Bryn have their own lessons to teach as well. Callum grooms her to become a leader. Ali helps her become strong and independent. Devon and Lake teach her loyalty, friendship, love, and support. Chase is her home, and he loves her unconditionally. Maddie and Lucas teach her that some people are too broken to be saved and that sometimes she just has to let go—she can't fix everyone. And Lucy, Katie, and Alex show her the joy and innocence of childhood, when the world around her seems dark and dangerous.

And the monsters in Bryn's world are also her teachers. They show her the face of evil and its tenacity and strength, forcing her to find the will and the strength inside herself to fight back, learning their strengths and weaknesses, and ultimately how to overcome and conquer them. Monsters help Bryn grow, change, and increase her power and her wisdom as she fights against them.

Notes

1. Parul Bavishi, "Interview: Jennifer Lynn Barnes," *Q Blog*, October 1, 2010, http://www.quercusbooks.co.uk/blog/2010/10/01/interview -jennifer-lynn-barnes/.

2. Jennifer Lynn Barnes, "Q&A: About the Books," http:// jenniferlynn barnes.com/qa.html.

3. Heather Butterfield, "Jennifer Lynn Barnes," Smart Pop YA, June 25, 2010, http://www.smartpopbooks.com/2890.

4. Jennifer Lynn Barnes, "Author Jennifer Lynn Barnes Guest Blog and Contest," Bitten by Books, August 26, 2010, http://www.bitten bybooks.com/29757/author-jennifer-lynn-barnes-guest-blog-and-contest -live-here/.

5. Barnes, "Q&A."

6. Butterfield, "Jennifer."

7. Butterfield, "Jennifer."

8. Barnes, "Q&A."

9. Bavishi, "Interview."

10. Butterfield, "Jennifer."

11. Butterfield, "Jennifer."

Bibliography

Barnes, Jennifer Lynn. *Raised by Wolves*. New York: Egmont USA, 2010.
———. *Trial by Fire*. New York: Egmont USA, 2011.

10

The Wolves of Mercy Falls Trilogy by Maggie Stiefvater

Maggie Stiefvater believes that supernatural creatures are intriguing to teens because they involve a "something more," something outside normal reality, that invokes a feeling of wonder and curiosity, akin to a "what if" scenario. This "something more" allows her to play with ideas and metaphors, and werewolves can be metaphors of all kinds of things. After Stiefvater had a dream about wolves in a snowy wood,[1] she decided she wanted to write a werewolf series. She chose Minnesota as its setting because it already had a wolf population,[2] and it was cold enough that it made sense that the low temperatures affected the wolves and forced them to change from humans to wolves for the duration of the winter. She also didn't think that the classic werewolf image was very sexy or scary—it was representative of something that is, for most people, no longer scary, since wolves are (sadly) rare and not seen as dangerous predators. Plus she wanted them to change for more than one day during the full moon, but without breaking the connection to the natural cycles of the earth, so it seemed right to her to link their change to the seasons, so they would be forced to stay in one form for several months. These werewolves don't fear giving in to the violent beast inside them, as classic werewolves do; they fear losing their identity when they shift to wolves in the winter.[3] Sam feels like he loses his "Samness" when he shifts to wolf every winter. Everything that makes him, him, is gone, buried beneath the wolf Sam, and he isn't sure it will all be there when he changes to his human body, months later.

Stiefvater decided she needed to make the series narrated by both male and the female protagonists in order to get into the heads of several characters, rather than writing a one-sided romance. *Shiver* is narrated by Grace and Sam, who have been aware of each other all their lives but don't meet until the novel opens. Sam rescued Grace when she was mauled by the wolves in the woods near her house when she was a small child, and since then he has watched over her, both as a wolf and as a boy, although he has only approached her as a wolf.

Grace is a strong personality, although she is neglected by her parents and lives essentially alone. Her physical needs are provided for, but her psychological and emotional needs are not. But her strength has allowed her to overcome this, and she has learned to be a survivor, to figure out how to get along on her own, and doesn't see herself as deprived of anything. Nor does she feel sorry for herself. Life is the way it is—and she deals with it. She has Rachel and Olivia, she has her books, and in the winter she has her wolf.

But Grace's life takes a major turn when she finds a wounded boy with yellow eyes lying on the back steps of her house—Sam, with a past he gives her only glimpses of, is instantly fascinating. Soon, her need to be with him leads her to desert her friends and defy her absentee parents. When she learns his secret, that he is her wolf in human form, she is willing to do whatever she can to keep him from changing and leaving her alone.

Sam was bitten when he was a small boy, and his parents tried to kill him to keep him from shifting to his wolf form. He was adopted by Beck, who is the alpha of the wolf pack in the woods, but as he has grown older, Sam has begun to yearn to be fully human, because he isn't himself as a wolf. He is an intelligent, quiet, creative boy who loves music, poetry, philosophy, and books, and he lives for the summers when he can enjoy these things. Wolves do not communicate in words as humans do, nor can they read minds. They can share simple images and ideas, but that's all. They are completely animal, without any vestiges of their warm-weather humanity, killing and eating other animals to survive, staying mostly in the depths of the woods to avoid the hunters that try to kill them.

When Sam is rescued by Grace and then gets to know her, he decides to fight off changing for as long as he can, because something inside him has told him that this is his last time to shift. Once he shifts this time, he will be a wolf for the rest of his life, without any access to the things that he finds so important and so vital as a human. Sam is deeply protective of Grace, and while they have an intimate relationship and he spends many nights in her bed, they are chaste until Grace is ready to take their relationship to the next level, and Sam is fine with this. He puts her needs before his own, always.

Linger has four narrators—Sam, Grace, Cole, and Isabel. When asked which one she liked the best, Stiefvater responded, "I like Sam for the way he sees people, Grace for the way she sees events, Isabel for the way she sees relationships, and Cole for the way he sees himself. As an author, all those provide endless challenges."[4] Cole is one of Beck's new wolves, a musical genius who became a rising rock star when he was still a teen, but he carries a lot of baggage about things he's done and the lives he's ruined, primarily Victor's, his best friend and the drummer in his band. He feels a deep sense of guilt and self-loathing and wants to get away from his life, so when Beck finds him on tour in Toronto, he decides becoming a wolf is the perfect way to essentially commit suicide, and he persuades Victor to come along. Cole reveals himself only in fragments: his early life, his decision to create a rock band, the band's overwhelming success, his drug addiction, and his gradual realization that while he's good at music and the band is known all over the world, he's even better at hurting those closest to him, who love him the most. Stiefvater originally created him as an "anti-Sam" character and had to give him a troubled backstory to give him a good enough reason to become a werewolf.[5]

Isabel is a minor character in the first book, bitter and angry about her brother's death from a wolf attack, not realizing that her brother didn't die, but was transformed into a werewolf and now lives in the woods with the rest of the pack. Her father is a wolf hunter, determined to rid the woods of wolves once and for all, and Isabel supports him, until she realizes he might shoot his own son. She's popular at school, and dangerous to those who cross her, and her voice is sharp, snarky, and sarcastic. Tall, beautiful, with perfect blonde ringlets, she looks like an ice princess, but that's just a mask to hide how she feels inside. She is a good friend to Sam and Grace, letting them see who she really is behind her façade, especially in the second book of the trilogy. She is stuck in her grief and hurt about her part in her brother's death, and as *Linger* opens, she has transformed her appearance to reflect what she feels inside. Drawn to Cole because she sees the same hopelessness and brokenness in him that she feels inside herself, she is still afraid to let him inside. She seems unable to accept that she did everything she could to save her brother—she gave him tainted blood so he would run a high fever and be cured of becoming a werewolf, a remedy she successfully used to save Sam. Her connection to Cole is what helps her begin to heal as they share their pain, and she begins to like herself and who she has a chance to become.

Isabel and Cole provide a foil for the sweet romance between Sam and Grace—their relationship is dark and dangerous, as they stand at a distance from each other, wanting to be together yet not trusting enough to come together. But as their trust begins to grow when they share their pain, their darkness begins to fade. Sam and Grace have a long-standing love; even though they only watched each other for years, their connection is deep and solid. Cole and Isabel are at the beginning of their relationship, when everything is new and difficult and scary, and there are no guarantees. In addition, there's the added complication of Isabel's dad hunting the wolves in the woods and killing Victor, Cole's best friend, who became a werewolf only because Cole talked him into it. However, seeing his friend's dead eyes in the body of a slaughtered wolf was the final stressor that allowed Cole to make the absolute decision to overcome his previous life and mistakes.

Sam and Cole also have a set of commonalities that connect them and allow them to understand and respect each other. They are both trying to hold on to a physical form—Sam wants to be human, Cole wants to be a wolf. They have both been damaged by life, and both show the scars of that damage. They are both musicians, and both write songs or poetry that reflect their experiences and their pain.

While in the hands of a less-skilled author, four narrators might be confusing, but Stiefvater has been careful to give each of them a unique voice that conveys the differences in their personalities. She notes that people either love or hate Cole and Isabel, reacting to them perhaps more strongly than to Grace and Sam because they are edgier characters.[6]

She also created whole personalities and characteristics for each of the characters. Sam's enjoyment of poetry, philosophy, and a variety of esoteric and classic works is something that grew from his personality as Stiefvater got to know him better, rather than something tacked on to make him seem more thoughtful or interesting. She ended up doing a great deal of research and threw out many of the quotes, songs, and poems she found because while she liked them, she didn't think that Sam would.[7] And the backstories for the other characters are equally detailed, even if they are only alluded to in the text.

But Sam was not an entirely predictable character. Stiefvater had created an entire backstory for him that he wasn't willing to go along with. She says,

> In the very first draft of *Shiver*, I was writing along and Grace was standing over Sam's hospital bed, and she noticed scars on his wrists. And I was like—"Wait, what? There are scars?" Because sometimes, as a writer, there are these weird moments where the story just unfolds without you, and you can go with it or you can chop it out and get it back on course. So I decided to go with it. I decided that surely Sam . . . had tried to kill himself. But when I went to type Sam's next line of dialog . . . he said, "My mother did this one. My father did this one. They counted backwards so they'd do it at the same time. I still can't stand to look at a bathtub.". . . I don't know where that line came from, but it changed the entire book. And the instant he said "I still can't stand to look at a bathtub," I knew I was going to do everything in my power to get that boy into one.[8]

But Sam isn't the only character that Stiefvater loved to torture—she took great pleasure in making all of them face their worst fears and abused them too much to actually want any of their lives to be real. While it's great in fiction, it could be difficult to go to through in reality.[9] Cole is a good example of that—virtually all of the glimpses of his past that readers see are dark and painful, and living through them has been so unpleasant that he's willing to become a werewolf to get away from his life and who he has become. Grace goes from being ignored by her parents to being smothered by their attention and their anger, from one extreme to another, with no hint of a more tolerant or flexible attitude in between.

Stiefvater also wanted to be able to bring in her characters' pasts and show how past events impacted their current personas, emotions, and actions. Past events in characters' lives even change their perception of current events, giving them a depth and reality that might not otherwise be achieved.[10] Sam, Grace, Isabel, Cole, Beck, and the other wolves are who they are because of what they have experienced and how they have interpreted and reacted to it. The way first Beck and then the other wolves accounted for Grace's never shifting to a wolf changed the way they saw her and themselves, giving them a set of rules that Cole later proved incorrect, sending the story off in a whole new direction. Even the parents in the books are shaped by events from their pasts: Isabel's father, Tom, is driven to eradicate the wolves at any cost; Grace's parents turn instantly from laissez-faire to overcontrolling when they find out she is doing something they disapprove of—a hallmark of guilt about the way they treated her in the past. And Beck tries to hide his past from Sam, even though it influences the way he sees his adopted son.

Stiefvater also wanted to make all her characters realistic, so her readers could recognize them and identify with them, so she was surprised about the negative reaction reviewers had to Grace's parents in *Shiver*, questioning their authenticity. She knows absentee parents like Grace's—well-educated upper-middle-class people who don't see themselves as bad parents, but as parents who have done their jobs—have gotten their kids into high school with good grades, eligible for college; have raised kids who are not into drugs, gangs, violence, or anything else addictingly negative—and who see their kids as being able to take care of themselves.[11] They don't feel the need to interact with their kids on more than a superficial level and may be closely connected to each other, as with Grace's parents, or may be just as independent from each other as they are from their children. These families might be seen as families from the outside, but they aren't really, because they don't have the close interactive connections that families require. Stiefvater compares them to solar systems, orbiting each other because of the "gravitational pull of the same last name."[12] The teens in these families get themselves up, make their own breakfasts, and get themselves to school. After school, they come home and decide what they will do with the rest of their day, including taking care of themselves, fixing meals, doing homework, talking to their friends, and getting ready for the next day.[13] Some may even have the house to themselves while their parents go to weekend or weeklong conferences, vacations, or second honeymoons. And Stiefvater also comments that she's seeing more and more of these kinds of families all the time,[14] something that is confirmed by a number of researchers.[15]

But there was another reason for making many of the parental characters unpleasant—a reason common to many young adult authors: Stiefvater wanted her protagonists to solve their own problems and learn from the process. Her trilogy is about their confronting the monsters in their lives and conquering them. That can't happen until the parents get out of the way. And in addition, not many teens see their parents as wholly positive and wise. Even Beck has his dark side in the book, as Cole shares a side of Beck that Sam has never seen or known about. Grace has a very clear view of her parents and what they have deprived her of. The fact that she doesn't wallow in it, but accepts it and moves on, doesn't mean she doesn't understand what kind of people and parents they are. Even Isabel and Cole have relatively clear-eyed views of their parents and the impact that they have had on their lives, both good and bad. Had Cole's father not taught him science and groomed him to work with him in his lab, Cole would not have been able to figure out the puzzle of Grace's illness. And Isabel's parents' frequent absences allowed her time to help both Sam and Cole.

While the intended audience of the trilogy is teen girls fascinated by the idea of having a supernatural boyfriend, Stiefvater didn't want to write a wimpy romance about a girl pining after a boy with supernatural powers; she wanted to make her female protagonists strong characters, able to take care of themselves. Both Grace and Isabel are able to do just that, with parental figures who are very much in the background of their lives. Grace's relationship with Sam is that of equals—he rescues her, and then she rescues him right back. He gives her what she needs, and when she gives him what he most wants, it shows exactly how well she knows him.

As one of the narrators of *Linger*, Isabel is able to reveal more of her thinking and perspective and to show herself as being more complex than the mean girl/ice princess that she is in *Shiver*. Even her appearance changes drastically from one book to another, including a new style and an edgier, tougher hair style—spikes instead of ringlets. While she is still grieving over her brother's death and angered by her father's attitude toward wolves and his slaughter of them, she is also instantly attracted to Cole, to his edginess and his bad-boy persona, even though he's a wolf. She gains strength as the story progresses, and her participation in the plan to save Grace is necessary to make the whole thing work.

Writing from a male perspective wasn't a problem for Stiefvater, since she has two brothers and grew up with a lot of quiet, creative guys and had no problem getting into the heads of boys like that.[16] In addition, she's a musician, like both Cole and Sam, which gave her a great deal in common with them.[17] Not only did she write lyrics for the songs in the books, she also created playlists for each volume, which she listened to while she wrote the books and are available on her website.[18]

While Stiefvater is a fan of werewolves, she isn't a fan of series and surprised herself a bit when she finished *Shiver* and realized she still had loose ends to tie up, that gradually resolved themselves into three story arcs, creating a trilogy. But she has promised that *Forever* is the end. The story of the Mercy Falls wolves will be over.[19]

When asked about what happens in *Forever*, Stiefvater has revealed very little. There will be happy things, there will be sad things, but there will be more happy than sad. Here are three hints she included on her website, along with the announcement of the contract for *Forever*:

1. Even though the series has been compared to *Romeo and Juliet*, none of the protagonists will commit suicide at the end.
2. Sam's and Grace's families don't hate each other.
3. It will involve kissing—lots of kissing.

Of course, some of the questions not answered in *Linger* will be answered in the final volume: What happened to Olivia? And what about the third wolf that Beck brought back from Canada? Will Sam find a genuine cure? What if Cole's identity is revealed to the world—what will that do to Mercy Falls and to the pack? If Sam does find a real cure, who will decide to remain wolf, and who will become fully human? It seems obvious that Sam and Grace will want to be human, but what about the others?

Notes

1. Prophecygirl, "Author Interview: Maggie Stiefvater," by *Wondrous Reads* (blog), September 7, 2010, http://www.wondrousreads.com/2009/06/author-interview-maggie-stiefvater.html.
2. Nikki, "Author Interview: Maggie Stiefvater," *YA Reads* (blog), September 29, 2009, http://www.yareads.com/author-interview-maggie-stiefvater/author-interviews/1928.
3. Melissa Montovani, "Interview with Maggie Stiefvater," *YA Book Shelf* (blog), http://www.yabookshelf.com/2010/07/interview-with-maggie-stiefvater-author-of-the-wolves-of-mercy-falls-series/.
4. Book Woman, "Book Woman Interviews Maggie Stiefvater," *Book Woman Reads YA* (blog), July 2010, http://bookwomanreadsya.webs.com/apps/blog/.
5. Brenna Yovanoff, "Brenna Yovanoff/Maggie Stiefvater: Author One-on-One," Behind Yellow Eyes, February 8, 2011, http://www.behindyellow eyes.com.
6. Paulette Suhr, "Interview: Maggie Stiefvater: *Linger* ing Possi bilities," The Trades, July 25, 2010, http://www.the-trades.com/article.php?id=12023.
7. Suhr, "Interview."
8. Frankie Diane Mallis, "Maggie Stiefvater *Shiver* Interview—Repost," First Novels Club, July 19, 2010, http://www.firstnovelsclub.com/2010/07/maggie-stiefvater-shiver-interview.html.
9. Mallis, "Maggie Stiefvater."
10. Montovani, "Interview."
11. thedarkphantom, "Interview with Maggie Stiefvater," *The Dark Phantom Review* (blog), July 22, 2010, http://thedarkphantom.wordpress.com/2010/07/22/interview-with-maggie-stiefvater-author-of-linger/.
12. thedarkphantom, "Interview."
13. Joni Richards Bodart, "Young Adult Authors as Trusted Adults for Disconnected Teens," *ALAN Review* 37, no. 1 (Fall 2010): 16–22.
14. thedarkphantom, "Interview."
15. Bodart, "YA Authors."
16. Montovani, "Interview."

17. Mallis, "Maggie Stiefvater."
18. Prophecygirl, "Author Interview."
19. Suhr, "Interview."

Bibliography

Bodart, Joni Richards. "Young Adult Authors as Trusted Adults for Disconnected Teens." *ALAN Review* 37, no. 1 (Fall 2010): 16–22.

Stiefvater, Maggie. *Shiver*. New York: Scholastic, 2009.

———. *Linger*. New York: Scholastic, 2010.

———. *Forever*. New York: Scholastic, 2011.

11

The Nightshade Series by Andrea Cremer

Andrea Cremer had always loved writing, but she never thought she could make a living at it, so she became a history professor instead, specializing in the early modern period, which is between 1500 and 1800, and in gender and sexuality studies during that time period. She teaches at Macalester College in St. Paul, Minnesota.[1] In 2008, she broke her foot in a horseback riding accident and was stuck on the couch for the summer, so she decided to try writing a book.[2] Calla was the only character she had to start with. Cremer knew she was a girl who was a wolf, she knew Calla was strong, but also in a difficult predicament from which it seemed there was no way out. The world of Nightshade was her answer to how Calla's problems came about.[3] From the moment that Cremer met her, Calla was unapologetically independent and in your face,[4] determined to do whatever she wanted to do and make her own way in the world. Cremer also saw her clearly in her mind's eye—a platinum blonde with golden eyes, very much like the girl on the cover of *Nightshade*.[5]

Calla is a girl growing up in a supernatural world, a strong person and a respected leader and warrior, destined since birth to be one of the alphas of a new generation of Guardians, or were-wolves. But she is also afraid, angry, and controlled by the rules of the society she lives in, even as she fights against them. Cremer's area of expertise (1500–1800) was a time of overwhelming and violent changes: witch hunts, the Inquisition, colonization of new continents, and other social transformations that changed the way life was lived across Europe and the Americas.[6] She researched how religion, gender, and violence interacted to shape culture and enforce hierarchies, and she brought much of this expertise and knowledge to creating the world of Nightshade, examining theories of how societies are created and managed and creating the political relationships between the packs and between the Guardians and the Keepers.[7] Creating the mythology of Nightshade was all about blending her interest in wolves, in the wilderness, in history, and in feminist politics into a backstory that would read as real and authentic to readers, and then sticking to the rules she set up for that world.[8]

Cremer was also deliberate about connecting the real world with the Nightshade world, and so they are layered on top of each other to some extent. References to Luna bars, the Denver Broncos, and other real-world things allow readers to relate to the Nightshade world more easily, because pieces of it are already familiar to them.[9]

Calla was already powerful, a Guardian and a wolf, so Cremer had to create a force that was more powerful than Guardians. Since the early modern period of history was about witch hunts and the abilities assigned to witches, she decided to make witches and witchcraft more powerful than the Guardians.[10] The history and mythology of Nightshade include some events and ideas from history as well as new twists she created for the series.[11] The fourth volume of the series, which is a prequel, is set during the 1400s and includes the history of the Witches Wars and how they came about.[12]

While Cremer's wolves are shapechangers, they are not classic werewolves because she doesn't really like the way she has seen werewolves portrayed in books and movies. She grew up in northern Wisconsin and was always fascinated by wolves—*real* wolves, the ones that lived in the forests of that area. She saw wolves as beautiful, intelligent, and graceful,[13] social creatures living in groups—nothing like the werewolves in books and movies, who were ugly creatures, ruled by rage and bloodlust while in their wolf form, unable to use any of their human abilities or knowledge, some of them half man, half beast and all of them hating their wolf. Lycanthropy was seen as a curse, and the best possible end for these werewolves was to free themselves of the curse and return to being fully human again.

Cremer, on the other hand, would love to be able to turn into a wolf, and the world of Nightshade reflects that. These wolves revel in the power and abilities that their wolf half gives them,[14] and they are able to be themselves, to think, to feel emotions, to make decisions and act upon them, whether they are in human or wolf form. In addition they live in packs, social groupings like families, and their loyalty is first and foremost to those packs. And like families, these packs sometimes change in membership and leadership—the wolves in Calla's and Renier's packs will unite when Calla and Renier are bonded. In the months leading up to the ceremony, the two packs begin to move from rivals to colleagues and even friends, and alliances develop between pack members.

Keepers are the only ones who can create new packs, like the one Renier and Calla will lead, and they have planned for its creation for years, even matching up Renier's and Calla's parents, the way that Renier and Calla have been matched since birth. Alphas are not allowed to fall in love—their mates are planned and specified—and while the Keepers take suggestions from the alphas about other matches within the pack, they retain the ultimate power to decide. The new pack will have ten members, five Nightshade and five Bane, and will be able to add new members as the alphas prove themselves as capable leaders and warriors. The Nightshade pack is Calla, or Cal; Bryn, who is her beta; Ansel, Cal's younger brother; Mason; and Fey. The Bane pack is Renier, or Ren; Dax, his beta; Sabine; Neville, or Nev; and Cosette.

Packs have very strong social bonds that revolve around intense loyalty to the alphas, just as real wolf packs do. Each alpha has a beta, a second in command, and the rest of the pack align themselves under the leaders. Their bonds of affection help to make them fierce warriors, a tightly knit group who work together smoothly. While there can be conflict between packs, intrapack conflict is rare. This is why Ren suggests that the ten who will become the Haldis pack begin to make friends with each other before the bonding takes place. And as the two packs get closer, the relationships among their members get more complex. Bryn and Ansel are in love, as are Mason and Neville, whose relationship not only crosses pack lines, but is also gay. Sabine has chased after Ren for years and is intensely jealous of Cal's position as his mate. She also protects Cosette, who is somewhat fragile, from Efron, Logan's father, by accepting the demands Efron makes on her. These demands are not made specific but seem to be sexual in nature, and not always pleasant, which helps explain Sabine's hostility in general. Dax and Fey, the two best fighters, also pair off.

Logan has been appointed by Bosque Mar, Shay's "uncle" and a Keeper more powerful than either Efron or Lumine, as the Keeper for the new pack, even though he is quite young for the job, and he may or may not allow any of these couplings, but after his first meeting with his new pack, he makes it clear that he doesn't want Mason and Nev together, since he wants Mason for himself. Mason manages to evade him by threatening to out Logan to his father and the other Keepers, but the danger to him and to Nev still remains. While the younger Guardians accept homosexuality, the adults in the community, Guardians and Keepers alike, do not, and will deal harshly with offenders.

Then Logan reveals that the young Guardians also have a special task—protecting Shay. He has been targeted by the Searchers already, and he must be kept safe—the Keepers have given it their highest priority. Since Shay is interested in Calla, she will be his primary bodyguard, but all the members of the new pack will be responsible for his safety as well. The Keepers have not revealed why Shay is so important to the Searchers, only that they believe him to be key to their success against the Keepers. The Guardians are to protect him without letting him know they are doing so, because Shay must not learn anything about their world.

Keepers are also the only ones who can give permission to create new Guardians by turning humans into Guardians using a bite and an incantation. Made Guardians are not as comfortable in both their forms as born Guardians are, although they do have all of the other powers that born Guardians possess, such as magical, healing blood. Made Guardians are created only in times of dire need, such as war, and only after careful consideration by the Keepers. This is why Shay's becoming a Guardian is so risky—he and Calla don't know how the Keepers will react to their breaking such a major rule, even if it is to save Calla's life.

The Guardians' shift from human to wolf and back is different from the classic werewolf, with pain, breaking bones, tearing muscles and tendons, and shredded clothes. The Guardians are warriors, and their shift needs to be as fast and smooth as possible, so they can function efficiently in either form. Nightshade wolves use a complex magic to shift that borrows the idea of multiple dimensions from string theory. As Calla explains to Shay, her body exists in both forms at the same time, but in different dimensions. She can choose which form her soul inhabits, bringing it into the real world. The other form is still there, waiting for her to inhabit it. When she shifts from human to wolf, all her clothes and other things she is wearing or carrying stay with her human form, waiting for her when she shifts back from wolf to human. And she can also pull parts of the other form to her if she needs to—and have sharp wolf teeth or claws when she is in her human body.[15]

Guardians exist only to protect the Keepers, who are witches and warlocks and are extremely powerful, not subject to any of the rules they enforce on the Guardians and the humans. Efron is the Keeper for the Bane pack and is greatly feared for his cruelty and malice. Lumine is the Keeper for the Nightshade pack and is a far more benevolent ruler, although she also keeps a close eye on her Guardians. Keepers rely on Guardians to protect them, but Guardians are also their servants and subject to their whims and commands. Keepers also depend on Guardians to protect their territory, guard their boundaries, and prevent Searchers from finding the sacred sites they need to work their witchcraft.

Both Keepers and Searchers are Old Ones, beings that look human but are both earthly and divine, witches full of magic power. They are able to move between the human and the spirit world and have existed since the beginning of time. Keepers are the wardens of the earth and have the power to protect it. When humans entered the world, Old Ones were charged with protecting them. But some of the Old Ones wanted power for its own sake and didn't want the job of protecting humans. The schism resulted in Searchers and Keepers; the former look for the sacred sites to rob them of their power and to control and enslave the humans, while the latter use the power of the sites to hide and protect them and the humans. The Searchers are a source of unbalance and chaos, the Keepers a source of balance and creativity, and the war they fight takes place in both the spirit and the earthly realms.

Place plays an important role in the series, and Cremer was very deliberate when she set it in Vail, Colorado, a mountain town with some very wealthy, celebrated, and elite residents. It seemed to her to be the kind of place the Keepers would prefer, where their wealth would allow them to interact with humans only in ways that they chose to. The setting also required mountains (not hills) and remote areas where the packs could live away from human contact, and where Keepers could build their huge mansions.[16] In addition, the West has mythos that Cremer wanted to include in her world, a spirit of independence, a need to explore and discover. She also wanted to connect the "Wild West" setting to the history of war and witchcraft in medieval Europe, and show how the present day world of Nightshade reflects the conflicts that have come before it and shaped it in ways she has not yet revealed to her readers. Because there is a past, a history, for the Nightshade world, Cremer was able to show how it complicates motivations and choices for those who live in it.[17] This history is the major focus of the fourth book in the series, a prequel that focuses on the Witches Wars that were the reason why Guardian/Keeper/Searcher society developed as it did.

The world of Nightshade is hierarchical to an extreme, with many rules that must be obeyed without question. It includes Guardians, or werewolves, who serve and protect the Keepers, witches and warlocks that rule the society and whose edicts may not be questioned. The Keepers are secretive and don't reveal the reasons behind their actions, decisions, or demands, even when they seem unreasonable or cruel. If they do reveal them, it is done with planned and careful attention to the results of sharing the information. It is in their best interests to keep as much as possible of their history and present-day activities away from the Guardians, and to do so, they have created layers of lies about themselves, the Searchers, and the Guardians. This dates back to the Witches Wars, and the destruction they caused. The Keepers are determined to keep the peace and have structured their society around that. The Guardians accept these strictures because they are part of the world they were raised in and have become part of the background of their lives.[18]

Calla accepts the fact that the Keepers decided when she and Ren were born that they would become the leaders of a new pack of wolves, and they would be mated as the two alphas of that pack. She also accepts that she must remain chaste, while Ren is able to have sexual encounters with anyone he wants to, even though it occasionally makes her wonder about his ability to be faithful to her after they are bonded. She and Ren both accept the Keepers' decision that Logan will be the Keeper and Master of their new pack, even though neither of them really like or trust him. Ren accepts that Shay will be under the protection of the Haldis pack, even though he is extremely jealous of and hostile to Shay. And all of the Guardians accept the rules that say that humans do not mix with Guardians or Keepers. While humans have great power in their own world, in the world of Nightshade they are at the bottom of the food chain, while the Keepers are at the top, and the Guardians are below them, above the humans.

Cremer has made Shay one of the most important characters in the book in several ways—there's a lot more to him than meets the eye. First, he is a member of the love triangle that is central to the story, which sets him and Ren at odds over Calla, who cannot make up her mind between them. Ren seems to be completely self-confident about his relationship with Calla and regards her as his property, but in reality he's somewhat unsure of himself and Calla's attraction to him. Shay's pursuit of Calla and her response to Shay infuriate Ren and make him more possessive of Calla than ever. Calla has been attracted to Shay from the first moment she saw him, drawn to him almost against her will, tempting her to forget her duty to the pack and to the Keepers. Ren and Shay are immediately at odds and create a tug-of-war with Calla caught in the middle.

Second, Shay is the focus on the online component of the book designed to attract readers and create excitement about the book before it was published. He has his own website (http://www .shaydoran.com/2010_08_04_archive.html) and narrates seven videos about his arrival in Vail, his uncle's house and library, and the puzzles he found there in the old books, strange words and images he is determined to decipher. Viewers are invited to join him on Facebook and help him solve the mysteries, which allow Shay to open a hidden cabinet and find an ancient book he believes was written by Thomas Hobbes, called *The War of All against All*. It contains old maps, one of them showing the area around the Haldis Cavern, which he is determined to explore.

The discovery of this book cements Shay as a central character because it allows him to begin to figure out who he is, why he's in Vail, and what the secrets of the Keepers are. It reveals the reasons behind the power structure of the Nightshade world and allows him and Calla to begin to question it. It is the Keepers' most secret and hallowed text, containing knowledge so powerful that no one but the Keepers could read it—it's forbidden for anyone else to see it, on pain of death. It's written in Latin, and Shay hasn't been able to translate much of it, focusing on the Haldis map instead. When he shows it to Calla, she reveals to him that he is in the middle of a supernatural war that has been going on for generations between the Keepers and the Searchers, and the book is the history of it.

Shay also has a tattoo of a cross on the back of his neck that he cannot see, probably because of a spell put on him by his uncle, and the last two lines in the Keepers' book refer to it: "May the Scion bear the cross. The cross is the anchor of life." Shay is the Scion, although he's not sure what that means. He also becomes a Guardian when he and Calla explore the Haldis Cavern and a huge brown recluse spider bites Calla, almost killing her, and she turns Shay to make his blood that of a Guardian, so it can save her life. When they explore the cave afterward, Shay finds a magical cylinder, the Haldis, which only the Scion can touch, and he takes it with him when they leave the cave. But Cremer doesn't reveal what being the Scion means, why the Searchers want Shay, or what the significance of the Haldis is, nor does she explain the layers of lies created by both the Searchers and the Keepers to keep the young Guardians ignorant and confused about what is happening around them, including which group are the good guys and which aren't.

In the next volume, Calla learns about some of these secrets and lies, and reaches out to control her own life and destiny and to discover if true love can withstand the trials she must go through to find it.

Teens will identify with Ren and Calla and the conflict between their loyalty to their society and their desire to break free of the complex array of rules designed to keep them subjugated to the Keepers. They are appealing figures, both powerful and yet controlled, leaders and yet followers. They are supported by the members of their packs, who also simultaneously submit and rebel in a variety of ways against the adults in their lives. But the pack members don't let their conflicts with the world around them endanger the pack bond of friendship and affection that they share. They are willing to do anything for each other, and their loyalty to their alphas and their packs is unswerving—which is also highly appealing to teens who share this kind of "pack mentality" with their friends. Cremer is able to pull on these connections to keep the tension high, pulling the reader through the story, as the characters are tugged this way and that. She also doesn't shy away from difficult issues, including sexual abuse, sexual repression, double standards for males and females, and marriage for politics rather than marriage for love, and she has created a beautiful and fantastical world as a setting for these and other very real issues in the lives of today's teens.

Notes

1. Valorie, "Interview with Andrea Cremer," *Truth be Told* (blog), October 15, 2010, http://www.truthbetoldblog.com/2010/10/interview-with-andrea-cremer-author-of.html.
2. YA Book Reads, "Interview with Andrea Cremer," *YA Book Reads* (blog), October 19, 2010, http://yabookreads.com/blog/2010/10/19/interview-with-andrea-cremer/.
3. Moonlight, "Exclusive Interview with Andrea Cremer!" Werewolves, October 24, 2010, http://www.werewolves.com/exclusive-interview-with-andrea-cremer/.
4. Pewter Wolf, "Nightshade Blog Tour: Interview with Andrea Cremer," *The Pewter Wolf* (blog), January 12, 2011, http://thepewterwolf.blogspot.com/2011/01/nightshade-blog-tour-andrea-cremer.html?spref=tw.
5. Kirsten Miller, "My Interview with Andrea Cremer!" *The Eternal Ones* (blog), October 15, 2010, http://theeternalones.wordpress.com/2010/10/15/my-interview-with-andrea-cremer/.
6. YA Book Reads, "Interview."
7. Brenna Yovanoff, "Interview with Andrea Cremer," *Brenna Yovanoff* (blog), October 8, 2010, http://brennayovanoff.livejournal.com/27600.html.
8. Maryann Yin, "Five YA Authors in One Interview," Galleycat, March 18, 2011, http://www.mediabistro.com/galleycat/five-ya-authors-interviewed-at-the-same-time_b25269.

9. Julia Keller, "Notes on *Nightshade*: Werewolves and Women's Power," *Chicago Tribune*, November 8, 2010, http://articles.chicagotribune.com/2010-11-08/features/chi-notes-on-nightshade-werewolves-110810_1_young-women-young-adult-readers-fantasy-world.

10. Pewter Wolf, "Nightshade."

11. YA Book Reads, "Interview."

12. Miller, "My Interview."

13. Nora, "Author Interview: Andrea Cremer," *The Bucket List* (blog), April 3, 2011, http://thebucketlist-gn.blogspot.com/2011/04/author-interview-andrea-cremer.html.

14. YA Book Reads, "Interview."

15. Peace, Love, Teen Fiction, "Andrea Cremer Interview," Facebook, January 16, 2011, http://www.facebook.com/note.php?note_id=140200272706008.

16. Keller, "Notes on *Nightshade*."

17. Miller, "My Interview."

18. Ann Nesbet, "Interview with Andrea Cremer about NIGHTSHADE!" *The Enchanted Inkpot* (blog), November 23, 2010, http://enchantedinkpot.livejournal.com/74798.html.

Bibliography

Cremer, Andrea. *Nightshade*. New York: Philomel, 2010.

———. *Wolfsbane*. New York: Philomel, 2011.

———. *Bloodrose*. New York: Philomel, 2012.

12

The Firelight Series
by Sophie Jordan

When Sophie Jordan began thinking about writing a paranormal YA novel, she didn't want to write another vampire or werewolf novel—she wanted something that was unique and fresh, and considered a number of paranormal elements. When she thought of dragons, and how they might have evolved over centuries, she knew she had the shapeshifter for a new paranormal world. She didn't want classical dragons—giant dinosaur-like creatures didn't appeal to her[1]—but she wondered how dragons might have evolved and changed in order to survive millennia while being hunted by humans. Since one way for prey to hide is to become like its hunter, she had dragons evolve into draki—shapeshifters that look human but can also exhibit some of their dragonlike characteristics when they want to. When the series begins, they are not really dragons any longer, but have evolved into a completely new species.[2] In addition, Jordan felt that making them look human made them more appealing and relatable.[3] There were never a lot of dragons to begin with, and not all the descendants exhibit draki characteristics, so they are actually a dying breed. And humans still hunt them for their gems and their ability to locate gems deep in the earth, their armorlike skin, and the magical healing powers of their purple blood. Jordan wanted her protagonist, Jacinda, to not only be a draki, but also unique among her kind, so she made her the last fire-breathing dragon, the first one born in over four hundred years.[4] Dragons have wings, and so draki do, too, although their laws allow flying only after dark and only in certain areas protected by a mist that prevents hunters from seeing them. Their ability to appear human is their greatest secret, and revealing it is their gravest sin.

But in spite of the fantastical elements in the series, it is very grounded in the real world,[5] making it easy for teens to identify with. Jordan was a high school teacher during her twenties, and she draws upon that experience when she creates her teen characters. Since she was closer to their age, they were far more open and frank with her than they were with older faculty members.[6] However, she didn't make any attempt to "write YA." She wrote in first person, so the reader can see inside Jacinda's head, but didn't dumb her down or use a lot of teen slang; she wrote Jacinda the same way she'd write any other heroine. Jordan also wanted to create a character-centered novel, in which characters grow and change because of the relationships they have with each other and the situations they encounter.[7] And some of those situations include conflict—in fact many of them do.

Identical twins Jacinda and Tamra fight constantly, because the draki pride almost venerates Jacinda as the last living fire-breather and shuns Tamra as a nonfunctioning draki who never manifested. Tamra's jealousy has festered for years, and when the family gets to Nevada and she is the one who is courted and accepted, she retaliates viciously against her sister, leading to Jacinda's revealing herself to the hunters in the book's final scene. Their mother has also become a nonfunctioning draki and is eager to get away from the pride, putting her in conflict with Jacinda. The relationships among the three of them are tense because there is no way the mother can support both her daughters.

Jacinda is conflicted about her relationship with the pride. She wants to embrace its traditions and values, but still chafes under its restrictions. Because she is a fire-breather, the pride wants to control her life and mate her to Cassian (the son of the pride alpha) as soon as possible, even though she's still sixteen, so she will breed a new generation of little fire-breathers.

Will is also in a contentious relationship with his father and extended family, who have hunted draki for generations, determined to eradicate the species. He hates the idea of killing such beautiful creatures, and when he finds Jacinda, he doesn't tell the other hunters. His rebellion is more covert than Jacinda's—he biding his time while still participating minimally in the hunts, waiting till he's out of high school and can leave his family.

Another theme in this title is lies and secrets—many of the characters have them, and their revelation drives the plot. Jacinda keeps her flying a secret when she flies without the pride, and when she flies at Chaparral. Her mother keeps secret Severin's (pride alpha) plan to punish Jacinda for flying after dawn, and the truth about her husband's death. Jacinda and Will both hide their relationship and their connection to each other, lying to their friends and families. And while her mother and her sister wait for Jacinda's draki to die, Jacinda hides the fact that being around Will rejuvenates it. Cassian is aware of what his father wants to do to gain ultimate control over Jacinda, and how devastating such a punishment would be, yet says nothing to her, even though he professes to love her.

Control is another issue that runs through the book, the need to control and the need to be free. Jacinda has fought the restrictive pride rules for years, her dragon nature yearning to live free, without rules that govern her actions. She is a rebel at heart, even though she loves the pride deeply and can't conceive of life without it. Once she manifested as a fire-breather, these restrictions became even more rigid, because of her value to the pride. Severin, the pride leader and Cassian's father, no longer sees her as an individual, only as "our fire-breather." He is willing mutilate Jacinda in order to control her. Cassian is his father's son and also wants to control Jacinda, seeing her only as one of his possessions, and even though he says he won't let the pride hurt her, his actions speak far louder than his words. When it's necessary to confront his father in order to save Jacinda, will he be able to do it?

Control is also an issue with the twins' mother. She is unable to control Jacinda and her draki urges to fly, so she leaves the pack and goes to the Nevada desert not far from Las Vegas, where the air is hot and dry and the earth is desiccated—exactly the opposite of what Jacinda needs. She wants to kill Jacinda's draki and seems amazingly unaware that this is as cruel a punishment as the one that Severin was planning on administering. She has never liked being draki, and she seems completely unaware that Jacinda loves her draki self, so killing it off would kill her as well.

Will's family is also very controlling, forcing him to do what he doesn't want to do. He has no choice about going on the hunts and is watched by his cousins Xander and Angus for the slightest sign that he is not adhering to the family's expectations.

Tamra is determined to control her mother and Jacinda, and she is willing to do anything she has to in order to stay in the human world. She doesn't care that Jacinda is miserable; she just cares about being part of the popular crowd and making the cheerleading squad. She finally has the chance to be the twin on the top and takes every opportunity to let Jacinda know it. It will be interesting to see how she develops in the next books, because at this point, she is a thoroughly unlikable character.

And Jacinda has her own inner control issues—she must keep her draki under control, and keep herself from manifesting when she is afraid or in danger. She must also work to keep from manifesting when she's around Will, who draws her draki to him.

Teens will be drawn to the Romeo and Juliet nature of Jacindas' and Will's relationship—an impossible romance between a hunter and his prey—and to the conflicts and connections that it sets up for the other characters. *Firelight* is followed by *Vanish*, and Jordan also plans on a third volume, as yet untitled. Much of *Vanish* takes place at the pride's home and gives the reader more insight into the day-to-day life of the pride.[8]

Notes

1. Prophecygirl, "Author Interview: Sophie Jordan," *Wondrous Reads* (blog), September 7, 2010, http://www.wondrousreads.com/2010/09/author-interview-sophie-jordan.html.

2. Lauren, "Firelight Blog Tour: Interview with Author Sophie Jordan," *I Was a Teenage Book Geek* (blog), March 11, 2011, http://iwasateenagebook geek.blogspot.com/2011/03/firelight-blog-tour-interview-with.html.

3. Prophecygirl, "Author Interview."

4. Lauren, "Firelight."

5. Eleni, "Author Interview: Sophie Jordan," *La Femme Readers* (blog), September 12, 2010 http://lafemmereaders.blogspot.com/2010/09/author -interview-sophie-jordan.html.

6. Eleni, "Author Interview."

7. Nicole, "Interview—Sophie Jordan," *Word for Teens* (blog), September 4, 2010, http://www.wordforteens.com/2010/09/interview-sophie-jordan .html.

8. Alex Bennett, "Author Interview: Sophie Jordan," *Electrifying Reviews* (blog), September 15, 2010, http://www.electrifyingreviews.com/2010/09/author-interview-sophie-jordan.html.

Bibliography

Jordan, Sophie. *Firelight*. New York: HarperCollins, 2010.
———. *Vanish*. New York: HarperCollins, 2011.

III

ZOMBIES: THE REANIMATED, RESURRECTED MONSTER

> They scare me more than any other fictional creature out
> there because they break all the rules. . . . Zombies don't
> act like a predator; they act like a virus, and that is the
> core of my terror. A predator is intelligent by nature, and
> knows not to over-hunt its feeding ground. A virus will
> just continue to spread, infect and consume, no matter
> what happens. It's the mindlessness behind it.
>
> —Max Brooks

Cultures around the world have long accepted the idea that those
who die don't always stay dead.[1] Family members return to their
homes, with real, solid bodies, unable to speak, communicating
only with gestures and facial expressions.[2] There are religious elements to this, in that many cultures look to the dead for help and
wisdom.[3] Jesus was able to raise the dead, and after his resurrection he invited "doubting Thomas" to feel the wounds in his body,
hands, and feet. At Pentecost, he also gave his disciples the power
to raise the dead, and many Catholic saints are also said to have
had this power.[4]

Another source for the belief in zombies might be instances in
the 1800s of catalepsy, a condition that caused the whole body to
become stiff and rigid so that it appeared to be dead. However it

was not a permanent condition, and when the person recovered, he or she could have been described as coming back to life. This is what happened to Constance Whitney, a noblewoman in the late 1800s. After an elaborate funeral, the corpse, dressed in her finest gown and jewelry, was placed in the tomb. A greedy church sexton waited until everyone was gone and then tried to steal one of her rings. When it wouldn't come off, he began amputating her finger, but the pain revived her, and the "corpse" sat straight up, terrifying the thief. She lived for several years afterward.[5]

Zombies are the only classic monster that is not descended from the gothic European tradition, as are vampires and werewolves, but from the folk cultures of Africa and Haiti and the practice of voodoo.[6] Voodoo is correctly called *vodoun*; the term "voodoo" is offensive to the practitioners of this faith because of the way it has been portrayed in Western culture.[7] It came to the New World with slaves who worked on cotton and cane plantations in the South. The areas most affected by this influx of slaves and voodoo were the slave ports of New Orleans, Louisiana, and Charleston, South Carolina, and in these and other areas of the South, many voodoo priests and priestesses were said to be able to raise the dead to do their bidding.[8]

The person whose writing did the most to make zombies a part of the American psyche was William Seabrook, who visited Haiti and wrote a book called *The Magic Island* that examined the various forms of voodoo that he found there. Published in 1929, it contained a description of zombies working in cane fields, with no thought or volition of their own, completely controlled by their sorcerer or master. There are still questions about whether or not the men in the cane fields that Seabrook saw were actually risen corpses; they could have been drugged or just doing work by rote and thus appearing to be under outside influence.[9] Some kind of powerful drug could have been used to put them into a trance or coma, making them highly suggestible and willing to obey the orders of someone in control. Such a drug could also have put them into a cataleptic coma, so they would appear to have died, and consequently to be buried, only to be "awakened" days later when they were dug up, still in a trance, but able to continue to work. This means that the process of "zombification" would be physical rather than psychic or perhaps psychological. A zombie will stay under the master's power until it eats salt or meat, because doing so will allow its consciousness to return, when it is most likely to seek revenge for its servitude, which explains why voodoo-created zombies are fed only a bland soup or gruel to keep them alive.[10] Others claimed that the Haitian zombie was an actual risen corpse, reanimated by magic, controlled by its animator, and needing neither food nor rest.[11]

Much of Seabrook's work is characterized by sensationalism rather than solid research, and his book includes a rather gruesome description of the rites of "Culte des Mortes," or Cult of the Dead, which involved possession and raising the dead. Whether or not it ever existed or existed as Seabrook described it is questionable, but excerpts of the book were widely reprinted in U.S. newspapers and magazines and formed the basis for the American conceptualization of the zombie as a living corpse connected in some way to the practice of voodoo. Seabrook's work also inspired the 1932 movie *White Zombies*, starring Bela Lugosi, which is considered to be the first full-length zombie film and has become a cult classic.[12] In spite of less-than-stellar reviews,[13] it made $8 million at the box office, an astounding feat for the time period.[14]

In its September 9, 1940, issue *Time* magazine claimed that Seabrook had introduced the word "zombie" into American culture,[15] but it had been included in the *Oxford English Dictionary* since 1819, in conjunction with slavery, and had been used in 1899 in a travel article on Martinique.[16] Nevertheless, there is no doubt that Seabrook is the person who popularized the name and codified to some extent the description of the zombie.

But the basis of the modern zombie—the shambling, rotting, flesh-eating monster—was the 1968 George Romero movie *Night of the Living Dead*, which was the first time zombies were depicted as cannibalistic. Romero's zombies were symbolic of mindless consumerism and the destruction of society, and the movie was set in everyday places like shopping malls, churches, or homes, places that should be safe but were overrun with creatures bent on the destruction of any humans they could find and eat.[17] A zombie cannot be killed, because it is already dead. It can't be distracted from its drive to eat living human flesh as soon as possible and as much as possible, just like a hungry shark following the taste of blood to its prey, attacking over and over again, stopping only when there is nothing left to feed on. These zombies have no thought processes or intelligence,[18] and the only thing they notice in their environment is their food—in other words, humans, and particularly human brains.[19]

Zombies also have a drive to reproduce, which they do just by biting someone; their saliva combines with their victim's blood, spreading the zombie virus and instantly creating another zombie eager to find food.[20] It is not surprising that the AIDS epidemic sparked a renewed interest in zombies[21] because of the similar transmission of infection.[22]

Ties of family and friends are nonexistent to zombies, and in Romero's *Night of the Living Dead*, a little girl zombie kills her mother with a trowel and then eats her father and a brother eats his sister.[23] It is easy to giggle at the start of that movie, but audiences are silent and shell shocked by the bleak finale. They have no idea where the movie is going to take them, and for most people it is far more horrifying than they expect,[24] as family bonds are broken and humans become nothing more than meat.

In Charlie Higson's *The Dead*, there is a brief thread that reprises this theme—zombies can't recognize the bonds of family or friendship. A man, who is not infected for some reason, is able to get a large bus started and heads for London with his son, picking up kids along the way, including the protagonists. But when the man finally does get sick just days later, he accidentally smothers his son during the night, holding him closely in spite of the boy's struggles. He is distraught when he sees his son's body the next morning, but after just a few hours, he has forgotten the boy entirely. He's no longer human and is consumed by his need for human flesh. It is a gruesome and disturbing scene, since the man had been almost obsessively devoted to the boy, and the reader is able to feel the connection between them, making the final disconnect all the more powerful.

Romero has made five other "Dead" films, including *Dawn of the Dead* (1978), *Day of the Dead* (1985), *Land of the Dead* (2005), *Diary of the Dead* (2008), and *Survival of the Dead* (2009), and he has been called the "Godfather of all Zombies." His movies have used zombies to depict a variety of societal problems or conditions, including consumerism, the conflict between science and the military, class conflict, and the stress and chaos of war.[25]

Zombies even moved into popular music with the production of Michael Jackson's *Thriller* music video, and they are featured in the video game *Resident Evil*.[26] Some of their appeal in the latter situation comes from the idea that zombies are around only to eat humans, making it easy to choose between good and evil. Zombies are evil, humans are good, and so zombies can be killed without guilt. This can be an extremely cathartic experience for someone who has not been allowed to express violent tendencies, or who is experiencing bullying or abuse.[27]

Like vampires and shapeshifters, zombies exist between, on the boundaries—not alive, but not yet dead. Both hold the same fascination, fear, and intrigue.[28] But while vampires can be said to represent the conflict between two different creatures—bloodsucker and human—zombies are two sides of the same coin: they have been alive and are now dead, but they have been human in both states, at least to some extent. This characteristic makes them more puzzling than their other two colleagues and gives them a flexibility possessed by neither of the other two.

They can be compared to the example from physics of Schrodinger's cat, in which the cat can be said to be both dead and alive at the same time. In the experiment, it is postulated that a cat is put into a sealed lead box, which is then closed and sealed. It can be said with certainty that at this point, the cat is still alive. However, if we open the box, verify that the cat is alive, put a vial of cyanide in the box with the cat, and close and seal the box as before, predicting the cat's viability becomes more complex. It could have played with and broken the vial and would therefore be dead. Or it could have ignored it and still be alive. It is both dead and alive. There is no way to know for certain unless we open the box. So it is with the zombie. It is in an undecided state, at the boundaries of life and death, as is Schrodinger's cat before the box is opened to reveal whether the animal is alive or dead.[29]

As a liminal entity at the boundary of life and death, zombies are a figure of horror, something that is neither this nor that, something impossible and yet present,[30] someone we recognize as having been like us, and therefore, someone we might become. This is the core of our fascination by and fear of the zombie. They are us, yet they are not. We may become them, although we have not so far.

They may have been friends or family, but they are no longer, even though we can see the resemblance, and that makes them innately horrifying. They may be eating someone, but they haven't grown fangs or changed into an animal, and they still look human to some extent. Romero once described zombies as just "the neighbors."[31] Death in the middle of life, unexpected, fascinating, horrible.

Romero's *Night* may have been the first zombie movie, but it was followed by many more, some inspired by his work, but others based on the zombie novels and novellas that appeared first as pulp fiction, but later as books in their own right. Richard Matheson's *I Am Legend* is not technically a zombie novel, but it was the source of Romero's inspiration for *Night* and has been filmed three different times, under three different titles, most recently as *I Am Legend*, starring Will Smith, which was one of the highest grossing films of 2007. The novel was the first to introduce the idea of a worldwide apocalyptic disaster caused by disease—which is a perfect description of Romero's film.[32]

Since 2000, there have been a flood of zombie novels written for adults, but enjoyed by all ages. It seems to have had a trickle-down effect that has produced some excellent fiction written for teens. Max Brooks wrote the hilarious and satirical *Zombie Survival Guide* in 2003 and followed it with *World War Z*, a more conventional novel that recounts the outbreak of a particularly nasty disease that is spread through bodily fluids. Zombies in his world are extremely durable, and in colder climates, they can freeze over the winter and thaw out in spring, going right back to their flesh-eating ways.[33]

David Moody's series Autumn is one of the more successful series and may be the darkest zombie fiction written yet. The books have an increasing sense of complete hopelessness as the survivors, who are immune to the disease that has created the zombies, struggle to cope with thousands of increasingly hostile walking bodies (Moody doesn't use the word "zombie," and they are not flesh-eating).[34] He seems to have influenced Jonathan Maberry, because Maberry's zombies are just as sensitive to sound as Moody's, and noise can bring them from surprising distances, searching for the human source of the sound.[35]

Jonathan Maberry has been fascinated by zombies since he was a child and writing about them for a number of years, becoming one of the best-known authors in the field. He has written two nonfiction books on zombies, including one on zombie forensics, *Zombie CSU: The Forensics of the Living Dead*, and a best-selling fiction series for adults, which opens with *Patient Zero*. He is well versed in the genre, which accounts for his knowledge of key points made by other important authors in the genre. His zombie series for teens, the Rot & Ruin series, has been well reviewed, and fans are eagerly awaiting more installments. (His view on writing for teens is included in chapter 13.)

It is also important to remember that each generation creates the monsters it needs or wants, and zombies are no exception. In 1968 *Night of the Living Dead* was an instant success, and it was also a year of revolution, antiwar protests, assassinations, and student protests. The Vietnam War was being played out on televisions across the country, and snipers or serial killers began to be all too commonplace.[36] (I still remember watching Charles Whitman firing from the University of Texas tower in August 1966, and seeing people across campus collapse, dead or wounded. We had just gotten our first TV exactly a year before, and that's the only thing I can remember seeing on it.) The old monsters seemed passé and zombies represented modern fears, and like other psychos of various kinds, they spoke to people who felt that civilization was collapsing around them.[37] And today, zombies run the gamut from terrifying to ridiculous, and even include real, living zombies, as crowds of people dress and act like zombies to go bar crawling, to a rave, or just to hang out and party. While vampires and shapeshifters have once again risen in popularity, this time the zombie is right there beside them, the newest of the horror archetypes and more than ready to make its influence felt any way it can.

Whether or not current authors subscribe to Romero's depiction of the rotting, cannibalistic zombie or not, they have given their zombies a chance to speak some of the same messages that Romero did. Daniel Waters's zombies are the ultimate minority, hated, feared, and discriminated against because of something they didn't cause and can't do anything about. Jonathan Maberry uses zombies to show us ourselves and to comment on the ways we treat each other, making us question just who the real monsters are. Charlie Higson creates incredibly dangerous zombies and then puts them into postapocalyptic London, setting them against defenseless and bewildered children who must kill or be killed. A. J. Whitten's zombies are from Haiti and have a variety of magical powers that enable them to capture their prey—humans, of course—more easily, but Amy Plum's zombies, while they have supernatural powers, are a kinder, gentler variety, acting as guardian angels who swoop in to save those in danger.

Zombies are a blank slate upon which the author can put an individual stamp. They can stand for anything. And while they have not replaced either vampires or shapeshifters, zombies have definitely moved into position alongside them as one of the most popular monsters of the twenty-first century.

Notes

1. Bob Curran, *Zombies: A Field Guide to the Walking Dead* (Franklin Lakes, NJ: New Page Books, 2009), 14.
2. Curran, *Zombies*, 14.
3. Curran, *Zombies*, 12.
4. Curran, *Zombies*, 17.
5. Curran, *Zombies*, 49.
6. Curran, *Zombies*, 80.
7. Shawn McIntosh and Marc Leverette, eds., *Zombie Culture: Autopsies of the Living Dead* (Lanham, MD: Scarecrow Press, 2008.), viii.
8. Curran, *Zombies*, 122–123.
9. Curran, *Zombies*, 147–149.
10. David Flint, *Zombie Holocaust: How the Living Dead Devoured Pop Culture* (Medford, NJ: Plexus Publishing, 2009), 10–11.
11. J. Webb and S. Byrnand, "Some Kind of Virus: The Zombie as Body and as Trope," *Body & Society* 14 (June 2008): 83–98.
12. Curran, *Zombies*, 147–149.
13. *Wikipedia*, s.v. "Night of the Living Dead," accessed June 23, 2011, http://en.wikipedia.org/wiki/Night_of_the_Living_Dead.
14. Flint, *Zombie Holocaust*, 16.
15. "Books: Mumble-Jumble," *Time*, September 9, 1940, http://www.time.com/time/magazine/article/0,9171,764649,00.html.
16. Flint, *Zombie Holocaust*, 11–12.
17. Webb and Byrnand, "Virus," 83–98.
18. Jonathan Maberry and David F. Kramer, *They Bite!: Endless Cravings of Supernatural Predators* (New York, NY: Citadel Press, 2009), 366.
19. Webb and Byrnand, "Virus," 83–98.
20. Webb and Byrnand, "Virus," 83–98.

21. Annalee Newitz, "War and Social Upheaval Cause Spikes in Zombie Movie Production," io9.com, http://io9.com/5070243/war-and-social-upheaval-cause-spikes-in-zombie-movie-production.
22. "Zombies," University of Michigan, http://www.umich.edu/~engl415/zombies/zombie.html#haiti; Robin Wood, "Fresh Meat: Diary of the Dead May Be the Summation of George Romero's Zombie Cycle (at Least until the Next Installment)," *Film Comment* 44, no. 1, 28–31.
23. Wood, "Fresh Meat," 28–31.
24. Jonathan Maberry, *Zombie CSU: The Forensics of the Living Dead* (New York: Citadel Press, 2008), 2.
25. *Wikipedia*, s.v. "George A. Romero," accessed June 24, 2011, http://en.wikipedia.org/wiki/George_Romero.
26. McIntosh and Leverette, *Zombie Culture*, 11.
27. McIntosh and Leverette, *Zombie Culture*, 13.
28. McIntosh and Leverette, *Zombie Culture*, 186.
29. McIntosh and Leverette, *Zombie Culture*, 189–190.
30. McIntosh and Leverette, *Zombie Culture*, 193.
31. McIntosh and Leverette, *Zombie Culture*, 195.
32. *Wikipedia*, s.v. "I Am Legend (novel)," accessed June 23, 2011, http://en.wikipedia.org/wiki/I_am_legend.
33. Flint, *Zombie Holocaust*, 165.
34. Flint, *Zombie Holocaust*, 166.
35. Flint, *Zombie Holocaust*, 167.
36. Flint, *Zombie Holocaust*, 11.
37. Flint, *Zombie Holocaust*, 7.

Bibliography

Brooks, Max. *Zombie Survival Guide*. New York: Three Rivers Press, 2003.
———. *World War Z*. New York: Three Rivers Press, 2007
Curran, Bob. *Encyclopedia of the Undead: A Field Guide to the Creatures That Cannot Rest in Peace*. Franklin Lakes, NJ: New Page Books, 2006.
———. *Zombies: A Field Guide to the Walking Dead*. Franklin Lakes, NJ: New Page Books, 2009.
Flint, David. *Zombie Holocaust: How the Living Dead Devoured Pop Culture*. Medford, NJ: Plexus Publishing, 2009.
Hardman, K. (producer), R. W. Streiner (producer), and G. A. Romero (director). *Night of the Living Dead*. Motion picture. Image Ten, Laurel Group, and Market Square Productions, 1968.
Higson, Charlie. *The Enemy*. New York: Hyperion Books for Children, 2010.
———. *The Dead*. London: Puffin, 2010.

Maberry, Jonathan. *Zombie CSU: The Forensics of the Living Dead.* New York: Citadel Press, 2008.

———. *Patient Zero.* New York: St. Martin's Griffin, 2009.

———. *Rot & Ruin* (Rot & Ruin, 1). New York: Simon & Schuster, 2010.

Maberry, Jonathan, and David F. Kramer. *They Bite! Endless Cravings of Supernatural Predators.* New York: Citadel Press, 2009.

McIntosh, Shawn, and Marc Leverette, eds. *Zombie Culture: Autopsies of the Living Dead.* Lanham, MD: Scarecrow Press, 2008.

Moody, David. *Autumn.* New York: St. Martin's Griffin, 2010.

———. *Autumn: The City.* New York: St. Martin's Griffin, 2011.

———. *Autumn: The Purification.* New York: St. Martin's Griffin, 2011.

Newitz, Annalee. "War and Social Upheaval Cause Spikes in Zombie Movie Production." io9.com. http://io9.com/5070243/war-and-social-upheaval-cause-spikes-in-zombie-movie-production.

Seabrook, William. *The Magic Island.* New York: Harcourt, Brace, 1929.

Wood, Robin. "Fresh Meat: Diary of the Dead May Be the Summation of George Romero's Zombie Cycle (at Least until the Next Installment)." *Film Comment* 44, no. 1, 28–31.

"Zombies." http://www.umich.edu/~engl415/zombies/zombie.html #haiti.

13

The Rot & Ruin Series
by Jonathan Maberry

Jonathan Maberry has always been fond of zombies, and seeing George Romero's *Night of the Living Dead* in October 1968, when he was ten years old, changed his life.[1] It was the first movie that completely terrified him, and he'd watched just about every monster movie that had been made and the monsters hadn't scared him at all—he thought of them as his friends and admits that he was a "weird little kid" back then.[2] But *Night of the Living Dead* was different. Yes, it was about the undead, but they weren't drinking blood or tearing out the occasional throat; they were eating the living, in huge mouthfuls! And nothing could stop them.[3]

Even at ten Jonathan already had planned carefully how he'd defeat the monsters he'd met so far, but what could he do against the hordes of mindless undead determined to eat him? There were so many dead people, and if they rose to eat the living, people everywhere would be totally overwhelmed. It didn't seem as if there was any way out, and it made him aware of how small and insignificant he really was.[4] He thought it was the scariest movie of all time. For years afterward he speculated about what he would do if he were one of the people in that house, sure that he would do something differently. Writing about zombies was a way to help figure that out.[5] Not to mention the fact that he wanted to scare the next generation just as badly as he'd been scared![6]

Maberry had always wanted to be a writer, and he says he doesn't remember a time when he didn't want to tell stories, but now he had a focus for his work—horror. He has also written thrillers, mysteries, and nonfiction,[7] and he prefers not to limit himself to one genre.

Maberry is well aware of how important good research is to good storytelling. The more solidly he grounds his story in the real world, the more likely it is that readers will be able to suspend their disbelief and identify with the characters in the book. But this needs to be balanced—they need to know only as much of the science behind the plot as is necessary to follow it.[8] One of the things Maberry enjoyed most was making the zombie world as real as possible. How would living your day-to-day life in a nonelectronic world be different because zombies lived there too?[9]

In *Rot & Ruin*, Benny has to get a job when he turns fifteen— what kind of jobs are available in his world? Fence testers make sure the fences that protect the town are strong enough to keep the zombies out, and spotters sit on the tops of tall towers near the town, looking for approaching zombies. Pit throwers toss all the body parts of zombies into the incinerator at the quarry, ash soakers wet down the ashes so they don't float all over town and pollute the air, and pit rakers rake out the ashes. None of the quarry jobs are easy or pleasant, even though they are necessary.

Erosion artists are important to the families of those who have become zombies, and they hire bounty hunters like Tom Imura, Benny's older brother, to help end their relatives' undead existence. Working from photographs, these artists make sketches of what a specific dead person might look like as a zombie so the hunters can identify that person more easily. Maberry's portrait on the dust jacket of *Rot & Ruin* was done by noted erosion artist Rob Sacchetto.[10]

Then there are bounty hunters, men who go into the Ruin to kill zombies, either for the bounty paid for every dead zombie or to fulfill a contract for a specific zombie's death. Tom is an ethical hunter, even gentle and respectful, but not all hunters are. Some are just as monstrous as those they mutilate and kill.

One of the inventions that Maberry most enjoyed creating became part of a job that Benny considered—carpet coat salesman. Carpet coats came from Maberry's research for one of his nonfiction titles, *Zombie CSU*. He interviewed a forensic odontologist (bite expert) about the effects of death on dental ligaments and how quickly they began to decay. Zombies are just not able to bite as hard as a human can.[11] So Maberry began thinking about what things a zombie wouldn't be able to bite through that a human could use for protection, and he came up with carpet.[12] It is relatively pliable, can be cut and sewn, but a zombie couldn't bite through it. Street clothes wouldn't protect you from a horde of hungry zombies, and even leather couldn't give really long-lasting protection. But carpet? Who's going to be able to bite through a carpet—especially with rotting teeth? Voila! Carpet coats! They could protect arms, torso, even legs, if they were long enough.[13]

Another real-world item that Maberry put into the story is Zombie Cards—kids love to collect cards, so why would a zombie apocalypse change that? But they weren't always just for kids to collect—in the beginning they were printed for bounty hunters going into the Rot & Ruin to look for zombies, to give them an idea about where to go and what the zombie looked like. But the printers wanted to make more money, so they soon made them more sensational and collectible. The front of each card has pictures of famous bounty hunters, heroes of First Night and the Zombie Wars, random famous people who had become zombies, and on the back is a biography of the person and the name of the artist who drew the portrait. The rarest cards are called the Chase Cards, and there are only six different ones, one of which is of the Lost Girl, who is rumored to live alone in the far reaches of the Rot & Ruin. When Benny gets that card in one of the packs he buys, he feels the world shift under his feet. He doesn't know it, but his life has careened off in a new direction because of the card and the face of the girl printed on it.

Maberry started learning martial arts when he was six, and he has maintained an interest in various forms of martial arts since then. He has studied jujutsu and kenjutsu (Samurai sword fighting) for forty-six years, and he holds an eighth degree black belt in jujutsu and a fifth degree in kenjutsu. This interest is reflected in Tom Imura's skill with a samurai sword in *Rot & Ruin* and is expanded upon in *Dust & Decay* when Tom trains Benny and his friends to be Samurai. The Samurai were skilled fighters, but the core of their belief system was a set of ethics called Bushido, seven standards of behavior about courage, honesty, loyalty, respect, benevolence, honor, and integrity. The katana, the Japanese Samurai sword that Tom fights with, is a favorite of Maberry's. It is light, durable, elegant, and practical, and when used correctly is very fast and extremely good at cutting through bone. It is also quiet so it doesn't attract a lot of attention from zombies and doesn't need to be reloaded.[14] Maberry's long years of experience using it ground Tom's skills and movements solidly in reality. Tom also reflects his creator's philosophy about martial arts: while they are important for survival and defense, violent confrontations are not fun and sometimes leave scars. Tom chooses not to fight when he doesn't have to, just as Maberry now prefers the meditative aspects of solo training with a katana.[15]

While Maberry has had to deal with dark issues at various times in his life, his sense of humor has allowed him to keep an optimistic outlook. So there is humor in all of his books, to relieve the darkness for a moment and give a glimpse of the good things in life. He thinks it makes his horror titles unique, and he says, "I'm a very happy guy living a great life. So, I laugh a lot, and so do my characters."[16]

While he has written about a variety of different monsters, he finds zombies to be one of the easiest to write about, which is one of the reasons why they are so popular right now. Zombies are a threat to the characters in the book—they are big and bad and dangerous, and there are hordes of them. Their presence puts the characters under stress, and how they react to that stress is the meat of the story. And there's no need for a long, complex backstory about where they came from or why they exist—not even Romero ever pinned it down. They're here and they're hungry, and that's enough. Instant horror. And that is the key to writing believable zombies—they have to be scary. They may be funny onscreen, but Maberry believes that doesn't work in fiction. Their very relentlessness means the characters facing the zombies go from shock and denial to deep-seated, genuine fear, and so does the reader.

In addition, zombies are very flexible monsters, able to appear in any genre, and an author can tweak the stereotype in any way he or she chooses to fit the characters and plot.[17] The monsters in the Rot & Ruin series are classic George Romero zombies—slow, shuffling, rotting, yet still looking like the people they were before they died and rose as zombies.[18]

They are unthinking, driven only by the smell of living human flesh or attracted by noise or rapid movements. There are a few zombies who are nomadic and travel from place to place, but no one has determined why they roam or how they decide where to go. Most stay near their homes, places where they lived or worked, and when they don't see or smell humans, they tend to stay in the same position without moving. During Benny and Tom's first trip into the Ruin, Benny sees a zombie standing in a front yard, wearing a bathrobe and overgrown with weeds and vines. Zombies are not "driven" to hunt except when they perceive living human flesh, and then they respond on an instinctive or biological level. Unless they are killed or "quieted" by severing their spinal cords, zombies do not die. They rot to a certain point, and then they just stop rotting—another thing no one has been able to explain. They attack only the living, animals as well as humans and even bugs. But they're slow and easily distracted, so most animals are able to get away, and if they don't, they do not reanimate. Only humans come back as zombies. As soon as a body starts to cool, the monsters stop feeding on it, which is why so many living dead are only partially eaten. Even if a group is locked inside a house for years, they don't attack or feed on one another or try to escape. They don't need to feed; they don't feel hunger; they just have an obsession with eating living flesh when they are able to find it. When they can't, they simply stop and just exist.

It is always dangerous to be around zombies, but spraying yourself with "cadaverine," a substance that is made from rotting bodies that smells like zombies, and moving very, very slowly means that you can escape notice. Zombies are not able to figure out any kind of mechanics, and most cannot even turn a knob to open a door or raise a window to get out of a room. When Benny thinks he and Tom are trapped in the house with a zombie, and zombies are banging on the front door and windows, Tom points out that the zombie inside is restrained and unable to hurt them, and the zombies outside won't think to go to the back door, so they will be able to sneak out the back and escape.[19]

No one knows exactly why zombies began to reanimate on First Night, although most people believe that it was some kind of parasite, virus, or disease. The only way to kill them is to destroy their brains (for instance, by a direct gunshot to the head) or cut their spinal cords at the base of their necks. Severing the spinal cord stops the activity of whatever brought them back to life and guarantees that they will never reanimate. It is called "quieting" and is practiced by ethical zombie hunters like Tom, and it is also done immediately after anyone dies to ensure that they will stay dead. Since beheading is another way to sever the spinal cord, this is also an effective way to kill a zombie, but it can be much more brutal. Usually when zombie hunters bring in zombies, they restrain them but don't behead them until after their bounty has been recorded for the hunter, to ensure that it is a real kill, not a dishonest hunter claiming someone else's kill. The bodies, some of them dismembered, are then taken to the quarry and burned. One of the more gruesome scenes in the book involves a group of bounty hunters who have trapped some zombies and are taking turns lopping off their arms and legs with swords and fancy martial arts moves before they dump the limbs and still-moving torsos into a wagon to take them back to be counted, so they can get their money. Once their bounty is paid, they will behead the zombies and take them to the pit to be burned.

Maberry wanted to write a series that was neither apocalyptic (about the destruction of humanity) nor dystopian (about the civilizations that have grown up many years after the apocalypse), but a combination of both. So he set the series just fourteen years after First Night—the night when suddenly, for some reason, the newly dead began to reanimate as zombies and humans had to figure out how to survive. The older generations remember First Night; the younger ones remember only the aftermath.[20] This is why Tom and Benny are so far apart in age—to give Tom the memories of the world before First Night and to set up a parental figure for Benny. Tom was sixteen when Benny's mother married their father, and she was more of a mother to him than his own mother had ever been. Benny was two and Tom was twenty and about to graduate from the police academy when First Night happened. Benny's first memory is of his parents, as he watched them through the window of their house as Tom took him away to safety. The relationship between Tom as parent and Benny as evolving teenager is crucial to the story.[21]

Maberry likes the intellectual challenge of setting his characters in a horrific landscape and letting them decide how to react to it. It gives him and his readers a chance to explore how people react to the stress and the situation, and to examine how their thoughts, actions, choices, and interactions are changed as a result. For Maberry, it's not a zombie story; it's a story of survival against crushing odds that include zombies.[22] It's a look at how heroes and villains and all too human monsters are created by what they choose to do, to say, and to believe about themselves, their world, and the zombies that threaten them. He writes about the battle between good and evil, and those who fight the monsters, oppose evil, and take a stand against the darkness.[23]

Although much of horror fiction is about harsh emotions—fear, anger, terror—Maberry wanted to include softer emotions to have more heart in his story. His characters feel love, hope, joy, loyalty, and trust, and they work to share their inner selves, even when it's awkward or difficult. They grow together, rather than tearing each other apart. The important part of the story of Tom, Benny, Chong, Nix, Lilah, and the others is how they react to the horror that they have to live through, how they survive and achieve. Maberry believes strongly in the power of friendship, and he allows Benny's love for his friends to give him great strength and courage. Benny doesn't know these things about himself until he is forced to face great danger and great fear.[24] Lilah, the Lost Girl, is based on some of the loners Maberry has known over the years,[25] people who have been very broken and have used their damage to find a way to heal and regain personal power. Lilah is very strong simply because she was very damaged.[26] Tom reflects Maberry's belief in the goodness in life, using his power and strength to protect the innocent, the unprotected.[27] He has been through great trauma in his life and bears the scars, but he hasn't been embittered by what he has endured and has remained true to the best part of himself—his love, courage, and loyalty. He is no doubt an old soul, a teacher and a caretaker as much as a warrior, knowing well that in order to give the good guys a chance to win, he must protect who and what is most important to him.[28]

Maberry also wanted to examine the nature of evil, and how and why it manifests. Some of the characters in the book are truly and deeply evil, genuine monsters.[29] It is those characters that give the book its darkest, edgiest, and most graphic and horrifying scenes. Who are the true enemies of humanity—the undead with their horrifying hunger for living flesh, or the living who take pleasure in their mutilation, mockery, and eventual death?[30]

Charlie Pink-eye is one of the most realistic characters in the book because he is based on some of the very abusive people Maberry has known. He is Tom's polar opposite, doing good for others only so he can take advantage of them later.[31] While Lilah was able to create a life for herself and heal, Charlie has let the events in his past twist and poison him until he sees only the worst in people. He wants to be the "big dog," the one everyone else looks up to, and he wants his own way, no matter what. He lives to hurt, to destroy, to manipulate others so he can get what he wants. He is willing to roll over everything in his path to achieve that goal. Written as the essence of pure evil, Charlie may be repulsive just because he is so realistic, far more of a monster than the zombies that he tortures and kills.

The series began with a short story called "Family Business" that Maberry wrote for Christopher Golden's anthology *The New Dead*. He sent it to his agent, and she convinced him that he had written the opening of a YA novel. He originally pitched it as a two-book deal but now plans to write a tetralogy.[32] He has completed the second volume, *Dust & Decay*, and has begun to work on *Flesh & Bone* and *Fire & Ash*. There is a lot going on in Benny's world that Maberry would like to explore, and the first two books cover a period of only seven months.[33] Maberry outlines each book and frequently writes the first and last chapters before he begins to write the whole book, but sometimes a character surprises him. For instance, Nix was not supposed to be one of the major characters, but she was determined to make herself heard and began taking on more and more of the action, until she became one of the central characters in the book and one of the leaders of the new generation.[34]

Maberry had not read much YA fiction before he began thinking about writing *Rot & Ruin*, and he was surprised when he began reading the genre. His agent gave him a reading list, and he was blown away. He realized that YA literature had finally grown up, and authors were able to respect the intelligence and life experience of teens without talking down to them or pulling their punches.[35]

Maberry has taught writing to teens for several years and is glad to join the ranks of YA authors who write the hard books teens need to read. He particularly enjoyed the fact that teens are more open to cross-genre stories than adults are, and he didn't have to restrict himself to one genre, but was able to just tell the best story he could.[36] He was able to experiment with edgy scenes and plotlines and take risks with character development. He not only enjoys the extra freedom in writing for teens, but also the responses of his readers, who are very enthusiastic about the series.[37]

The adults in this world, including Benny's older brother, Tom, remember what it was like before, when the world was like the one we live in today. They remember First Night, its horror and terror, and how hard they had to struggle to survive. They share a post-traumatic stress disorder as a result of what they have had to endure, and while some have begun to recover, many never will—they have forgotten the value of life. Their humanity has been stripped away.[38] They hate and fear the zombies outside the fence that surrounds their town and refuse to go beyond it to reclaim more land so they can grow more food, even though rations are always short. Theirs is a culture of fear and denial and routine. They have trained themselves to think of life as existing only inside the fences of their towns—it makes them feel safe and gives them a routine.

The younger generation, who were born after First Night or were babies when it happened, don't remember much about it at all. Their world today is all that they know. It's a primitive existence, without electricity or technology, because in the minds of many adults, perhaps even most, technology is somehow blamed for everything that happened—creating the zombies and destroying most of humanity. This younger generation, Tom believes, will be able to make the decision to leave the town, reject the fear, and begin to reclaim their country. He and a few of the adults have tried to make changes, but it has been an uphill battle, fighting the fear and the fourteen-year-old rut that people have settled into, content to live as if they were in the 1800s.

But Benny and his friends are ready to challenge the adults—they don't believe that the world is completely ruined and broken. They refuse to believe that there is no chance for a different future; they just aren't sure how to create it.[39] The world they live in is all about death and the living dead, and these children are going to have to reevaluate it and determine how to conquer it. And that is going to involve figuring out what to do about the zombies. They can be controlled—either killed or imprisoned—with planning and preparation, but it's going to be important how those things are done, whether with respect for the people they once were or disregard and scorn for the monsters that they have become.

First Night is talked about as if it was just one night, but it took weeks for civilization to fall. There were lots of fights, big ones with the military and small ones with families or neighborhoods struggling to defend their homes. In the end, it wasn't so much that the zombies won but that the living lost, surrendered to fear and panic and poor decisions. Nuclear bombs were dropped on large cities and urban areas to kill the zombies—and they did kill some. But they also killed humans, who arose as more zombies. The radiation was so intense that zombies who had been infected killed more people just by getting close to them. Everyone who died, no matter how they died, arose as zombies, driven to eat living flesh. When it was all over, humanity was nearly gone. Now there are only about thirty thousand people left alive, living in small settlements along the Sierra Nevada in central California.

Tom estimates that there are over 300 million zombies in America, about 30 million in Canada, and 110 million in Mexico. He's not sure about Europe, but the zombie virus was thought to have spread worldwide. There may be other enclaves of survivors elsewhere, but without electricity or gasoline-powered engines, there is no safe way to find them. Nix believes that there may be some survivors on the coastal islands off California, or if those islands have zombies on them, they could be eradicated with careful planning and the islands cultivated to provide food. She is sure the risk to find out is worth taking.

Benny is the central character in the Rot & Ruin series and the one Maberry most enjoyed writing. He is fifteen when the novel opens, facing the necessity of getting a part-time job or having his rations cut. The only thing he is unwilling to do when his search begins is to go into the "family business" and apprentice himself to his brother, Tom. He hates Tom for not saving their parents and believes him to be a coward. Not until Benny faces the reality of the great Rot & Ruin, the world outside the fences that protect his town, does he begin to understand what his life is all about. Benny must learn the value of human life and to see the world from points of view other than his own. He must learn about the history of his world and understand the importance of facing the challenges of the future and the changes that it might bring. It is more than a coming-of-age story; it is a story that examines what makes us human, what happens to us after death, and what that means. He begins with a fierce, glowing hatred of zombies and ends with an appreciation of who they were in life and what they meant to the people who loved them. Benny moves from adulation of a cruel man for his exaggerated and self-aggrandizing stories to a realization that his brother's lack of bragging does not mean that Tom is without honor or courage. Discovering that the world is not as he had assumed or imagined it to be is shocking to him, as his flat, single-layer world is replaced by a more complex, multidimensional one where very little is as it first seems to be.

Tom is well aware of Benny's hatred, but he continues to love and accept his brother anyway. His patience and methodical teaching methods allow Benny and his friends to understand the importance of living with purpose, the respect that should be given to both the living and the dead, and the futility of evil. Tom is a tragic figure, who has borne great and overwhelming loss, yet maintains his honor and idealism. He is a warrior, but a peaceful one who knows and understands himself and his world.

Lilah was a child when First Night happened, and she and her little sister almost didn't survive it. But they did, only to be captured and tortured by sadistic men who forced humans, especially women and children, to fight zombies bare handed for profit. She escaped into the Rot & Ruin and left humans behind forever. She is about sixteen and has had no contact with anyone for many years. Tom has seen her twice from a distance, as have some other zombie hunters. No one knows how she has been able to survive for so long.

Charlie Pink-eye and Motor City Hammer are classic bad guys—tough, charismatic, and dangerous. They have their own agenda and will stop at nothing to accomplish it, and their actions and motivation are solidly grounded in real life. They surround themselves with like-minded followers and feed on the adulation of boys like Benny. As the series continues they and others like them will continue to provide a dark counterpoint to the group that surrounds Tom and Benny.

Dust & Decay begins six months after the battle with Charlie and Motor City Hammer. Benny, Chong, Nix, and Lilah have spent those months in Samurai training with Tom, preparing to go out into the Ruin in search of a better life than they can have within the confines and fences of Mountainside. But as soon as they leave the town behind, they are pursued by zombies, wild animals, and vengeful humans, and they must face the horrors of Gameland first-hand. In addition, evidence is mounting that points to Charlie Pink-eye being alive, instead of dead, as they all believed. Could he have survived his horrific fall? Going into the Rot & Ruin is a dangerous thing to do, and not all the endings they find are happy ones, nor will all of their group survive.[40]

Notes

1. Jonathan Maberry, *Zombie CSU: The Forensics of the Living Dead* (New York: Citadel Press, 2008), 3.

2. Maberry, *Zombie CSU*, 3.

3. Prophecygirl, "Author Interview: Jonathan Maberry," *Wondrous Reads* (blog), March 16, 2011, http://www.wondrousreads.com/2011/03/author-interview-jonathan-maberry-rot.html.

4. Sideshow, "Interview with Jonathan Maberry," Sideshow Collectibles, August 5, 2009, http://www.sideshowtoy.com/?page_id=7264.

5. Jonathan Maberry, "FAQ," JonathanMaberry.com, http://jonathan-maberry.com/faq.

6. Thomas A. Erb, "Ty-ing Up the Genre—An Interview with Jonathan Maberry," Hellnotes, http://hellnotes.com/ty-ing-up-the-genre-an-interview-with-jonathan-maberry.

7. Julie, "Interview with Jonathan Maberry, Author of *Rot & Ruin*," Manga Maniac Café, November 11, 2010, http://www.mangamaniaccafe.com/?s=maberry.

8. Darren, "Author Interview: Jonathan Maberry #YAD2," *Bart's Bookshelf* (blog), October 29, 2010, http://www.bartsbookshelf.co.uk/2010/10/29/author-interview-jonathan-maberry-yad2/.

9. Heather Zundel, "Interview—Jonathan Maberry, Author of *Rot & Ruin*," *Secret Adventures of WriterGirl* (blog), January 26, 2011, http://thesecretadventuresofwritergirl.blogspot.com/2011/01/interview-jonathan-maberry-author-of.html.

10. Julie, "Interview."

11. Darren, "Author Interview."

12. Zundel, "Interview."

13. Zundel, "Interview."

14. Reading Rocks, "Interview with Jonathan Maberry and Excerpt from *Rot & Ruin*," *Reading Rocks* (blog), November 13, 2010, http://www.reading rocks4me.com/2010/11/interview-with-jonathon-maberry-and.html.

15. Nicholas Yanes, "Comics Interviews: An Interview with Jonathan Maberry," *SciFiPulse* (blog), May 25, 2009, http://scifipulse.net/?p=8536.

16. Dennis Tafoya, "*Rot & Ruin* by Jonathan Maberry," The Big Thrill, August 30, 2010, http://www.thrillerwriters.org/2010/08/jonathan-maberry-is-making-the.html.

17. Zundel, "Interview."

18. Darren, "Author Interview."

19. Zundel, "Interview."

20. Darren, "Author Interview."

21. Jenn, "Jonathan Maberry, author of *Rot & Ruin*," *Jenn's Bookshelves* (blog), October 14, 2010, http://www.jennsbookshelves.com/2010/10/14/author-guest-post-jonathan-maberry-author-of-rot-ruin/.

22. Zundel, "Interview."

23. Zundel, "Interview."

24. Zundel, "Interview."

25. Zundel, "Interview."

26. Zundel, "Interview."

27. Julie, "Interview."

28. Amy P., "*Rot & Ruin*, by Jonathan Maberry," book review, *YA or STFU: Young Adult Literature without Apology* (blog), February 27, 2011, http://alanis.simmons.edu/blogs/yaorstfu/2011/02/27/rot-and-ruin-by-jonathan-maberry/.

29. Zundel, "Interview."

30. Tafoya, "*Rot & Ruin*."

31. Prophecygirl, "Author Interview."

32. Darren, "Author Interview."

33. Tafoya, "*Rot & Ruin*."

34. Nicole, "Interview: Jonathan Maberry," *Word for Teens* (blog), December 7, 2010, http://www.wordforteens.com/2010/12/interview-jonathan-maberry.html.

35. Prophecygirl, "Author Interview."

36. Jenn, "Jonathan Maberry."

37. Prophecygirl, "Author Interview."

38. Zundel, "Interview."

39. Darren, "Author Interview."

40. "*Dust & Decay*: Product Description," Amazon.com, http://www.amazon.com/Dust-Decay-ebook/dp/B004INH9PY/ref=sr_1_1?ie=UTF8&qid=1304902421&sr=8-1.

Bibliography

Maberry, Jonathan. *Zombie CSU: The Forensics of the Living Dead*. New York: Citadel Press, 2008.

———. *Rot & Ruin* (Rot & Ruin, 1). New York: Simon & Schuster, 2010.

———. *Dust & Decay* (Rot & Ruin, 2). New York: Simon & Schuster, 2011.

14

The Cellar by A. J. Whitten

A. J. Whitten is actually adult romance writer Shirley Jump and her teen daughter Amanda, and *The Cellar* is their second collaboration. It has been included here because of some of the unique aspects of its depiction of zombies.

These are magical Haitian zombies who can remember working in the cane fields before their zombie master used his Arcane Knowledge to make them immortal zombies. While they do live on human flesh, they are not mindless eating machines. In fact, in the goriest of the scenes in the book, Marie and Adrien imprison their victims in the basement and eat bits and pieces of them, slicing off fingers or chunks of flesh and skin to nibble on while the victim remains alive. These scenes contain some of the worst horror in all of YA literature. But the cellar is not just where they keep their "dinners"; it is also the storage place for their coffins, which are handy places to stash upcoming dinners or the occasional unwelcome guest who is resisting being broken to Adrien's will.

The zombies do get hungry and when deprived of flesh for long are ravenous and rather messy eaters, but when fed regularly, they seem to have appetites more the size of human ones. They can eat things other than living human flesh, but they do prefer to have their dinners alive and human, although when a victim dies more quickly than anticipated, they are also willing to eat the recently deceased. Brains are a delicacy because they hold the intelligence and the soul of the victim, which can be passed on to the zombie, and Adrien believes they should be consumed with reverence and appreciation rather than gobbled down quickly.

However, their bite doesn't turn the victim into a zombie, and it is possible for the human to survive even a severe bite. Changing someone into a zombie is a magical rite, with incantations and spells, and can be done only by someone who has been taught the proper steps and rituals, including sucking out the life and breath and breathing zombie breath back in. The victim becomes a zombie immediately.

With enough food, zombies can look very human, although the longer they go without food, the worse they look and the more they age and decay. They can move their consciousness from one body to another when their current body wears out. Adrien treats his bodies well, so they last a long time, but Marie is more careless about hers, and they wear out quicker. The ability to move their consciousness is called The Knowledge, and it is known only by older zombies, who are frequently reluctant to share the skill with others.

Adrien appears to be a teenager, shops at Abercrombie & Fitch, drives a red Camaro, and has a sophisticated sense of style, with his tailored suit coat and jeans combination, topped off with Ray-Bans he never takes off. He has the magical power to ensure that every girl in school is instantly in love with him, except it doesn't work on Meredith. She thinks there's definitely something creepy about him, especially after she gets a glimpse of his eyes behind the sunglasses—he has worms and beetles crawling around in his eye sockets.

Marie is Adrien's mother figure, or mentor, and the head of their small two-person family. She looks ancient and can no longer hunt, so Adrien must provide for her. She is in desperate need of a new body, and this time wants one that is young and strong and likely to last for a long time. She will not share the magical secret of how to create a new zombie until Adrien has found her a new body.

Even if their bodies do not appear to be in very good shape, zombies are supernaturally strong and powerful. They do not feel physical pain, and when ordered to fight by their leader, they do so until they are torn apart or killed. Zombies fighting each other don't try to eat their enemy, just to tear him to pieces. They can be killed by being torn apart, by a bullet to the brain, by beheading (either having their head ripped off or cut by a knife or other weapon), by having their spine broken, or by being hit with acid, which causes them to melt.

Zombies are able to feel emotions, including tenderness and love. Adrien feels intense loneliness, which leads him to first fall for Heather and then send her away because he doesn't want her to have the same kind of pointless existence that he has had. He urges her to remember him as someone who loved her and not a monster. Heather and Meredith's father still cares about his daughters, even though Marie raised him as a zombie, and in the final battle he first reassures Heather and Marie of his love and forgives Heather for causing the accident that killed him, and then kills Marie to prevent her from getting to his daughters.

These zombies are neat about their kills most of the time. They live with fish tanks of piranhas and small carrion-eating fish to clean the last bits of flesh from the bones of their victims after they have finished the flesh and the organs, and the bugs and insects that surround them in swarms have taken care of the scraps. They are also accompanied by hyenas that hunt with Adrien and by vultures eager for leftovers. Once all the creatures have fed, there is little left to bury but the bones, which Adrien takes care of in the backyard, leaving no crime scene for police to investigate.

These scavenger creatures are under the zombies' control and can be sent out to follow humans and report back on their activities or attack them. When Meredith is not doing what he wants her to do, Adrien sends beetles and insects after her. Even though she and he are in class at the time with many other witnesses, Meredith is the only person who sees them.

Marie is cold and her emotions are violent—anger, hatred, jealousy, rage. She is determined to keep Adrien subservient to her because she feels that she owns him, and she is far more powerful than he realizes. He is tiring of eternal life and longs for another just like him to relieve the loneliness that is beginning to overcome him. He also wants to get away from Marie and start his own zombie family, where he will be in control and not under Marie's thumb. It is unfortunate that they both fixate on the same person—Heather, Meredith's sister, who was driving the car and caused the accident that left her scarred and their father dead. Marie wants her body, Adrien wants to turn her into a zombie and be with her forever—but not with Marie living inside her.

When Adrien refuses to hunt for Marie because she is determined to have Heather's body, she goes to the cemetery, digs up graves, dines, and creates a zombie army to take Adrien down. This sets up one of the final scenes, the required zombie-human battle for survival, and for once the humans win. Marie's head gets torn off, and Adrien sprays acid all over the zombies, including himself, and they all melt.

The uniqueness in this book is based upon the characteristics of its zombies—magical, intelligent, able to strategize and plan, able to control humans and animals with their thoughts, immortal, manipulative, selfish, and emotional. Whitten has left the Romero stereotype far behind and created zombies who can be murderers yet sympathetic, revolting but sexy. They commit crimes and do evil things yet yearn to be good and get the girl.

Bibliography

Whitten, A. J. *The Cellar*. Boston: Graphia, 2011.

15

The Enemy Series by Charlie Higson

Charlie Higson is the son of an accountant, but he has never held a proper job and isn't at all sure he could actually do it. He has always been interested in writing and acting, something that his father couldn't understand, but he sent Charlie to a rather avant garde school where they taught creative arts, including how to create television shows. He worked in comedy television for a number of years. Just as that was coming to an end, Higson got a proposal from the company in charge of the James Bond franchise, asking if he would like to write a series of books for boys on the young James Bond when he was about fourteen and just getting into solving crimes. He wrote five books for the series and then realized that because James was getting older, he might have to write some sex into the books, and that wasn't something he really wanted to do,[1] so he began to look around for another kind of book to write.

Higson wanted to write in another genre and had loved horror as a kid, so he began to turn in that direction. His youngest son, Sid, was about ten at that point and was obsessed by zombies—they both intrigued him and scared him to death and gave him nightmares. Higson had also loved zombie movies in the 1960s and '70s, so he decided to write about these monsters. Violence in kids' books is sometimes questionable, but zombies seemed to be a safe monster—they weren't real, and so he could smash them to bits without a problem.[2] He wanted his zombies to be truly frightening in both their appearance and their actions. He said he felt that he owed it to the children of Britain to "scare the living daylights out of them."[3] To make sure he was creating a story that could do just that, he read it aloud to Sid as he was writing it. He kept pushing the horror and the gore as he went, trying to really scare his son. But Sid just kept taking it without getting scared, so Higson pushed some more. Finally, Sid came downstairs at four thirty one morning, newly awakened from a nightmare about the book, and he was really scared. Higson was elated—he'd finally done it! The book was scary enough to scare Sid and would be scary to other kids as well.[4]

But adults have expressed concern about the effect of the gore and the violence in the books, causing Higson to comment that the kids who read the books enjoy them while still keeping them firmly within the fantasy realm where they are set.[5] After all, in the real world, a plague isn't going to strike all the adults in the world, making them into cannibalistic zombies eager to eat their kids. Kids understand that and so can enjoy being scared from within the safety of a book. Higson notes that sometimes having the pants scared off you by a good book can keep you from getting terminally depressed about the very real and scary and dangerous world around you. Adults can be very frightening to children. They are big, and strong, and powerful, and loud, and occasionally smelly. What better way to counteract this than by giving children carte blanche to fight back[6]—and win, at least part of the time. This is what Higson's books allow children to do.

When Higson started to work on *The Enemy*, he decided to give it a setting he knows and loves—the city of London. He knew he was writing a fantastical book, so he wanted to ground that fantasy in reality just as completely as he could. The streets, the buildings, the museums, the highway and subway systems—all are real. Readers living in London could actually trace the movements of the characters in the books through the streets and the buildings. Higson mused that someday someone might do walking tours of the locations in The Enemy series.[7] The only part of the series that he didn't create from whole cloth was Rowhurst, the school from which the boys escape in the beginning of *The Dead*. It is based on his old school, six-hundred-year-old Sevenoaks in Kent.[8]

The Waitrose supermarket that is the setting for the opening scenes of *The Enemy* is Higson's own market on Holloway Road, where he and his wife shop. Other places in the books are his favorite places in London, including the Imperial War Museum, the Tower of London, and the Natural History Museum. In order to write the sections of the books set in Buckingham Palace, he visited the palace on the Queen's birthday, when she had a big party based on British children's books, and was able to see quite a lot of it behind the scenes, such as the large park behind the palace. When he was a child, Higson fantasized about going into public buildings and doing anything he wanted[9]—trying on armor, getting into displays of various kinds, playing with anything he wanted to—and setting the series in some of those places allowed him to do that. The series was launched at yet another well-known London location— The London Tombs, where the skeletons of over 380 plague victims were found—and perhaps a location that might be included in one of the future volumes.[10]

Higson also included many references to popular culture in the books to further help ground them in the real world. He isn't particularly worried that those references will date the books, because he hates imprecise or vague references—that isn't how people speak and act in real life. He wrote the books for teens of today, not teens of tomorrow, and that demanded current references.[11] Not all books or movies with popular culture references will be inaccessible even if they are dated—the characters, their actions and emotions, and the lessons they teach will still be there for readers to identify with.

The Enemy takes one group of children from a suburban supermarket to Buckingham Palace and is set about a year after the adults first began to get sick. *The Dead* is actually its prequel, set in urban London immediately after the disease began to spread. Although some of the characters in the books overlap, the books end before the two groups, one in the palace, the other in the Tower of London, actually meet. The two groups meet for the first time in the third volume, *The Fear*.[12] Higson has given no hints about what will take place in the last three volumes planned for the series, although he has not closed the door to the possibility of additional volumes if demand warrants.

There is no explanation in the series for the disease that either kills the adults or turns them into zombies, because it is written from the point of view of the kids who are trying to survive. They don't know why it happened, only that it did and they have to figure out some way to survive it. Higson plans to let them discover more information about the disease in future volumes, once he figures out what it is.[13] He has talked to doctors and researchers to try to find out how such a disease might actually work and why its effects would be intensified by sunlight—a detail that gives his zombies something in common with vampires.[14] The third book, *The Fear*, also reveals whether or not the kids in the series will get sick when they get older—a real threat since at the end of *The Enemy*, Ollie is just one day away from his fourteenth birthday. Higson's contract with Puffin is for six books, and a large part of the three that have not yet been written will be focused on finding out more about the disease. There are a number of questions that have to be answered: Will the kids all get sick when they get older? Is everyone in the whole world infected, or is it only a British phenomenon? Is there a cure? Higson predicts that these and other questions will be answered gradually, and that the sixth book will reveal the secrets of the disease—assuming anyone is left alive at that point.[15]

While it is inevitable that the series would be compared to *Lord of the Flies*, Higson says that he believes it is more accurate to compare it to the Lord of the Rings, in which a group of creatures bands together to go out and fight the monster. They are friends, and they work together so they can all survive. William Golding didn't like children, so he had them destroy each other when they were left to their own devices, but he failed to acknowledge the fact that adults can be far worse than children.[16] Higson thinks that teens get a lot of bad press, and he wanted to help balance that out.[17] For him, adolescence is layered, often cruel, but sometimes also enlightened,[18] and never one dimensional. So when his groups of mismatched teens and children set out, they don't squabble and fight among themselves; instead they cooperate and work together to ensure that they can all survive[19]—at least the ones that Higson doesn't decide to kill off. He also wanted a certain epic adventure quality to the story, like the Lord of the Rings, in which they go on a journey or quest, and at the end of it, have a chance to see how much they have done and how far they have come.[20]

This series has a huge cast of characters who are well fleshed out and differentiated based on their jobs and purposes within the community. Higson wanted to have as wide a range as possible for his characters, so he included older and younger children, leaders and followers, fighters and nonfighters, those who are good with technology, or medicine, or scavenging. He worked hard to make them all believable, walking, talking people who came alive in his head and on the page, even though he knew from the beginning that he was going to have to kill off many of them. It wasn't something he wanted to do or enjoyed doing, but it was necessary to keep the tension and the suspense high. Some characters revealed their flaws and had to be killed, others pushed their way to the front of the line and demanded more time and space. When he finished, he discussed the characters with his sons and found that they recommended that he kill off a couple more people, which was quite difficult but which worked better in the end.[21] From the first page of the series, the reader feels the pressure, the tension, knowing that at any point time may run out for one of the children and in seconds he or she will be gone. Nothing can be taken for granted; no one can be considered safe.[22]

He based his characters on his sons' friends and other teens he knows, but several of them, even the girls, have some of his own characteristics. He is like other authors who draw on the person they know best—themselves—as a base for their characters.[23] He created characters that were both good and evil, trying to balance out those qualities. He also created characters that succeeded because of brains rather than brawn,[24] and ones that survived not by fighting, but by being clever, or fast, or small, or good at hiding—survival doesn't just depend on mindless violence.[25]

Characters also have traits that allow them to grow and share their lessons with the reader. Small Sam is often underestimated because of his size, but he learns that courage and bravery are not always dependent on one's stature. Maxie assumes leadership reluctantly but grows into the role, bringing to it a tenacity, toughness, and determination tempered by tenderness and understanding that perhaps would not have been present had she been a boy. Achilleus, a warrior in every sense of the word, realizes that force is not always the best way to win a battle. Circumstances bring out the best in these characters but bring out the worst in others, such as David King, who rules the group at Buckingham Palace and wants to set himself up as the new king.

These children are at war, and the leaders of each of the groups must make decisions that seem cruel, cold, and unfeeling, in order to save those who are under their protection. Jordon refuses to let anyone stay with his group at the Imperial War Museum because he has stockpiled supplies only for his group. If he shares, his group will die. He is willing to help Ed's group, to supply them with weapons, but no more. He is not being mean or selfish, but realistic.

Higson's main groups of children (one in each book) create their own communities or societies, with jobs, leaders, soldiers, even medical clinics.[26] They look out for one another, work together, share their food and other supplies, and protect the littlest of them, who aren't old enough to fight when the going gets rough.[27] Because of their unity and their friendship and their willingness to do whatever is necessary to survive, this main group is ultimately stronger than the other groups of kids struggling to survive.[28] Their leaders rule not just by might but with heart, inspiring the intense loyalties of the followers in the groups. They also consult their lieutenants before making decisions, winning their allegiance and enhancing the group's solidarity. There are "bad" kids that must be fought against, but Higson's communities of kids deal with them and then get back to the business of survival.

Higson was brutal about eliminating characters. He deliberately set up the beginning of *The Enemy* so the reader wouldn't know who'd survive and who wouldn't, who the important characters were and who played more minor roles.[29] Several times he knowingly set up a character to engage the reader only to kill off him or her a few pages later.[30] Not all these characters are minor—one of the most unexpected and startling deaths in *The Enemy* is that of a leader, one of the most charismatic and sympathetic characters the reader has met to that point. Another time, a character is saved at the last minute, over and over, only to finally go down just when the reader has decided it's safe. Higson defends himself by saying his work shows kids that good people, people you love, die too—and sometimes enemies survive and friends perish.[31]

He learned from his Young James Bond series that much of the tension was lost because readers always knew that James would survive. He wanted to make sure from the beginning that the readers of The Enemy series would have no such reassurance. Continually pulling the rug out from under his readers, Higson made the books much more tense and frightening. In doing this, Higson set himself up as an untrustworthy author and kept his readers involved and on edge. He also acknowledges that his sons are bored with a thriller/horror book or movie in which no one dies.[32]

To Higson, the threat from the zombies is very real and very visceral. What could be more frightening than people you love and trust wanting to kill and eat you—or eat you before killing you? The kids refer to grown-ups as "mothers" and "fathers," which makes the whole thing even more creepy.[33] Granted, if the disease had infected everyone above the age of fourteen (British edition) or sixteen (American edition), there are zombie teens out there who aren't parental figures, but the mass of zombies are parents and referring to them in familial terms certainly heightens the horror.

The adults versus kids scenario is not new to Higson, who notes it has been played out over and over as far back as Greek mythology, when kings and gods were warned that a child had been born who would one day grow up and overthrow them. It's unavoidable—if the child is going to grow up and find his or her place in life, the child has to get rid of the parents. And if a parent/adult is going to hold on to his or her place, the child has to die.[34] (Banishment doesn't work all that well—the child ultimately comes back, and the prophecy comes true.) It is a theme in fairy and folk tales as well—"The giants, the ogres, the witches, the grown-ups, they all want to eat the children. In the end though, the kids always win."[35]

Fiction for teens is a lot harder, grittier, and tougher than it used to be, and that means a higher body count, something at which Higson doesn't flinch. He wanted the series firmly in the horror genre, frightening enough that sometimes he himself was scared writing it, which helped convince him that he would be scaring his readers as well.[36] Nevertheless, the series isn't ultimately about zombies; it's about kids who are trying to survive a zombie apocalypse.[37] The zombies are there simply to provide the threat and danger. The real story is what the kids do in response to the zombies.

Notes

1. Aiden Smith, "Interview: Charlie Higson, Author," Scotsman.com, September 21, 2010, http://news.scotsman.com/features/Interview-Charlie-Higson-author.6539240.jp.

2. Claire Armistead, "Charlie Higson Reads from *The Enemy*," *The Guardian* Books Podcast, October 30, 2009, http://www.guardian.co.uk/books/audio/2009/oct/30/charlie-higson-enemy-samantha-harvey-wilderness-jackie-kay.

3. Zencat, "First Look at *The Enemy*," Young Bond Dossier, April 6, 2009, http://youngbonddossier.com/Young_Bond/Danger_Society_News/Entries/2009/4/6_First_look_at_The_Enemy.html.

4. Armistead, "Charlie Higson."

5. Smith, "Interview."

6. Charlie Higson, "Charlie Higson Explains Why He Wrote *The Enemy*, a Zombie Book for Children," *The Times*, August 29, 2009, http://entertainment.timesonline.co.uk/tol/arts_and_entertainment/books/fiction/article6812377.ece.

7. Teenreads.com, "Charlie Higson," Teenreads.com, May, 2010, http://teenreads.com/authors/au-higson-charlie.asp.

8. Selena Wang, "Selena Wang Interviews Charlie Higson," *The Great Raven* (blog), April 26, 2011, http://suebursztynski.blogspot.com/2011/04/interview-with-charlie-higson.html.

9. First News, "Sometimes You Scare Yourself," First News, October 30, 2010, http://www.firstnews.co.uk/discover/first-news-interviews-charlie-higson-i505.

10. Devin Zydel, "Charlie Higson's *The Enemy* to Be Launched at the London Tombs," CommanderBond.net, August 28, 2009, http://commanderbond.net/7024/charlie-higsons-the-enemy-to-be-launched-at-the-london-tombs.html.

11. Teenreads.com, "Charlie Higson."

12. Wang, "Selena Wang Interviews."

13. Armistead, "Charlie Higson."

14. Wang, "Selena Wang Interviews."

15. First News, "Sometimes."

16. Teenreads.com, "Charlie Higson."

17. Charlie Higson, "Charlie Higson on the Differences between Writing for Kids, Teens, & Adults," *The Guardian*, posted by PETA on April 5, 2011, http://www.insertliteraryblognamehere.com/index.php/ya-author-charlie-higson-on-the-differences-between-writing-for-kids-teens-adults.

18. Brian O'Connell, "Fast Adventures of an Accidental Author," *Irish Times.com*, December 28, 2010, http://www.irishtimes.com/newspaper/features/2010/1228/1224286356923.html.

19. Teenreads.com, "Charlie Higson."

20. Teenreads.com, "Charlie Higson."

21. Teenreads.com, "Charlie Higson."

22. My Favourite Books, *"The Enemy*—Charlie Higson," book review, *My Favourite Books* (blog), January 2, 2010, http://myfavouritebooks.blogspot.com/2010/01/enemy-charlie-higson.html.

23. Wang, "Selena Wang Interviews."

24. Jill Murphy, *"The Enemy* by Charlie Higson," The Bookbag, September, 2009, http://www.thebookbag.co.uk/reviews/index.php?title=The_Enemy_by_Charlie_Higson.

25. Teenreads.com, "Charlie Higson."

26. Peeptastic, *"The Enemy* by Charlie Higson," book review, *Attack of the Book* (blog), December 16, 2010, http://attackofthebook.com/2010/12/16/enemy-charlie-higson/.

27. Armistead, "Charlie Higson."

28. Teenreads.com, "Charlie Higson."

29. Armistead, "Charlie Higson."

30. Murphy, *"The Enemy."*

31. Armistead, "Charlie Higson."

32. John Butler, "Young Blood," *Irish Times*, October 3, 2009, 14, http://www.irishtimes.com/newspaper/magazine/2009/1003/1224255478130.html.

33. Teenreads.com, "Charlie Higson."

34. Teenreads.com, "Charlie Higson."

35. Teenreads.com, "Charlie Higson."

36. First News, "Sometimes."

37. Peeptastic, *"The Enemy."*

Bibliography

Higson, Charlie. *The Enemy*. London: Puffin, 2009.

———. *The Dead*. London: Puffin, 2010.

———. *The Fear*. London: Puffin, 2011.

16

The Generation Dead Series by Daniel Waters

Daniel Waters realized he wanted to be a writer when he was six years old and never changed his mind.[1] *Generation Dead* was his first novel, and the inspiration to write it came from a newsmagazine TV show on violence in schools, showing how taping random acts of violence or planned confrontations to post online was becoming increasingly popular. There were many clips of kids hurting other kids, and the one that hit him the hardest was of a little boy in a coat that was much too big for him, waiting for a bus to arrive, when a much bigger boy ran up and punched the boy, who fell to the pavement crying and bleeding from the nose and mouth.[2] The show scared Waters to death, and when he couldn't get the images out of his head, he knew he had to write about them.[3] The zombies were his way of coping with the horror of what he had seen,[4] because confronting it head-on was far too depressing. The reality of a kid hurting another kid just for entertainment was horrifying to Waters and, as the show pointed out, distressingly real.[5] Zombies allowed him to inject some humor into his books and treat the subject with a lighter touch.[6] They came to him out of the blue as he was thinking about cruelty, prejudice, and discrimination, and it occurred to him that if zombies were real, they'd be the most discriminated against group ever. For instance, what would happen if a zombie wanted to date a living girl and take her to the prom?[7]

Waters began with an outline,[8] but the book took on a life of its own as he wrote it so the first and last drafts looked very different.[9] Minor characters ended up becoming much more central to the story,[10] and one of the point-of-view characters was completely cut out when Waters realized he was adding nothing to the story and was subtracting from it in significant ways. Even so, writing him out of the book made him feel "oddly guilty and criminal."[11]

Waters's decision to avoid the voodoo and Romero-type zombies was almost instinctive, but it made more and more sense as he began to write. He wasn't interested in body counts, like most zombie books and movies are,[12] and he wanted to look at the idea of discrimination and how we treat those who are different from us, those who are marginalized in a variety of ways.[13] Since *Generation Dead* was published, he has been very gratified by the positive reader response to the issues and situations in it, including race, gender identity, gay rights, handicapped rights, and even feeling isolated and alone. Readers find much to identify with in characters and in situations.

The series is set in America, because in this story it is only American teens who are coming back from the dead. No one knows why, but a variety of things, including all the additives in fast foods, mold spores, first-person shooter games, global warming, childhood inoculations, and even microwaved food, have been blamed.[14] There are no zombie children, or parents, or grandparents. And not all teens come back to life. Pete's overwhelming anger and hatred of zombies stems from the fact that the girl he loved, Julie, died and didn't come back.

The zombies in this series are dead, have no heartbeat, don't eat or sleep, and don't need to breathe other than to talk. They aren't rotting and they don't smell. They move and think more slowly than the living and have pauses in their speech while they struggle to come up with the next words. Some of them look more like the living than others, and as the series opens, no one knows why they have different abilities, but gradually it becomes obvious that one thing that brings zombies back from the dead is love and loving—love of family, love of friends, and the ability or opportunity to express the love they themselves feel. Karen and Tommy, the two dead kids who appear most alive, have families who love them just as unconditionally as they did when they were alive. Before they died, they were surrounded by people who cared about them and supported them. Their deaths didn't change that. Tommy's only family is his mother, but her love is openly expressed and consistent. They don't have much, but they do have each other, and his mother's faith in him has given Tommy the self-confidence that helped him become the leader of the local dead kids and that took him on his journey to Washington to advocate for the rights of zombies all over America.

Karen is the only suicide to come back to life, and no one is sure just why she has, but it could have to do with her unwillingness to leave the love of her life, the love she believed she could never acknowledge, the one person she could never have. She may have killed herself because of the depression that always surrounded her, but her desire to be with her soul mate may have given her the strength to come back. Karen lives with her parents, who love her and moved to Oakvale so she could continue to go to school and be with her little sister, who was born nine months after Karen died and who adores her big sister with all her heart. Most zombies, even the "fast" ones, look like zombies, but Karen is able to pass as human, get a job at the mall, and even go undercover and date Pete, the Oakvale High bully who hates zombies and is part of a movement to destroy them all. Karen hopes she can find out what he has planned and stop it. She has always been unique among the zombies, but in *Passing Strange* she seems to be becoming less dead, and this could set up a new premise for the next volume in the series, which could very well examine the question of what makes us human. Zombies can think and speak and move and feel emotions, but they don't have a beating heart—is that what keeps them from being human? What other things separate the living from the dead?

Adam, who takes a long time to come back, has grown up in a hostile environment with a mother who doesn't support him, a mean stepfather who abuses and scorns him, and two older stepbrothers who yell at him and put him down. When he comes back, although his stepfather tries to be supportive and affectionate, his stepbrothers' attitudes have grown worse, and his mother refuses to be around him more than is absolutely necessary. While Phoebe has realized she loves him, she is unable to give him the consistent loving support and affirmation that he needs. It is only after his karate teacher urges him to go back to the dojo and work to get control of his mind and body that Adam slowly begins to improve.

Colette, who was Phoebe's and Margi's best friend, comes back after she drowned, but after she walks home from the hospital morgue, her parents won't let her in the house and neither will Margi or Phoebe. She stays in the woods until Tommy finds her and takes her to his mother. After his mother does all she can (she is able to help the dead kids but Waters doesn't explain how), Phoebe goes to live in the Haunted House with the other zombies who don't have a home. She continues to go to school and wants to be friends with Phoebe and Margi, although they are unable to accept her at first, feeling guilty about her death and their subsequent rejection of her. She is one of the slowest zombies until Margi's parents invite her to come and live with them, and surrounded by love again, she begins to improve her mental functioning, physical movements, and appearance. For every parent who is able to love and accept their zombie kids, there are many who reject them.

Waters looked at the zombie books and movies from the past, and it seemed to him that their scariness came from the fear of being assimilated into a faceless, mindless horde, of losing one's individuality and identity. Today this has been replaced to some extent by the fear that an individual can make him or herself as unique as possible and still not have anyone care. One might be a fully realized individual yet be unseen and unheard by society.[15] Teens, with their lack of power to impact the adult world around them, can easily identify with these ideas as well.

Waters also used a variety of terms for the zombies in his book, pointing out that they are perceived differently by different groups. Politically correct adults prefer the terms "differently biotic" or "living impaired." The dead kids in the series refer to themselves both as dead kids and as zombies and don't mind their friends using the same terms with affection, but object to some of the other pejoratives, like corpsicles, dead heads, worm food, shamblers, and the living dead, that are used to be deliberately hurtful. Examples of hate speech highlight the status of the dead kids as a marginalized minority throughout the series, and point out that sometimes it is not the word but the emotion and intent behind the word that makes it a pejorative. However, the zombies have their own words for the living that are no less hurtful. They are blood bags, bleeders, beating hearts, or breathers—all referring to things that are no longer characteristic of the zombies.

Waters also decided to use different stylistic techniques to keep his writing fresh. In *Generation Dead*, he spent a great deal of time figuring out where the pauses would go when the dead kids were speaking, how long they would be, and whether they would be consistent for each character or change when the character was feeling stressed, rather than calm or relaxed.[16] The pauses eventually came to indicate how high functioning each person was and how "far back" they had come. Waters enjoyed writing Adam's point of view in *Kiss of Death* because he had to change Adam's internal dialogue and speech as he came back more and more.[17] In *Passing Strange* Waters used Karen's internal dialogue to inform the reader of events from the past that were still having an impact on her and to make her depression more real. Future volumes may feature different narrators, including Tommy, as he continues his travels to advocate for equal rights for the differently biotic.[18]

The focus of this series is the question "How do we treat those who are different from us?" and the social and political implications of asking it. Waters's zombies can stand in for any minority or group that is discriminated against, whether it is because of race, gender identity, mental or physical disability, appearance, or personal preferences like what kind of music someone listens to or what kind of person someone chooses to date. In the Generation Dead world, zombies are like everyone else—they just want to fit in and enjoy the same privileges the living kids have, including a driver's license and a library card. In fact, they are just like we are—only a bit slower.[19]

Waters has also brought Tommy's website and blog to life online, written by Tommy, Phoebe, Margi, and a few others. It has posts from Tommy about his travels, a zombie meme to which several characters contribute, and an eclectic variety of bits and pieces. In January 2011, Margi revealed that there had been reports of zombies in Europe and Asia, so the phenomenon is spreading worldwide. The blog has almost over 2,800 followers, many of whom comment regularly.

There are different groups of zombies that are introduced gradually, as the scope of the Generation Dead world expands. There are the kids who go to high school and try to fit in, the kids who live at the Haunted House in the woods, and the Sons of Romero, whose bodies show the violent ways they died—Takayuki, or Tak, is missing part of his face and hand; George has patches of flesh missing from his torso so that his ribs show, and one ear and half of his nose are gone. Tak is one of the fast zombies, but George is one of the slowest. Popeye is another of the Sons of Romero; he is a zombie artist, creating several scenes or displays around town to support zombies. He has also decorated his own body in various ways to enhance his zombie appearance—he has no eyelids and has removed patches of skin so his muscles show through. He is aware that other people think he looks repulsive, but he likes the way he looks and seems to be a fairly upbeat person most of the time.

Some of the zombies agree with Tommy that they should fight for their rights; others aren't at all interested in being part of the living world, seeing life as far too dangerous or hating the living for being alive. It is the latter group that Tak takes into the lake to keep them from being hunted and killed after they are framed for the murder of a lawyer and his family.

The living have equally diverse opinions of the zombies. Zombies are treated as African Americans were treated in the 1950s and '60s and have no civil rights or privileges at all[20]—they can't drive, vote, or get a library card or a social security number, and they have no access to health care. Zombies can't leave the country because they have no passport, but the military is glad to have them, and they can be drafted into the armed forces. Radical hate groups want them exterminated, and there is no penalty for killing zombies because they aren't alive. Pete is not punished for killing Adam because he came back immediately, and while Adam is no longer a human, he is alive in some sense of the word. During the second and third volumes of the series, Nathan Mather, a radical antizombie preacher, and his followers become more and more powerful, trying to frame the zombies for a variety of crimes, including the murder of the lawyer who defended Pete and his family. If they can stir up enough antizombie sentiment, they can win followers to their cause and have legislation enacted against the zombies.

There are all kinds of subplots: romantic ones; political ones concerning zombie rights and snippets from Tommy's blog; minority rights ones that involve not only Mather's group but also the Hunter Foundation created to study and advocate for the dead kids; and newspaper stories about zombie persecution. There are also subplots that involve friendship and what it means, coming of age and how to cope with it, and a wide variety of different kinds of families and their interactions.

The series also has a wide variety of settings: the high school; Lake Oxoboxo, where Tak hides the zombies when the zombie riots start; the woods near the lake; the Haunted House in the woods where several of the dead kids live, which is the gathering place for the local zombie community and their friends; the Hunter Foundation where the Undead Studies classes meet and work and where scientists try to solve some of the mysteries of the zombies; Mather's compound in Arizona where his followers are trained; the mall where Karen works; and the homes of individual characters. Particularly interesting is Aftermath, the zombie club in New York City. Because zombies like a lot of intense stimuli, it is a mix of bright colors, comfortable furniture, pulsing lights, and loud music with a lot of bass, all of which makes it easy for even zombies to dance to the beat. Each location is distinctive and drawn in detail.

Characters are also very detailed and reveal themselves gradually throughout the series. One example is Pete, who steps onstage in *Generation Dead* as the "lead alpha" on the football team, a bully who enjoys beating up boys on and off the football field. He has anger issues and is vitriolic in his hatred of zombies. His parents are divorced, and his mother has remarried a weakling whom Pete despises. His father lives in California and ignores his son for the most part, although he does invite Pete to stay with him over the summer and occasionally throws money at him. Pete is desperate for his love and attention and approval and reacts with anger and resentment when he doesn't get them. But by the third book, *Passing Strange*, we have begun to understand why Pete is so hateful, especially toward zombies. He fell in love with a girl in California, and when she died and didn't come back, he was deeply wounded and started to lash out in response. It is doubtful that he will ever be a likable character, but Waters shows the reader enough about him that Pete is at least understandable and perhaps even a little sympathetic.

Karen is another character who moves from being a bit player to a more central one, as is Takayuki. While Tak hasn't yet become a narrator, he has become the leader of the dead kids, determined to keep as many of them safe as he can. Tommy, on the other hand, has moved from being one of the central characters in the first book to a more distant role as he remains offstage, seen only through the comments from his blog and e-mails to his friends. It will be interesting to see how Waters develops these and other characters and takes the series in new directions. His kinder and gentler zombies have many more stories to tell.

Notes

1. Falcata Times, "Daniel Waters," *Falcata Times* (blog), August 5, 2009, http://falcatatimes.blogspot.com/2009/08/interview-daniel-waters.html.

2. Kyle, "An Awesome Author: Daniel Waters (Day 1),"*Book Review Maniac* (blog), July 16, 2008, http://bookreviewmaniac.blogspot.com/2008/07/awesome-author-daniel-waters-day-1.html.

3. Monster Librarian, "Interview with Daniel Waters," Monster Librarian, http://www.monsterlibrarian.com/interviews.htm#Daniel_Waters.

4. Kyle, "Awesome Author."

5. Monster Librarian, "Interview."

6. Daniel Waters, "Stupid Theory of the Day," *My So-called Undeath* (blog), April 14, 2008, http://mysocalledundeath.blogspot.com/search?q=microwave.

7. Tina, "Author Interview: Daniel Waters," *Fantastic Book Review* (blog), May 13, 2009, http://www.fantasticbookreview.com/2009/05/author-interview-daniel-waters.html?showComment=1243185458486.

8. Falcata Times, "Daniel Waters."

9. IB Teen, "IB Teen Talks to Dan Waters," *Imperial Beach Library Teen Blog*, May 1, 2009, http://ibteens.blogspot.com/2009/05/were-here-were-dead-get-used-to-it.html.

10. Tina, "Author Interview."

11. IB Teen, "IB Teen Talks."

12. IB Teen, "IB Teen Talks."

13. Helen, "Review and Author Interview: *Generation Dead* (Daniel Waters)," *Helen's Book Blog*, January 2, 2010, http://www.helensbookblog.com/2010/01/review-and-author-interview-generation.html.

14. Daniel Waters, "Without Armor," *The Horror Library* (blog), March 11, 2008, http://horrorlibrary.blogspot.com/2008/03/can-you-say-second-tuesday-guest.html.

15. IB Teen, "IB Teen Talks."

16. Tina, "Author Interview."

17. Falcata Times, "Daniel Waters."

18. Ezmirelda, "Interview with Author Daniel Waters!" *Dreams of a YA Writer* (blog), July 2, 2010, http://parafantasy.blogspot.com/2010/07/interview-with-author-daniel-waters.html.

19. J. G. Faherty, "Book Review: *Generation Dead* by Daniel Waters," *Fear Zone* (blog), November 27, 2007, http://www.fearzone.com/blog/generation-dead.

20. Faherty, "Book Review."

Bibliography

Waters, Daniel. *Generation Dead*. New York: Hyperion, 2008.
———. *Kiss of Life*. New York: Hyperion, 2009.
———. *Passing Strange*. New York: Hyperion, 2010.

17

The Revenants Series by Amy Plum

Amy Plum was inspired to write a paranormal series when she read the Twilight series and loved it. But she wanted a new twist, a new monster, a new setting. It was to be set in the real world, but with just a tinge of magical realism hiding under the realistic surface. She came up first with her heroine—someone independent and smart, both intellectually and emotionally. Someone who had had some hardship in her life to temper her and give her maturity.[1] Her parents have just been killed in a car accident, ripping away all her plans and all her security. Her future is totally up to her—a terrifying place to be.[2]

Kate has a lot of Plum in her, but she is the person the author wishes she had been at sixteen,[3] stronger and wiser than her creator actually was.[4] In a scene in which Vincent quizzes Kate, all of her answers are the same as Plum's would be—they both love wearing jeans, T-shirts, and Converse low-tops.[5] Plum used the memory of her grief when her own mother died to help her write Kate's reaction to her parents' unexpected deaths, and Kate herself gave her the first sentence of the book: "Ten days after I got my driver's license, my parents died in a car wreck." Even though the prologue that contained the sentence was eventually cut, for Plum that was the inspiration that gave the book its focus and direction.[6]

Her favorite scene in the book is the fight at the end. It was the most fun to write, she says, because she could see the whole thing in her head and had to rush to get it down on paper.[7] Later, when she read it aloud to her husband while he was driving, he ran off the road because he was so surprised.[8]

Plum didn't want Kate to be completely on her own, so she gave her a party girl of a big sister, Georgia, who is very close to her although Kate is a loner. She also gave the girls wonderful French grandparents who are very involved in the world of art and very close to their granddaughters. This meant the story had to be set in Paris, a city where Plum had lived for five years in her twenties, a city that still seems magical to her. As a young writer, she was told "write what you know," and she knew Paris.[9] Paris is not only a romantic city, but also a city with a lengthy and dark history of crime, betrayal, and intrigue. Its streets have run with the blood of martyrs and rulers alike; its walls have hidden their mysteries for centuries, so it seemed like a good place not only for romance but also for a supernatural battle between good and evil.[10]

Once she had her heroine firmly in mind, Plum began to consider what kind of monster she would like to include, so she made a list of all the different kinds of supernatural monsters, but none of them really appealed to her.[11] She ended by crossing everything off her list except "gods" and "zombies," and then she wondered if she could combine them. As a historian, she was drawn to the idea of the undead because it would give her an opportunity to create a long backstory for each of the characters, but she was puzzled about how to make zombies into romantic heroes.[12] That was when she realized she would have to invent her own monster, and her version of zombies, which she called "revenants," was created. She started the book with only an outline of what revenants were and began to put the pieces together as she wrote. When she was stuck, she'd take time off and go for a walk, considering the problem as she exercised. Sooner or later the answer would come to her, as if she were just uncovering something that had always been there. She just had to give herself the time and space to find it.[13] Stephen King once referred to this process as "excavating fossils," and the phrase resonates for Plum as well.[14] In fact, much of the information Plum "discovered" about the revenants and their world wasn't used in the first book and may or may not be used in the future. But even if it doesn't appear in the story, it's still there as a foundation and a support, giving historical perspective and depth.[15]

While Plum used zombies in the first draft of the book (she wrote three), she soon realized that she would need a different term. "Zombie" creates too many assumptions in the reader's mind, and her monsters needed a name that wasn't so strongly connected to shambling, rotting, flesh-eating monsters. One day the word "revenant" popped into her head, a rarely used French word meaning ghost, or someone who returns from the dead. Since that is exactly what her monsters do, she decided that that was the term she would use to create beings who were historical figures as old and immortal as vampires, werewolves, and zombies.[16] Her revenants are humans who were killed while saving someone's life. They can reanimate, coming back to life with an implacable urge to save the lives of other humans who are about to die, sometimes dying themselves in the process. When they come back from death, they come back the same age they were when they were killed for the first time, so they are essentially immortal.

The city of Paris is not only the setting for the book, it is a character in its own right.[17] Plum was able to use lush and sensual descriptions in the book to introduce the city, and she also posted a map of Paris on her website,[18] with her own photos of locations in the book. Many of these locations are places she enjoyed when she lived in Paris, and others are ones she selected specifically for the book. She deliberately chose places she wouldn't have to research.[19] She lives three hours south of Paris, in a small town in the Loire Valley, the name of which she will not reveal. There she shares a rambling farmhouse that is over two hundred years old and in a constant state of renovation, with her husband and two children and a large red dog.[20] While she was writing the book, she went back to Paris and wandered the streets looking for places and buildings that she could use in the book.

For instance, the building she wanted to use for Kate's grandparents' apartment house, with the art restoration studio on the top floor, was in the wrong place, so she just moved it a few blocks away and plopped it down where she wanted it, facing a small park. Jean-Baptiste's *maison particulier*, where the kindred (the revenants) live, is in real life the Maillol Museum. Plum once lived in the building that houses Jules's art studio and loved going to the shops at the Village St. Paul, just down the street. The restaurant where Vincent and Kate went on their first date was one of her favorites, and the building next to the Sorbonne where Vincent and Ambrose died in 1968 was her old apartment building. Plum has ridden through the streets of Paris on a scooter, her arms around a handsome boy; kissed a boy on the Pont des Arts Bridge; and basked in the sun on the cobblestone quay of the Ile St. Louis.[21] In fact, the only place she created is the café where Kate first saw Vincent, the Café Sainte-Lucie, although she admits it could be any pretty café along the Boulevard Sainte-Germain.[22] Her pictures and her prose bring all those places to vivid life for her readers—in fact, such vivid life for some readers say that they've seen Kate and Vincent around Paris, and sent pictures of them to Plum, some of which she posted on her blog on May 17, 2011![23]

Just as she wanted to set her story in a real place, she also wanted to have real historical backgrounds for the revenants who help save the people who live there. She based Vincent's story on her husband's grandfather, who was a member of the Maquis in the south of France and told her his story one Christmas, much to the shock of the rest of the family, who hadn't heard it before. Ambrose is based on Plum's husband's grandfather, Sergeant Warren G. H. Crecy—"The Baddest Man in the 761st"—and Lucien is based on Philippe Henriot, "The French Goebbels," a politician killed by the Maquis. Most of the backstories of the revenants were based on her historical research.[24] Charlotte and Charles's story is set in occupied Paris during World War II, which was easy for Plum to imagine since she has read *Is Paris Burning?* by Dominique Lapierre and Larry Collins many times and was familiar with the era. She had to research mustard gas for Jules's story, and Gaspard's story was the most difficult to create, but when she started checking dates and places, she discovered that the background she had created for him fit right into place, just like there'd been "this little Gaspard-shaped hole in the fabric of history just waiting to be patched in."[25] Plum has also considered setting some historical fiction in the revenants' world, going back in time to tell the stories of their former lives, leading up to the present,[26] once she finishes the Die for Me trilogy.

Plum's writing style is somewhat organic. She began *Die for Me* not sure where it was going to go, but when her agent asked her to come up with a story arc for a trilogy, she realized she had to do an outline in order for the story to make sense.[27] Then when she was writing *Until I Die*, she realized that she needed more information to tie the books together and had to stop writing to figure it out. So while she knows where book three will end, she isn't sure how her characters will get there—or how they'll surprise her before they do.[28] The series will grow darker as Kate finds out more about Vincent and the other kindred, and readers can look forward to "love, heartbreak, mistrust, deception, [and] shock."[29] While three books are all she has planned now, she doesn't rule out the possibility of there being more.[30]

Revenants have existed for centuries, just as vampires, werewolves, and zombies have—they are just better at keeping humans unaware of their existence. They are dead but appear to be alive. They were killed saving someone else's life and according to the "law of the universe" in the revenants' world, if someone dies in place of someone else, he or she will come back to life three days later. Then they will be awake without sleeping for three weeks, and after that their bodies shut down and they appear to be dead for three days, before awaking to three more weeks of sleepless animation. It is simply a different kind of life cycle. They call their down periods dormancy, and while there is neither mental nor physical activity for the first twenty-four hours, after that the individual is mentally alert and able to travel outside the body and communicate with other revenants mentally. This state is called volant. When the revenants go on patrol, looking for humans who might be in trouble, there are usually two present physically and one volant, because being present only in spirit gives one a certain amount of prescience, which can be handy when rescuing humans. The afternoon when Charlotte saves Kate from being crushed by falling masonry at the Café Sainte-Lucie, Vincent was volant and let Charlotte know that it was about to fall.

The kindred reanimate to save human lives, lives that are about to end by accident or by design. It is their fate, and they are driven to accomplish it—to sacrifice themselves over and over to save the lives of humans. It is something that can be put off for a while, but the longer one waits, the more intense the compulsion to rescue a human becomes. The pressure builds up until it is impossible to resist doing something to get relief. It is the whole reason for their existence, and they are bound to that mission for eternity. Most members of Jean-Baptiste's family die several times a year—as Jules says, there are a lot of people who need to be saved.

In addition to a changed life cycle, revenants also have a number of special powers. When they reanimate for the first time, they are not just alive but also beautiful and charismatic, so humans are attracted to them as soon as they meet and are very willing to trust them. This is necessary to help revenants do their jobs—saving the lives of humans in danger. Revenants also have the power to control human emotion to some extent, and their touch can be soothing and comforting to a human, something that helps them in their rescues. But although they can communicate mentally with other revenants while volant, they can't communicate with humans in any way but human speech. Jules and Ambrose take advantage of women's attraction to them and date as many women as they can, but they are masters of the casual relationship, knowing how dangerous it would be for both humans and revenants if their worlds were to overlap.

It is also possible for a volant to possess the body of a revenant who is dying or dead. This is what happens when Ambrose is stabbed at the club and bleeds out immediately. Jules is there and able to possess him so they can get the body away from their enemies. If a revenant's body is killed and then burned, death is final. This is another reason they patrol with one volant member, so that person can let Jean-Baptiste know that there is a body that needs to be rescued when one of them takes a human's place. It needs to be kept safe at their home, away from any enemies who might steal it. This ability to possess another's body is only possible between revenants—for a revenant to possess a human mind and body produces severe mental and physical trauma from which the human may never recover, resulting in total insanity.

Revenants eat and drink like humans, although they don't sleep except when they are dormant. They do have great speed and strength, and Gaspard trains everyone who lives at Jean-Baptiste's home in various kinds of fighting, including swords, guns, and a variety of other weapons, and different forms of martial arts. Vincent's rock-hard and sculpted abs are no accident—he's earned them, and so have the rest of the family members, including Charlotte.

They must always be prepared, for they are not the only kind of revenant on Earth. There are also their enemies, the numa, and their fate is not to be driven to save human lives, but to take them. They are murderers who became immortal not just by taking lives, but by betraying someone to their death. Numa are dangerous, and they never die because they keep killing. They encourage humans to commit suicide, to become addicted to various substances, to lie, cheat, gamble, and steal—always driving them closer to death. Unlike humans, who can change their minds and turn away from evil, numa are totally corrupted by evil. The only option is their death, because they will stop at nothing to kill the revenants who save lives instead of taking them.

When they are animated, revenants age just like everyone else does. However, when they die, they reanimate at the age at which they originally died. Jean-Baptiste appears to be in his sixties, although he died at thirty-six, because he has decided to care for the revenants who live with him and also to care for other groups around the country. The urge to save a life can become overwhelming to a younger revenant, but it becomes easier the longer someone is a revenant, and Jean-Baptiste has had several hundred years of experience. Vincent was born in 1924, and he died when he was eighteen, in 1942. Since he hasn't died in a year, he's nineteen when he meets Kate. The oldest he has been is twenty-three; he has never been married or had children. He has lived for eighty-seven years yet nothing has happened to him to make feel older than he is right now. As he puts it, "I get to act like a guardian angel with a death wish, and in exchange I get a certain version of immortality."[31] In his mind, he and Kate are basically the same age, despite the difference in their birth dates.

When a revenant is wounded or dies, it is just as painful and difficult as any human's wound or death is, so it takes a certain amount of willpower to sacrifice oneself. This is why the compulsion to rescue a dying human is so necessary. Dying isn't easy, especially when you have to do it over and over again. Having experienced being stabbed or beaten or run over, the revenant is invested in that human's life and wants to be sure that the sacrifice was appreciated. So revenants are frequently somewhat obsessed with following their rescues and keeping tabs on them, although it is frowned on when it continues for too long. Vincent and Charlotte have snapshots of their rescues on the walls of their rooms—their Wall of Fame. Jean-Baptiste permits the revenants to go back and photograph their rescues and return to visit them twice while volant, but after that they must let their rescues go about their own lives.

Kate fears involvement with Vincent just as much as she is drawn to him. She almost didn't survive her parents' deaths, and he dies over and over. Knowing that in three days he'll be back doesn't lessen the trauma she feels and leads her to reject him. But Vincent has given her his heart and soul in a way he never has before, and while he respects her wishes and stays away, he begins to die, eaten up with regret and guilt. When his kindred urge Kate to consider returning to him, she agrees, hurting too badly to stay alone any longer. Vincent agrees to resist the urge to die as long as they are together and to work something out about the three days a month when he is dormant. Kate loves him too much to resist saying yes. Theirs will not be an easy love nor an easy life, but they are determined to have as much time together as they can manage in spite of the obstacles.

The characters are so complex and nuanced that the story rises above this somewhat stereotypical story line, and also because Plum is clever enough not to let the story end here. She has not yet dealt with the numa and their leader's plan to kill the last of those responsible for his own death many years ago. Lucien is determined to kill Vincent at any cost and burn his body. He has been working in the background, manipulating Kate's sister Georgia so he can get close enough to Vincent to end his existence forever. Had Kate not been as determined, intelligent, and courageous as she showed herself to be, he would certainly have won. But Kate is not going to let anything come between her and Vincent, no matter the cost, and she agrees to a dangerous experiment that could doom them both but instead results in the infamous fight scene that Plum so enjoyed writing. It opens the door to the developments sure to come in the next books.

Characters who change and grow, try and fail, then continue to try and succeed; who face the pain and the risk of loving deeply and chancing loss; who are willing to risk themselves to save those they love; who trust and believe and have faith in themselves and those they love; and who confront the monsters in their lives and refuse to let them win, no matter the odds—these are the role models teens today are searching for. Here is a story of family, of friendship, of loyalty, of trust, and of courage—things far too hard to find in today's society. Kate and her family, Vincent and his kindred, and the great city of Paris herself have much to offer, much to teach. There's little doubt girls will take the opportunity to reach out for a real world, with just a little tinge of magic.

Notes

1. Amy Plum, "FAQ," Amy Plum Books, http://www.amyplumbooks .com/faq/.
2. Ravenous Reader, "Author Interview with Amy Plum," *Tales of the Ravenous Reader* (blog), May 8, 2011, http://www.lushbudgetproduction .com/2011/05/author-interview-with-amy-plum.html.
3. Plum, "FAQ."
4. Bungle, "Author Interview with Amy Plum," *Midnight Readers* (blog), March 20, 2011, http://themidnightreaders.blogspot.com/2011/03/ author-interview-with-amy-plum.html.
5. Kelsey, "The Blog Tour: Amy Plum Interview," *The Book Scout* (blog), April 25, 2011, http://thebookscout.blogspot.com/2011/04/blog -tour-amy-plum-interview.html.
6. Me, My Shelf and I, "Interview with Amy Plum," *Me, My Shelf and I* (blog), April 20, 2011, http://www.memyshelfandi.com/2011/04/inter view-with-amy-plum-part-1-giveaway.html.
7. Heidi Bennett, "Author Interview: Amy Plum," *Miss Literati* (blog), http://blog.missliterati.com/2011/04/author-interview-amy-plum.html.
8. Me, My Shelf and I, "Interview."
9. Mandy, "Interview & Giveaway with Amy Plum," *Embrace Your Oddities* (blog), March 24, 2011, http://embraceyouroddities.blogspot .com/2011/03/interview-giveaway-with-amy-plum.html.
10. Cait, "Author Interview: Amy Plum (Die for Me)," *The Cait Files* (blog), March 30, 2011, http://thecaitfiles.blogspot.com/2011/03/hey -guys-last-weekish-i-review-die-for.html.
11. Cait, "Author Interview."
12. Plum, "FAQ."
13. Plum, "FAQ."
14. Mandy, "Interview."
15. Plum, "FAQ."
16. Plum, "FAQ."
17. Ravenous Reader, "Author Interview."
18. "Map of Paris," Amy Plum Books, http://www.amyplumbooks .com/map-of-paris.
19. Ravenous Reader, "Author Interview."
20. Amy Plum, "Blog: Where the Hell Is Montreuil-les-Vignes? (or: Why Didn't You Move to Cannes?)," Amy Plum Books, http://www.amyplum

books.com/2010/12/where-the-hell-is-montreuil-les-vignes-or-why-didnt
-you-move-to-cannes/.

21. Plum, "FAQ."
22. Me, My Shelf and I, "Interview."
23. Amy Plum, "Blog: Is Paris the Make-Out Capital of the World?" Amy
Plum Books, May 17, 2011, http://www.amyplumbooks.com/2011/05/is
-paris-the-make-out-capital-of-the-world/.
24. Plum, "FAQ."
25. Cait, "Author Interview."
26. Plum, "FAQ."
27. Plum, "FAQ."
28. KM, "Interview: Amy Plum, Author of *Die for Me*," *One Page at a
Time* (blog), May 3, 2011, http://one-page-reviews.blogspot.com/2011/05/
interview-amy-plum-author-of-die-for-me.html.
29. Book Butterfly, "Interview with Amy Plum, Author of Die for
Me," *The Book Butterfly* (blog), May 4, 2011, http://thebookbutterfly
.com/2011/05/die-for-me-by-amy-plumb-my-life-had.html.
30. Mandy, "Interview."
31. Amy Plum, *Die for Me* (New York: HarperTeens, 2011), 179.

Bibliography

Plum, Amy. *Die for Me*. New York: HarperTeens, 2011.

IV

ANGELS, UNICORNS, DEMONS: THE UNEXPECTEDLY DEADLY MONSTERS

Be not forgetful to entertain strangers, for thereby some
have entertained angels unawares.

— Hebrews 13:2

It would be absurd if we did not understand both angels
and devils, since we invented them.

—John Steinbeck, *East of Eden*

Unlike those who pretend to be immaculate, fallen angels
are usually more intriguing because their earthliness is
heavenly.

—Carl Polloi

A truly wise man never plays leapfrog with a unicorn.

—Anonymous

When choosing which monsters, beyond the Big Three, to include
in this book, it was important to look at the plethora of supernatural
creatures that populate much of YA fiction these days and decide

which of them are truly monsters and which are not. Many are paranormal—fallen angels, demons, ghosts, witches, warlocks, faeries, changelings, and so on—but not really monsters, in that they are humorous or romantic rather than evil or deadly. Others do not have the rich backstories and high quality writing that qualify them for inclusion. Three series stand out from the rest, starring killer angels, unicorns, and demons.

Diana Peterfreund's Rampant series is based on historical unicorns, rather than the white, sparkly, rainbow-hued creatures that currently populate little girls' bedrooms. These are killer unicorns, determined to slaughter every human they can get their horns on. Their horns are poisonous and also emit a venom that in the largest of these creatures can kill from yards away. L. A. Weatherly's angels are also not the kind that show up so often on greeting cards. Although they look like stereotypical angels, these are actually aliens who feed off human energy and are determined to take over Earth. Sarah Rees Brennan's Demon's Lexicon trilogy is set in a world where magic exists, if you know how to look for it, and stars two brothers who have been running from evil magicians all their lives.

Angels—The Celestial Monster

The term "angel" is derived from the Greek word *angelos*, which means messenger, a being which carries messages between God, gods, or celestial entities and humans.[1] Angels, in various forms, are found in most world religions and are generally considered to be semidivine immortal beings superior to humans.[2] In the Bible, they are considered to be corporeal, such as the angel that fought with the patriarch Jacob,[3] because the scribes and poets who wrote the Old Testament didn't know how to describe spiritual beings other than as humans. So, when King Nebuchadnezzar (Daniel 3:25) threw three men into the fiery furnace and later saw four forms walking around inside it, he realized one was an angel.[4] Later, however, they were seen as spiritual beings, so appeared as noncorporeal entities, apparitions or ghosts that could be seen and heard but not touched or felt. Other theologians took the middle ground, believing that angels were spiritual, noncorporeal beings who were able to assume corporeal human form in order to accomplish certain tasks.[5]

Angels reveal divine truth to humans, and also help them to attain salvation or receive special blessings. Sometimes they also mete out justice of various kinds, destroying the wicked who prey on their fellow man, supporting the weak, rewarding the just, or punishing the unjust. Angels also accompany the souls of the dead to their final resting place and announce the birth of spiritual leaders. Angels announced Jesus' imminent birth to Mary, and later to Joseph, and still later to the shepherds in the hills on the night he was born.[6]

The Christian concept of angels comes from the Jewish interpretation, which most likely came from the Egyptians. By the late fourth century, Christian theologians had divided angels into different categories, with different duties and missions.[7] There are a number of different kinds of angels described in the Old Testament, and there was no way the huge six-winged being described in Isaiah could be mistaken for a human,[8] so obviously there are different types of angels for different tasks or situations. There are seven ranks or orders of spiritual beings listed in the New Testament—angels, archangels, principalities, powers, virtues, dominions, and thrones. The Old Testament mentions only two kinds of angels, the cherubim and the seraphim, and all these together make up the nine choirs of angels mentioned in later Christian theology.[9]

Many Christians consider angels to be asexual, and images show them looking like human males with male names.[10] While early depictions of angels portray them in a variety of clothing, including soldier's uniforms or the vestments of an officer of the church, the standard garb is a full-length white robe or gown.[11] Traditionally, they are dazzlingly beautiful, attractive and even magnetic to humans, with a shining blue-white aura.

Wings are not seen in the earliest images of angels, which appeared around the third century, but they have been winged since the fourth century, when wings were added to indicate their journey from the celestial realm to interact with humankind on Earth. The seraphim and cherubim have more than one set of wings to indicate their higher status, and these creatures are generally seen only in celestial contexts, as opposed to earthly ones. The Bible records many interactions between humans and angels, and the Roman Catholic Church emphasizes the role of angels in Catholic teachings.[12]

Today, many Christians believe that angels are present with humans on Earth, to help and guide them in any way they can. Therefore, they say, it is prudent to be kind to those around you, because one of them may be an angel, ready to reward or to punish. This belief is based on the statement in Hebrews 13:2 about "entertaining angels unawares." The song "Angels among Us," written by Don Goodman and Becky Hobbs, and performed by Alabama on their 1993 *Cheap Seats* album reflects this belief, as a young boy walking home from school in the winter takes a shortcut and loses his way. He is scared and alone and it is getting dark, when a kind old man appears to hold his hand and lead him home. But when they get there, his mother can't see the old man, even though he is standing right there in front of her, and that's when the boy realizes he has been with an angel all along. Several other verses recount similar events, and the chorus repeats that angels are among us, sent from God to help us in our darkest hours, "To show us how to live, to teach us how to give / To guide us with the light of love."

A 2002 study from the United Kingdom[13] was based on interviews with people who claimed to have seen angels or had various kinds of experiences with them, including visions of angels in a variety of forms, such as unusually beautiful or extraordinary-looking humans who vanish when their task is done—traditional angels with wings, white robes, and beautiful auras, or noncorporeal beings of dazzling light. Others had a sense of being touched or pushed to avoid a dangerous situation or were given guidance when lost. This study was published in *Seeing Angels* by Emma Heathcote-James as part of her PhD research,[14] and was reprinted in 2009, including more than fifty case histories of ordinary people who have seen angels and had their lives changed as a result.[15]

Many Americans also believe in angels, particularly guardian angels. In 2008, Baylor University did a poll of 1,700 people, 55 percent of whom responded affirmatively to the statement, "I was protected from harm by a guardian angel." The responses were the same across denominations, level of education, and geographical region, although they were slightly lower (37 percent) for those making more than $150,000 a year. The significant part of these findings is that the question was not whether or not the respondents believed in guardian angels, but whether they believed that they had had an actual, experiential encounter with a guardian angel.[16]

Teens also believe in angels and are doing so in increasing numbers. In a 1994 Gallup Youth Survey on "Teen Belief in the Supernatural" 76 percent of more than five hundred teens ages thirteen to seventeen indicated that they believe in angels, a higher percentage than those who believe in astrology, ESP, witchcraft, vampires, and other supernatural events or creatures. The number of teens who believe in angels has been growing steadily, from 64 percent in 1978, to 69 percent in 1984, to 76 percent in 1994, while at the same time, belief in other supernatural figures or ideas has declined.[17]

It is no surprise, then, that there has been a major increase in YA fiction featuring angels. In the spring of 2010, as Vanessa Thorpe noted in her April 4, 2010, article "Angels Become the New Vamps," in *The Observer*, seven new series were begun, including two that depict angels that are in no way traditional. L. A. Weatherly's Angel Burn series stars an Angel Killer and killer angels, who are aliens from another world or dimension, determined to take over Earth. They look like blazingly beautiful traditional angels but feed off humans, sucking their energy from them, leaving them mentally and physically broken. British author Bryony Pearce's novel *Angel's Fury* looks at an equally dark and grim scenario inspired by the evil and malevolent Nephilim of the Old Testament. A fallen angel is walking the earth looking for ways to bring mankind to its ultimate destruction. It is determined to turn all good to evil, all love to hate, all hope to despair.

It is interesting, and perhaps ominous, that in the twenty-first century, books for young people have turned these messengers of God, traditionally pure creatures of goodwill and light, into harbingers or purveyors of evil.

Unicorns: The Horned Monster

Unicorns were first reported by the ancient Greeks not as mythology but as natural history, since they believed unicorns to be real. The first to mention unicorns was Ctesias, a Greek physician at the Persian court[18] in about AD 398,[19] when writing about the animals he saw in India.[20] He described the unicorn as being like a wild ass,[21] bigger than a horse[22] with a white body, a dark red head, deep blue eyes, and a single horn that was red, black, and white.[23] This horn was able to cure disease when made into a drinking cup.[24] They were very fast, and impossible to capture.[25] Pliny said the unicorn was a fierce beast, with the head of a stag, the body of a horse, the tail of a boar, and the feet of an elephant, with a deep bellow and a single black horn.[26] It was also called a monoceros, which could be a form of the Arabic karkadann, or rhinoceros.[27] Even Aristotle believed that the unicorn was real, an animal with a single hoof (not cloven) and a single horn. And five hundred years later, the Roman scholar Aelian confirmed the existence of the unicorn just as Ctesias described it but went on to say that in the mountainous interior regions of India there was a beast called a kartajan, which is Sanskrit for Lord of the Desert. It was the size of a horse, with a tawny mane, feet like an elephant, the tail of a goat, and a single sharp black horn. It was said to be gentle around other animals, but fought fiercely with those of its own kind and preferred to live where there were no other animals around.[28]

An animal called the re'em is mentioned in the Greek translation of the Old Testament, a wild oxlike animal with incredible strength and agility and a huge horn, impossible to tame. Translators of the King James Version of the Bible express "re'em" as "unicorn."[29] There are also several Jewish folktales that concern unicorns. When Noah built the ark, he was instructed to include two of every kind of animal, including the unicorn. However, the unicorns refused to board,[30] and so were not saved. Shel Silverstein, noted children's poet, shares the reason in his poem "The Unicorn Song," published in *Where the Sidewalk Ends*, in 1974. The unicorns were simply having too much fun playing in the rain and hiding from Noah, so finally he had to close the door, leaving them behind. It was recorded in 1967 by the Irish Rovers, as the title song for the album *The Unicorn*, and was popular in the United States, Canada, and Great Britain.

Other Jewish folktales have different endings to the story, however. The unicorn was considered to be among the fiercest of beasts, able to kill even an elephant with one thrust of its horn. On board the ark, unicorns demanded so much time and trouble that Noah kicked them off.[31] They either drowned or swam as long as they could, and a few may have survived to evolve into the narwhale, known as the "sea unicorn."[32]

In Alexandria, during the second century AD, a book called *The Physiologus* was written, containing the descriptions of all the animals on Earth and allegorical stories about them.[33] The unicorn was included, but the description of it was much more like the unicorns described in the Middle Ages. It was said to be about the size of a goat, with the requisite long, single horn, and very fierce—impossible to catch. The only way it could be captured was for a virgin to be left alone where unicorns were known to be. She was to wait until a unicorn came up and put its head in her lap and fell asleep. Then the hunters could capture it. There were various requirements for the virgin—some sources stipulated that she must be a nun, or of noble birth, or pure of heart, or a virgin in the strictest sexual sense of the word. It was said that the unicorn would be able to tell if the girl was a virgin or not, perhaps by smell or some other more magical method.[34]

While Western unicorns were wild and impossible to tame, Eastern unicorns were meek, quiet, and thought to bring good luck.[35] The Chinese unicorn, called a kilin, had the body of a deer, the tail of an ox, the hooves of a horse, and a single short horn. Its fur combined the five holy Chinese colors of red, white, black, blue, and yellow.[36] Seeing it was supposed to be a sign of good fortune, which perhaps explains why none have been seen recently.[37] Unicorns appeared to several Chinese emperors to bring them good luck or good news. One of these was Emperor Yao, who was the fourth of the five emperors who shaped the Chinese world. The kilin was also believed to be able to foretell the birth of great men, and in 551 BC Confucius's mother encountered a unicorn in the woods near her home. It approached her and gave her a piece of jade and put its head in her lap. The inscription on the jade indicated that her unborn son would be a man of great wisdom, a prophecy that came true, because Confucius is respected as a philosopher and scholar all across the world.[38]

The Japanese unicorn, called a kirin, looked rather like a bull with a shaggy mane. It was supposed to be able to tell the difference between guilt and innocence, and judges used them in legal disputes. The unicorn would stare at both parties and then stab the guilty one in the chest with its horn.[39]

In Arabia, the unicorn is called the karkadann and is said to have magical powers—eating its meat would banish demons.[40] It lived on the grassy plains, and its horn was believed to be poisonous.[41]

During the Middle Ages, the description of the unicorn from *The Physiologus* became widely known and accepted, although there were still some questions about its size and appearance. Was it more the size of a goat or a horse? Did it have a mane? What did its tail look like, and were its hooves split or solid? The descriptions varied by region and source.

Unicorns were frequently associated with kings and royalty, and the royal throne of Denmark was constructed out of unicorn horns, which were most likely narwhale tusks. Narwhales were Arctic mammals with a long, spiraled, pointed tusk, which was actually a single long tooth.[42] The depiction of spiraled unicorn horns in art comes from these narwhale tusks.[43] In the third century BC Alexander the Great bragged about riding a unicorn into battle,[44] and some have speculated that his great war horse Bucephalas might have been one of the larger forms of unicorns. The animal was a gift from his father, King Phillip of Macedonia, because Alexander was the only person who could ride it. He didn't try to break its will, but instead stroked it and talked softly to it, persuading it to let him ride, not forcing it to.[45]

There are many animals, including antelopes, oryx, and eland, that could have contributed to the legend of the unicorn, but it is interesting to note that the current depiction of the unicorn, with its white coat, goat's beard, and flowing mane and tale, is much closer to these more gentle and tame animals than some of the fiercer and more dangerous animals that have been called unicorns in the past.

Demons: The Possessing Monster

While the word "demon" conjures up a supernatural being of pure evil and malevolence, bent on making life miserable for whatever human it chooses to torment, they have not always been thought of that way. To the ancient Greeks, demons were minor deities, not necessarily good or evil. The Greek word *daemon*, from which "demon" and "daimon" are both derived, means genius and intelligence and was used for all kinds of spiritual beings, whether they were good or evil.[46] Homer used the terms "gods" and "demons" interchangeably, and Plato described them as "supernatural beings between mortals and gods, such as inferior divinities and ghosts of dead heroes."[47] Socrates described his daimon as a spirit that helped him seek the truth,[48] warning him when he was about to make a mistake, but never telling him exactly what to do.[49] Some demons were said to be intermediaries between humans and gods, similar in function to angels,[50] but the word was gradually used more and more to describe diabolical supernatural spirits who put pressure on humans to do things that were not good for them.[51]

In seventeenth-century Europe, the various demons were classified according to their level of power and the specific kind of impact they made on the humans they attacked. There were, among others, demons who caused nightmares, sexual demons, and demons who made people think that they were able to fly.[52] This was a time of intense interest in demons and demonology, and a list was compiled in 1589 by a demonologist named Binsfield that included the seven archdemons and the evil or quality that made them demonical, based on the seven deadly sins. The list included Lucifer (pride), Mammon (avarice), Asmodeus or Ashmodai (lechery), Satan (anger), Beelzebub (gluttony), Leviathan (envy), and Belphegor (sloth).[53]

Demons were also thought to be gods or spiritual beings who were overcome or cast aside when the culture that created them was conquered by another culture, and new gods were set in place. Often continuing to practice the old religion would be considered witchcraft, which also helped support the idea that demons were malevolent and evil.[54]

During the Middle Ages, demon worship became popular, and many practiced the Black Mass, during which an inverted cross was placed on the altar and the mass was said backward. It is somewhat amusing that a fragment of this mass survives today as part of magicians' spiels—"Hocus-pocus" is an abbreviated form of "Hoc est corpus meum" ("This is my body"), part of the Eucharist.[55]

Some early historians also connected upheavals in society with increased demonic activity, the way current thinking explains similar occurrences by looking at economic and other factors.[56] Today we cite the increased interest in supernatural beings in books and visual media as a reaction to the increased stress and tension brought about by global warfare, economic crisis, and threats of environmental disasters.

Demons have also long been feared for their ability to possess humans and control their thoughts, emotions, and behavior.[57] This was seen many times in the New Testament, when Jesus was empowered by the Holy Spirit to cast out demons. These demons were purely evil, servants of Satan, and manifested themselves as mental illness, physical illness, blindness, deafness, paralysis, and more. It is important to note that even before his death, Jesus empowered his disciples with this healing power as well, and they continued this work after his resurrection.[58] The Roman Catholic Church teaches that angels and demons are real beings, not just symbolic constructs, and has a group of officially trained and sanctioned exorcists who perform exorcisms. They also believe that demons can be overcome by the prayers of the faithful.[59]

Demons have also been seen as fallen angels who fell from the grace of God, and who may or may not ever be reconciled with him, and as evil spirits, supernatural beings with the power to control humans whenever they choose to do so. They can even be the "inner devils" we face on a daily basis—greed, pride, fear, anger. Demons can be summoned, conjured up, and required to do the bidding of the one who summoned them. They can be controlled, conquered, or cast out. They can seem to be pure evil, extremely dangerous, or the spawn of Satan. It all depends on the individual's perception, which is always subject to change.

Notes

1. *Encyclopaedia Britannica*, academic edition, s.v. "Angels and Demons."
2. *Wikipedia*, s.v. "Angels," accessed June 12, 2011, http://en.wikipedia.org/wiki/Angels.
3. *Britannica*, "Angels and Demons."
4. Angels: An Online Resource, "History of Angels," Angels: An Online Resource, http://www.cyodine.com/angels/History.htm.
5. *Britannica*, "Angels and Demons."
6. *Britannica*, "Angels and Demons."
7. *Wikipedia*, "Angels."
8. Angels, "History."
9. *Britannica*, "Angels and Demons."
10. *Wikipedia*, "Angels."
11. *Wikipedia*, "Angels."
12. *Wikipedia*, "Angels."
13. *Wikipedia*, "Angels."
14. Emma Heathcote-James, *Seeing Angels: True Contemporary Accounts of Hundreds of Angelic Experiences* (London: John Blake Publishing, 2002).

15. Amazon, *Seeing Angels*, Amazon.com http://www.amazon.com/Seeing-Angels-Contemporary-Accounts-Experiences/dp/1844547868/ref=sr_1_1?ie=UTF8&qid=1308261235&sr=8-1.

16. David Van Biema, "Guardian Angels Are Here, Say Most Americans," *Time*, September 18, 2008.

17. Hal Malcovitz and George Gallup, "Introduction," *The Gallup Youth Survey: Teens and the Supernatural and Paranormal* (Broomall, PA: Mason Crest Publishers, 2005), cited in *Wikipedia*, "Angels," note 78.

18. Review of *The Natural History of Unicorns* by Chris Levers, *New Yorker* 85, no. 28 (September 14, 2009).

19. *Encyclopedia Mythica*, online edition, s.v. "Unicorn," accessed August 15, 2011, http://www.pantheon.org/articles/u/unicorn.html.

20. Review of *The Natural History*.

21. Elmer G. Suhr, "An Interpretation of the Unicorn," *Folklore* 75, no. 2 (1964): 94.

22. *Mythica*, "Unicorn."

23. Suhr, "Interpretation."

24. Review of *The Natural History*

25. *Wikipedia*, s.v. "Unicorns," accessed June 10, 2011, http://en.wikipedia.org/wiki/Unicorn.

26. Suhr, "Interpretation."

27. *Wikipedia*, "Unicorns."

28. Matthew Webber, "The History of the Unicorn," Unicorn Dreams, http://www.unicorn-dream.co.uk/unicorn2.html; The Guard House, "Britannica: The Unicorn," The Guard House, http://www.novareinna.com/guard/unicorn.html.

29. *Wikipedia*, "Unicorns."

30. Guard House, "Britannica."

31. Dianne Stephens, "Unicorns in the Bible," The Unicorn Collector, http://www.unicorncollector.com/legends.htm.

32. Guard House, "Britannica."

33. *Wikipedia*, s.v. "Physiologus," accessed June 12, 2011, http://en.wikipedia.org/wiki/Physiologus.

34. Webber, "History."

35. *Mythica*, "Unicorn."

36. Guard House, "Britannica."

37. The Equinest, "A Brief History of the Unicorn," The Equinest, accessed June 12, 2011, http://www.theequinest.com/a-brief-history-of-the-unicorn/.

38. Guard House, "Britannica."

39. Guard House, "Britannica."

40. Guard House, "Britannica."

41. *Wikipedia*, s.v. "Karkadann," accessed June 12, 2011, http://en.wikipedia.org/wiki/Karkadann.

42. "Here Be Wonders," *The Economist*, January 31, 2009.

43. *Wikipedia*, "Unicorns."

44. Stephens, "Unicorns."

45. Kevin Owens, "Unicorns and Warriors," All about Unicorns, http://www.allaboutunicorns.com/warriors.php.

46. Essortment, "The History of Demons," Essortment: Your Source of Knowledge, http://www.essortment.com/history-demons-21320.html.

47. D. J. McAdam, "Demonology," D. J. McAdam: Where the World Goes for Free Advice, http://www.djmcadam.com/demons.htm.

48. *Britannica*, "Angels and Demons."

49. *Wikipedia*, s.v. "Daemon (classic mythology)," accessed June 12, 2011, http://en.wikipedia.org/wiki/Daemon_(classical_mythology).

50. *Columbia Electronic Encyclopedia*, 6th ed., s.v. "Demons."

51. *Britannica*, "Angels and Demons."

52. *Britannica*, "Angels and Demons."

53. *Columbia*, "Demons."

54. *Britannica*, "Angels and Demons."

55. *Britannica*, "Angels and Demons."

56. McAdam, "Demonology."

57. *Wikipedia*, s.v. "Demon," accessed June 21, 2011, http://en.wikipedia.org/wiki/Demon.

58. Paul S. Minear, "Demons," in *The Oxford Guide to People and Places of the Bible*, ed. Bruce M. Metzger and Michael D. Coogan (London: Oxford University Press, 2001), found at Oxford Reference Online, Oxford University Press, San José State University, http://www.oxfordreference.com.libaccess.sjlibrary.org/views/ENTRY.html?subview=Main&entry=t97.e84 (accessed June 5, 2011).

59. *Wikipedia*, "Demon."

Bibliography

Heathcote-James, Emma. *Seeing Angels*. London: John Blake Publishing, 2002.

"Here Be Wonders." *Economist*, January 31, 2009.

Malcovitz, Hal, and George Gallup. "Introduction." In *The Gallup Youth Survey: Teens and the Supernatural and Paranormal*. Broomall, PA: Mason Crest Publishers, 2005.

Minear, Paul S. "Demons." In *The Oxford Guide to People and Places of the Bible*, ed. Bruce M. Metzger and Michael D. Coogan. London: Oxford University Press, 2001. Oxford Reference Online. Oxford University Press. San José State University. http://www.oxfordreference.com .libaccess.sjlibrary.org/views/ENTRY.html?subview=Main&entry=t97 .e84 (accessed June 5, 2011).

Pearce, Bryony. *Angel's Fury*. London: Egmont, 2011.

Review of *The Natural History of Unicorns* by Chris Levers. *New Yorker*, September 14, 2009.

Suhr, Elmer G. "An Interpretation of the Unicorn." *Folklore* 75, no. 2 (1964): 91–109.

Van Biema, David. "Guardian Angels Are Here, Say Most Americans." *Time*, September 18, 2008.

Weatherly, L. A. *Angel Burn*. Somerville, MA: Candlewick Press, 2011.

———. *Angel Fire*. London: Usborne Publishing, 2011.

18

Killer Angels: The Angel Burn Trilogy by L. A. Weatherly

L. A. (Lee) Weatherly is the author of more than thirty books of children's and middle grade fiction, but *Angel Burn* is her first YA novel[1] and includes "high speed car chases, angel smack-downs and witty banter."[2] She grew up in Little Rock, Arkansas, and has lived in Hampshire with her British husband, Peter, since 1995.[3] She's always wanted to be a writer and feels very lucky that she can do it full time.[4] Choosing to write for children was easy, since she loves reading children's fiction and always tries to write the kind of books she'd like to read herself.[5] But Alex and Willow's story seemed to be made for teens for many reasons—the paranormal aspect, themes of isolation and alienation, the lure of something forbidden or un-known—all are intriguing to teens, who are facing similar feelings and situations.[6] In addition, both Alex and Willow have grown up isolated from mainstream society, and in Alex's case extremely isolated, something that many teens can identify with easily, and something that allows the two characters to be drawn together im-mediately, as each recognizes the "aloneness" in the other.

They also both have parents that have been damaged by angels. Alex's father Martin was a CIA operative and was one of the first to learn about angels and the dangers they presented. He established the first Angel Killer training camp in southern New Mexico, and took Alex and his older brother Jake there to live when Alex was only five. Although Martin was greatly respected by the CIA as their most expert Angel Killer, by the time Alex made his first solo kill when he was twelve, Martin had started to become mentally unbalanced, perhaps because of his wife's death years before when an angel ripped away her life force, or because of the angel fallout from the number of angels he'd killed over the years. He died about five months before the Invasion, killed by an angel when he was lost in his madness.

Miranda, Willow's mother, was never the same after her encounter with an angel. She was able to keep herself together until Willow was about five or six, but then she began to slip away into her own world. Willow had to cook, keep house, brush her own hair, and take care of herself so no one would ever know that her mother couldn't do any of those things and take her away. When she was nine, Willow and Miranda moved in with her mother's sister, and Miranda gradually became catatonic. When Alex reads Miranda's energy for the first time, he immediately recognizes the symptoms of severe angel burn, the result of an angel feeding from a human. He doesn't realize at the time that the angel didn't just feed from her; he had sex with her as well, and Willow is the result.

Weatherly has known Alex for almost twenty years, but when he first showed up in her mind he was a thief in a fantasy novel and an expert with knives instead of guns. Willow came to her about the same time, but her name was Jhia, and Weatherly didn't really get to know her until she started considering a contemporary setting. Suddenly, her name changed to Willow, she was really good at fixing cars, and she was psychic. At that point, Weatherly had the basic idea for her plot: Willow has seen something psychically that she shouldn't have, and Alex is the teenage hit man assigned to kill her, but instead, they fall in love.[7] A hunter—an assassin—in love with his prey; it was romantic.[8] The problem was that it couldn't have a happy ending if Alex was really a hit man—and Weatherly likes happy endings. Every so often, Weatherly would mentally take the idea out and play with it a little, still unable to figure out how to make it work, and then return it to the back of her mind.[9] She did know that Alex was from New Mexico and Willow was from upstate New York, and that their story would involve a journey from one place to the other.[10] She began thinking about including a paranormal twist to their story. One day while looking at a display of nonfiction books on angels, she began to wonder about what might happen if angels weren't the loving and friendly beings who helped humans, distributing blessings on all they met, and were instead creatures to be feared—beings with their own agenda.[11] What if they hated humans instead of loving them, and only wanted to use and manipulate them? The story fell quickly into place from that point, and she finished the book in about eight months.[12] Willow became a half-angel to explain her psychic ability and why the Church of Angels wants Alex to kill her—half-angels are an impossibility, but she exists anyway, and the church believes that somehow she has the ability to destroy all of angelkind.

But that doesn't mean that the writing process was always smooth sailing. Weatherly had always known that the road trip would involve kidnapping. However, Alex and Willow had minds of their own, and Alex objected when Weatherly wanted him to kidnap Willow and take her to talk to his old mentor, Cully, at the camp where he grew up and learned to be an Angel Killer, in the desert of New Mexico. They went along with it but were so sullen about it that the road trip simply didn't work.[13] The physical realities of how to keep someone confined on such a long trip made Alex so unpleasant that there was no way Willow was going to fall in love with him. Willow had to have a reason why she would want to go with him willingly—putting her in danger from angels who wanted her dead as soon as possible provided that reason. Listening to the characters and what they wanted was the only way for Weatherly to make all the pieces fall into place.[14]

And that was not the only surprise Weatherly got—she didn't have any idea that Alex spoke Spanish until she wrote the scene where he suddenly started speaking it! She had not written it into his backstory, and it changed not only the first book, but the other two as well.[15] Characters need to develop on their own, organically, she says, and writing about them is simply getting to know who they are, their likes, dislikes, flaws, and strengths.[16] It's their faults that make them interesting.[17]

The first book is narrated by both characters, Willow speaking in first person, Alex in third. Weatherly wanted both of them to have a say in the book because their voices speak so strongly in her mind, and she wanted to present both their perspectives. She also notes that while she believes that she could have written Willow's story in third person, she couldn't have written Alex's in first person—it simply isn't how he sounds to her.[18] One of her favorite books is Sylvia Engdahl's *Enchantress from the Stars*, which also has the girl's voice in first person and the other characters' in third. Its structure and doomed romance were a real influence on *Angel Burn*.[19]

Even though the journey between the two characters' homes was a part of the plot from the very beginning, it included parts of the country that Weatherly had never visited, and she wanted to make sure she got the settings correct. So she and her husband drove from Maine to New York to New Mexico, following the route Willow and Alex took, ending up in California.[20] Most of her descriptions of the countryside were fairly accurate, although she had not realized how dramatic and mountainous eastern Tennessee was,[21] nor that the panhandle of Texas was so much more than it had been described to her—hot and flat—and had sweeping expanses that allowed one to see for miles and miles, clear out to the horizon, peaceful and pure.[22] They spent several days in New Mexico, since Weatherly wanted to get a feel for Alex's home state. She also wanted to find a place in the desert that could have been the location of the Angel Killers camp where he grew up. When she found it, she knew it immediately from the chills she felt. She stood there taking pictures of it and letting it soak into her.[23] The trip definitely contributed to her ability to make the different locations come alive, recognizable to someone familiar with the different areas. Thirty of the photos Weatherly took are posted on her website, including the one of the Angel Killer camp. (And speaking of pictures, she loves the cover of *Angel Burn* so much that she has a picture of it on her phone so she can show it to anyone she meets![24])

Weatherly always knew that Alex and Willow's story would be so long and complex that it would require a trilogy, and she knew from the beginning what the end would be. She describes it as "very sad, but hopefully really lovely, too" and can hardly wait to write it.[25] The second volume, *Angel Fire*, is set mostly in Mexico City and introduces several new characters, one of whom Weatherly has been dying to write about, who creates a love triangle and tests Alex and Willow in ways they didn't expect, challenging their love for one another.[26] The story is darker than the first volume, since the situation with the angels is getting worse and the stakes for humanity are higher than ever. *Angel Fever* will be the third and final volume, including a showdown with the angels and more complications on the romantic front.[27]

Weatherly says she knows authors aren't supposed to have favorites from among their books, but *Angel Burn* is "incredibly special" to her, because she's known and loved the characters for so long.[28] She's in love with Alex just as much as Willow is, and loves Willow because she's a strong female character who's totally capable of making her own decisions.[29] Writing it was an intense experience,[30] as was sending it out into the world and wondering how other people would respond to it.[31] Alex has been in her mind for so long, nagging her to write his story, that she's not sure how she'll get along without him.[32] Her long acquaintance with these two characters means that both of them are complex and three dimensional.

Identity and the masks we all wear is a recurring theme in Weatherly's work and is clearly a central part of this trilogy, as both Alex and Willow have secrets to hide. What do their masks look like, and how much do they reflect the real person inside? Much of their road trip is spent getting to know each other and letting those masks slip away as they reveal their long-kept secrets. When they have to spend several days at a motel while their car is getting fixed, they begin to share what their lives have been like.

Both have been very isolated, Alex because of his upbringing as an Angel Killer, living in a small compound with only about thirty or forty other people in the middle of the desert (an idea that came from the movie *Terminator 2*[33]),and Willow because of her psychic ability, her strange family, her appearance, and her talent for fixing cars. She has never fit into the high school scene, while Alex knows nothing about being a teenager, except for what he's seen on TV. He was tutored intermittently, but never went to school—his English textbook was the Sears catalog. They will have to know each other's true selves and trust each other in order to survive the angels' attempts to kill both of them.

Weatherly's angels are utterly unique. They come from a different world or dimension, and some of them have been visiting Earth for centuries, to feed off humans, gorging on their life force, their energy, instead of feeding from the ether of their own world, like the majority of angels do. It has always been considered rather a coarse and rough way to feed, and it is extremely addicting, for both angels and humans. It is also quite dangerous for humans, causing insanity or disease, and even death when they are fed from too frequently.

In the Angel Killers' world, schizophrenia, cancer, multiple sclerosis, depression, Parkinson's disease, AIDS, and almost any other mental or physical ailment are all symptoms of angel burn. They are inevitable, whether or not they show up quickly or take years to develop. Once infected, humans with angel burn have a steadily declining quality of life and an increasing obsession with angels. However, these humans don't seem to notice their debility, because the angels promise peace and serenity and joy when they feed and leave the victim with a cherished memory of a gloriously radiant, beautiful angel who made them feel more wonderful and amazing and cared for than they'd ever felt. It's this memory that is so addicting for the angels' victims and the reason why they become so obsessed and are driven to experience being with an angel over and over again. It is also one of the reasons why the Church of Angels has grown so amazingly fast.

But two years ago, the angels discovered that their world was dying and could no longer be a source of the life-sustaining ether they require. Suddenly, feeding from humans was a much more attractive prospect. The First Wave was sent in (humans called it the Invasion), and after two years, it was declared by the Seraphic Council to be an outstanding success. Preparations for the Second Wave began immediately.

Angels have both a human and an angelic form. When in human form, they are quite attractive, even magnetic, and humans respond positively to them, trusting them instinctively. Their angelic forms are dazzling, radiating blue-white energy; they are seven feet tall or more, with huge feathered white wings and glowing halos. Their voices sound like the ringing of cathedral bells, and their faces are beautiful beyond belief. They can only be seen by the human they intend to feed from, and since they are feeding on only energy, there are no traces on their victims, so no discernable cause for the aftereffects.

Not long after the Invasion, the Church of Angels sprang up spontaneously, as humans became more and more enamored of the beautiful beings that promised so much. Just the touch of an angel caused people to become obsessed with them, and the church members had a cultlike zeal about angels.[34] As a result, the Church began to grow quickly. Soon, every Church of Angels congregation had an angel or two attached to it, enjoying the adulation of its members and feeding from whomever they chose to. However, not all angels fed from church members—some preferred to stalk their prey on the streets, just as they had done for centuries.

There are, however, other angels who believe that angels should help and protect humans, rather than use them for food. They are called "marshalers," and are able to put a small amount of psychic resistance in humans' auras, so they don't "taste good" to other angels. Under certain conditions, the resistance can also be passed from one human to another if their auras come into contact. They have been fighting the killer angels covertly for years, working through the Angel Project at the CIA, but since the agency was compromised four months ago and all the Angel Killers (AKs) were terminated, they have been forced to become more overt and are searching for Willow to see if she can help them stop the Second Wave from happening. (Alex was left alive because he was the best of the AKs, and the angels had a special job for him.) Killer angels call the marshalers "traitor angels," and they are executed whenever they are found out, by secret methods, methods so secret that even the assassin doesn't know what he has done, a solution in which Raziel, de facto head of the Church of Angels, takes a rather gleeful, evil pleasure.

As the Church of Angels became larger and more popular, the angels took it over and expanded its influence immeasurably through television, publishing, and Internet channels. Humans embraced the Church, eager for angelic blessings, not seeming to notice the high instance of illness, insanity, and deaths among its members. A wide variety of government offices, from local to national, were also taken over by the angels, even though the humans in them are unaware of the change, since many of them suffer from angel burn and angel obsession.

Many humans work for angels; some do it unwittingly, some consider it a huge honor to work for these glorious creatures who provide so many blessings for humans. One of these humans is a character who became one of Weatherly's favorites, moving from a minor part to a major one, simply because he insisted on more time onstage.

Jonah is an executive assistant to Raziel, who is not only head of the Church of Angels, but also the most senior angel who reports directly to the Seraphic Council. Jonah sees himself as weak, but he actually has the moral courage to look for answers—when he notices that angels may not be as beneficial as he has always believed—and then act based on what he's learned. He is at first intensely loyal to the angels, and particularly to Raziel, but then begins to question their motives when he sees the results of their actions. Like Jarel in *Enchantress from the Stars*, when Jonah realizes that everything he believed about angels and their treatment of humanity is not what it seems to be, he decides to betray the relationship that he has had with them and fight against them.[35] He plays a big role in the final confrontation at the Church of Angels cathedral in the first book, and Weatherly intended to kill him off at that point, but he absolutely refused to die, and so he appears in both of the other volumes. His story arc is interesting, and the author is delighted that he was so determined to live and be a bigger part of the story.[36]

The only opposition the angels have, other than the "traitor angels," is a small group of AKs who are passionately devoted to eradicating them from Earth. However, after the Invasion the AKs were taken over by the CIA, and many changes had to be made. The CIA required that each AK had to work alone, rather than in a group, and never contact any of the other AKs or their families. The AKs simply respond to anonymous text messages about where to go and whom to kill. Even between jobs they must remain alone, waiting for the next text to tell them they have a new assignment. Alex has spent eternities in cheap hotel rooms, watching endless hours of daytime TV. They are extremely well paid, but it is a difficult lifestyle, with few benefits other than the knowledge that they are doing all they can to rid Earth of angels. Alex has had no contact with any other AKs for twenty months, and he wonders sometimes if he is the last AK left alive, although he assumes that Cully is continuing to train new recruits at the New Mexico camp where he grew up. In the five years since his first solo kill, Alex has lost track of the number of angels he has killed but thinks it must be over two hundred. Until Jake was killed by an angel about a year ago, they'd kept a running tally, a brotherly competition, but since then, it has seemed pointless. He just does his job, and then waits for the next one.

But killing angels is not without its dangers, and every time he makes a kill, Alex must deal with the fallout from the energy exploding from the angel when it dies. He gets an intense headache and a major adrenaline surge that forces him to work out for hours until he can feel the rush begin to fade and give way to welcome tiredness. He used to go running after a kill, but it wasn't ever enough to completely exhaust him, which is the only way to work off the adrenaline so he can rest or sleep. Afterward he's always starving, needing to replenish his body after all the stress, but sometimes he is almost too tired to eat. It's his job, the only thing he's ever been trained to do, but it isn't easy.

Angels can't be hurt while they are in their human form, so the AKs must wait until they are ready to feed on a human and transform to their angelic form. AKs are trained to raise themselves to a higher level of perception where they are able to see humans' auras and angels in their angelic form. The angel's soul resides in its halo, so in order to kill the angel, its halo must be destroyed. A bullet is the safest and most effective way to do this. Once the halo is gone, the angel vanishes in an explosion of light and a shock wave of energy. However, if the halo is only nicked, the angel will be incapacitated for a brief time, but not killed. Death occurs only when the halo is completely gone. AKs learn early to be excellent shots. For them, the only good angel is a dead angel.

Notes

1. Kati Lear, "Giveaway: Angel Burn by L. A. Weatherly," *Princess Reviews* (blog), April 1, 2011, http://5678princessreviews.blogspot.com/2011/04/giveaway-angel-burn-by-la-weatherly.html.

2. Darren, "Review: Angel by L. A. Weatherly," *Bart's Bookshelf* (blog), August 9, 2010, http://www.bartsbookshelf.co.uk/2010/08/09/review-angel-by-l-a-weatherly/.

3. "L. A. Weatherly," Fresh Fiction, http://freshfiction.com/author.php?id=26565.

4. Darren, "Review."

5. Dwayne, "Author Interview: L. A. Weatherly (Part I)," *Girls without a Bookshelf* (blog), August 9, 2010, http://withoutabookshelf.blogspot.com/2010/08/author-interview-la-weatherly-part-i.html.

6. Jill Murphy, "The Interview: Bookbag Talks to L. A. Weatherly," The Bookbag, September 30, 2010, http://www.thebookbag.co.uk/reviews/index.php?title=The_Interview:_Bookbag_Talks_To_L_A_Weatherly.

7. Usborne Publishing, "L. A. Weatherly—about the Author," Usborne, http://www.usborne.com/angel/.
8. Lear, "Giveaway."
9. Usborne Publishing, "L. A. Weatherly."
10. Dwayne, "Author Interview."
11. Dwayne, "Author Interview."
12. Lear, "Giveaway."
13. Dwayne, "Author Interview."
14. Lear, "Giveaway."
15. Murphy, "Interview."
16. Lear, "Giveaway."
17. Murphy, "Interview."
18. Dwayne, "Author Interview."
19. Christin, "Author Interview: *Angel Burn* by L. A. Weatherly," *Between the Covers: A Book Review Blog*, May 20, 2011, http://www.betweenthecovers blog.net/2011/05/author-interview-angel-burn-by-la.html.
20. Christin, "Author Interview."
21. Christin, "Author Interview."
22. Dwayne, "Author Interview."
23. Christin, "Author Interview."
24. Lear, "Giveaway."
25. Murphy, "Interview."
26. Darren, "Review."
27. Christin, "Author Interview."
28. Usborne Publishing, "L. A. Weatherly."
29. Lear, "Giveaway."
30. Murphy, "Interview."
31. Usborne Publishing, "L. A. Weatherly."
32. Murphy, "Interview."
33. Christin, "Author Interview."
34. Christin, "Author Interview."
35. Christin, "Author Interview."
36. Darren, "Review."

Bibliography

Weatherly, L. A. *Angel Burn*. Somerville, MA: Candlewick Press, 2011.
———. *Angel Fire*. London: Usborne Publishing, 2011.

19

Killer Unicorns: The Rampant Series by Diana Peterfreund

Although Diana Peterfreund had always wanted to be a writer[1] and had authored the Secret Society Girl/Ivy League series since 2007, the Rampant series is a far cry from that hilarious insider glimpse of the secret society culture of Ivy League universities. The Rampant series began with a dream, a dream in which Peterfreund says she was being chased by a killer unicorn. When she woke up, she decided to research unicorns to figure out what the dream meant and discovered that there is a whole other side of the unicorn legend that has nothing to do with the sweet, fluffy, rainbow-hued creatures that populate toy stores and little girls' bedrooms. Since unicorns and virgins have long been thought of together, and Peterfreund had been wanting to write something about how virginity is seen in our society, it seemed natural to write a book on killer unicorns and the virgins they are drawn to, who are the only ones who can hunt and kill them. In the beginning, she had that premise and a heroine named Astrid, with long blonde hair and a lack of enthusiasm about killing unicorns. It was an amazing coincidence that the model on the covers of *Rampant* and *Ascendant* looked exactly like the girl Peterfreund imagined, complete with dark eyebrows, no makeup, and slightly messy hair, as if she'd just gotten back from a practice session or unicorn hunt.[2]

When asked to compare the two series, Peterfreund talked about their similarities as well as their differences. While one is set in the real world and is funny and one is set in a fantasy world and is action packed and more than a little gory, they are both about camaraderie, teamwork, and friendship, about girls and young women who are dealing with old and secret organizations and the limits they place on their female members.[3]

In this new series, Peterfreund wanted not just tough unicorn-killing heroines, she also wanted to include several social issues, like conservation and environmentalism, and what virginity is and how it is seen in our and other societies.[4] This makes for an interesting juxtaposition in the books, as one of the unicorn hunters, Philippa, or Phil, is an environmentalist not in favor of hunting unicorns to extinction, even though she realizes just how dangerous they are to both people and animals. So, while she is training to be a hunter, she is also searching for a way to protect the unicorns, perhaps relocating them to an isolated and uninhabited area.

The concept of virginity is also prominent in the novels, as characters question how to define it and what it means. The only characters that never question are the unicorns themselves—with them, it's crystal clear. When Phil returns to the Cloisters where they live after having been raped, Bonegrinder, the "house zhi," the smallest form of unicorn, immediately attacks her, just as she does any other nonhunter. (Orders of hunters usually keep a pet zhi to test the new recruits and verify that they are actually virgins.) The zhi doesn't question whether or not it was consensual, whether or not it was intentional, or how sorry Phil is that it happened. This is another interesting juxtaposition, because, of course, the human characters do ask all these questions and more. Phil was attracted to Seth, but she didn't intend for petting to get any further, told him no, and pushed him away, but it was too late. The situation gets even worse when it is revealed later in the story that he was paid to have sex with her and take her virginity and had planned ahead of time how to do it, knowing full well what it would mean to her. The situation isn't resolved, though, because Seth suddenly vanishes, leaving Phil to deal with the pieces of her now impossible dream.

Peterfreund struggled with this issue, because she wanted to write a realistic rape scene, and she wanted it to show a particular scenario—date rape or acquaintance rape or boyfriend rape, with someone the victim really likes, when things get beyond her control and way outside her comfort zone. This kind of rape is much more common and much more confusing, because other people don't treat it like rape. Phil's confusion about what happened and whether or not she was raped if there was no violence or fighting is typical of this scenario. Peterfreund wanted to bring it out in the open and promote discussion about it, so girls would know what rape is—even when it's with someone you care about. Astrid's powerful affirmation that it absolutely was rape—Phil's choice was taken away from her, and that makes it rape—is one that Peterfreund hopes her readers hear loud and clear, whether they have been raped, their friends have been raped, or they realize they might be raped sometime in the future. It's a sticky topic, and she deals with it masterfully.[5]

Another minor thread in the second book revolves around an intimate relationship between two of the hunters, although it isn't revealed how physical their relationship has become, and both are still virgins as defined by Bonegrinder, who still accepts and reveres both of them. This thread is not followed up, however, because the latter part of this volume centers primarily on Astrid.

Virginity is viewed differently across cultures and across time, and Peterfreund knew she had to define what it means in her universe. For instance, a virgin could be defined as an unmarried woman, a woman who possesses a hymen, or someone who has not participated in a specific kind of sexual act—is X defined as sex or not sex?—or virginity can be defined magically, because virgins have some special characteristic about their blood or their smell. It is a completely artificial construct and can be whatever the culture says it is.[6] After investigating the different meanings and significances of virginity, Peterfreund decided that since in her world the magic was created by Diana, goddess of the hunt, it should be defined the way Diana herself would have defined it: as having sex, whether it was consensual or not, brief or lengthy.[7]

The trilogy (Peterfreund assures her readers in the FAQ section of her website that there will indeed be a third volume, and that she hasn't deserted Astrid) is set in Europe, and mainly in Rome, where the Cloisters of Ctesias, built in the fourteenth century and home to the Order of the Lioness, to which unicorn hunters belong, is located. An interesting aside is that Ctesias, a Greek traveler to India, was the earliest person to describe unicorns—wild asses who were so swift they couldn't be captured alive, with red, white, and black horns on their foreheads—so Peterfreund was making a historical reference in naming her cloister.[8] Peterfreund went to Italy to visit the locations in the first volume; although it was a difficult trip, she was able to visit all the locations in the first novel, including the Galleria Borghese, the Etruscan City of the Dead, and cloisters with mosaics of unicorns and columns shaped like spiral horns, that could have been the same cloisters where the unicorn hunters lived. That experience gave her descriptions an extra layer of realism.[9]

Peterfreund had to do a lot of research for this trilogy, including the history and mythology of unicorns, the history of sword fighting and bow hunting, ancient weapons and how they were made and used, and the historical and current meanings of virginity in various societies. In addition, she studied with one of the top female bow hunters on the East Coast, learned about bow hunting and archery, and examined her large collection of ancient weapons. Peterfreund's descriptions of the centuries-old weapons the hunters used from the Wall of Weapons in the Cloister, including Clotilde's claymore, knife, and bow, are based on her research, and similar weapons could actually have existed.[10]

Peterfreund is well aware that when worldbuilding, the author must have rules, and those rules should not be broken. It doesn't matter if the reader knows the rules or not, but they must make sense and be consistent. There must be a reason for all of the rules that defines why they are important. If an author decides to break a rule, there must be a reason, and it must be major, significant, essential, and game changing. Peterfreund also knew that she couldn't have magic swarming all over the place willy-nilly, so she limited it to unicorns and hunters and the relationship between them.[11]

Her unicorns are based on "reality," or at least real historical writings from all over the world. There are five different kinds of unicorns that vary in size and appearance, but all are poisonous and all are deadly. They are based on unicorn mythology from all over the world, which Peterfreund explains on her website under "Unicorn Research."[12] And on killerunicorns.org, she describes the different types or breeds of unicorn.

The zhi are the smallest form of unicorn and are about the size of a goat. They have white fur, a short tail and mane, and blue eyes, and appear very gentle and affectionate. Bonegrinder is a young zhi. They are said to be able to separate the guilty from the innocent.

Most chapters of the Order of the Lioness keep a house zhi to test new hunters' virginity.

Einhorns look like classic Judeo-Christian unicorns, white, the size of a deer or horse, with a long, twisted horn, long mane, and a tail like a lion's, tufted at the end. They are very shy, preferring the woods or forests, so they aren't frequently seen.

Kirin are thought to be the most dangerous breed of unicorn because of their violent and destructive nature. They are about the size of a zebra and are black or some other dark color, very difficult to see. Their horns are not twisted like the zhi and einhorn, but are every bit as deadly. They are fierce in battle and easy to lose track of, allowing them to sneak up on their opponents.

Re'em are the only unicorns without a mane and are about the size of a bull or a buffalo. They are generally tan or fawn colored, and their fighting style depends on brute force. They are not often seen, because they are solitary creatures and live in desert or plains areas.

Karkadann are huge beasts, at least as large as an elephant, with a huge, massive horn. They are rare and are hardly ever seen. However, they are the most deadly—their venom emanates from their horn in a poisonous fog, allowing them to kill even at a distance. They have also been known to trample their prey to death. It is said that karkadann are able to communicate mentally and that this was the source of the connection between Alexander and Bucephalas.

Peterfreund wrote a synopsis and several proposals, finally decided that Astrid's point of view was the most effective, wrote the book, plot-boarded it (she describes how to do this on her blog—links are under "Writing and Publishing"[13]), and then began to write and revise. By the time the book was published, she had been talking about it for years, and her friend Justine Larbalestier had been teasing her about it online, so there was already a "Team Unicorn" waiting when it finally came out.[14]

When it came to naming her characters, Peterfreund decided to take her cues from their families' unicorn hunting heritage. Llewelyn means lion, and it is not only the name of Astrid's family but also the source for the name of the Cloisters. Philippa means horse lover; Cornelia means horn; Dorcas means deer; and Rosamunde means horse protector. Zelda comes from the Valkyrie name Griselda, and Astrid is also a Valkyrie name. Seth means darkness, and Brandt reflects that he was the first person in the book to be "branded" by a unicorn horn.[15] Bonegrinder is Peterfreund's favorite name, because it describes the little zhi so well and has a fairy-tale quality. Giovanni was not only a difficult name to come up with, but he was also a difficult character to create and went through several names and incarnations. He didn't come to life until he shared his own story with Astrid, which is when Peterfreund began to realize what he and Astrid mean to each other and how dangerous their relationship is.[16] This is interesting, since the last time Giovanni appears in *Ascendant* he is walking away from Astrid at a time when she needs him more than ever, even as she is pushing him away. Readers will be eager to see if or when he shows up in the final book and what role he will play.

When Peterfreund began to create the characters of her unicorn hunters, she assigned them very different motivations. Astrid is forced into becoming a hunter by her mother, Lilith, and wants to be a doctor or scientist. If she has to be part of the hunters, she'd prefer to work in a laboratory looking for the Remedy for their venom. There's no way that she (or any of the other hunters) could just walk away, because unicorns are magically attracted to them, and anyone near them could also be in danger. Learning that she is a hunter and finding out about the responsibilities that go with it has changed Astrid's life forever. By the end of the first book, she has recognized that there's no way for her to go back, to find her dream, and as much as she hates her magical powers at times, she also takes great pleasure in what they allow her to do. She is now part of an ancient organization that must work together to achieve their goal, and she has no way to go but forward. She truly has become Astrid the Warrior.

Cory hates unicorns because she watched them kill her mother. In the early chapters of *Rampant*, she is responsible for the first of several violent scenes, when she grabs Bonegrinder by one leg and her horn, swings her in a wide arc, and throws her as hard as she can off a balcony onto a cobblestone floor two stories below. It is Cory who began doing research into unicorns and their Reemergence after her mother's death and began contacting girls and their families who were descendants of Alexander the Great, because the goddess of the hunt, Diana, bestowed on him and all his descendants the powers of the virgin unicorn hunter. Some accounts have even said that Bucephalas, Alexander's great war horse, was actually a Persian species of unicorn called a karkadann, and it was Diana's powers that allowed Alexander to tame him, and Bucephalas's unicorn magic that allowed Alexander to become the conqueror of most of the known world.

Philippa isn't really interested in unicorn hunting—she's a vegetarian, a conservationist, and into practicing responsible culling techniques to control the unicorns and make sure they aren't a danger to humans. She's at the Cloisters mostly because it was a free trip to Rome, although she changes her mind fairly quickly once she comes face-to-face with a kirin. Even after she is no longer able to be a hunter, Phil wants to be actively involved in the Order.

Dorcas, Zelda, Rosamunde, Melissende, Ursula, Ilesha, and Grace are all hunters Cory found through her genealogical research of the twelve families of hunters. Peterfreund created lengthy backstories for each of the hunters, but since the trilogy is Astrid's story, she can't focus too much on them. She hopes to be able to write some short stories on the individual hunters and publish them in anthologies or on her website as surprises or extras for her fans.

Peterfreund has written two short stories so far, both set in the Rampant world but not part of Astrid's story. The first of these, "The Care and Feeding of Your Baby Killer Unicorn" from *Zombies vs. Unicorns*, is set in today's United States, and it involves "carnies, Sunday School, illicit kissing and a whole lot of blood." The second, "Errant," is from *Kiss Me Deadly* and is set in the eighteenth century and includes not only a *lot* of killer unicorns, but also nuns, fair ladies, and evil, manipulative lords.[17]

Giovanni is Astrid's love interest, an American who was expelled from school because he was at a fraternity party where things got out of control. His parents didn't know what to do with him, so he ended up with his mother's family in Rome. He is a complex character and seems to be a genuinely nice guy who likes Astrid in spite of the fact that she could easily overpower him. They have an electric and intense attraction to each other, although both of them acknowledge that having sex is not a possibility. Brandt, Astrid's boyfriend in the first scenes of *Rampant*, reappears in *Ascendant* and is still the same selfish, thoughtless person he had been.

Peterfreund, like many other young adult authors, has created few adult characters, which forces her teen characters to figure out their own answers to their problems. Three of the adult characters are particularly despicable—Lilith, Astrid's mother; Marten Jurgen, head of Gordian Pharmaceuticals; and Isabeau, who is in charge of the Gordian headquarters in France.

Peterfreund's website is huge, and she stays in close contact with readers who visit it and make comments on her blog. She is willing to respond to questions about the books, explaining details about characters, settings, plot twists, and, of course, unicorns. She also created a little website for the book trailer she wrote about the series, which is available at killerunicorns.org. She wrote it, filmed it, and even stars in it. She makes a great hunter, maintaining control over the killer unicorn (probably Bonegrinder) inside the crate sitting at center stage.

Notes

1. Melissa Buron, "Interview with Diana Peterfreund," *Melissaburon* (blog), March 18, 2010, http://melissaburon.livejournal.com/9718.html.

2. Angiegirl, "Interview with Diana Peterfreund + *Rampant* Giveaway!" *Angieville* (blog), August 24, 2009, http://angieville.blogspot.com/2009/08/interview-with-diana-peterfreund.html.

3. Buron, "Interview."

4. Malinda Lo, "Interview with Diana Peterfreund," *The Enchanted Inkpot* (blog), November 4, 2009, http://enchantedinkpot.livejournal.com/34406.html.

5. Diana Peterfreund, "Rampant Spoiler Thread," Official Website of Diana Peterfreund, August 26, 2009, http://www.dianapeterfreund.com/rampant-spoiler-thread/.

6. Lenore Appelhans, "Author Interview: Diana Peterfreund Discusses *Rampant*," *Presenting Lenore* (blog), August 21, 2009, http://presentinglenore.blogspot.com/2009/08/author-interview-diana-peterfreund.html.

7. Lo, "Interview."

8. Review of *The Natural History of Unicorns* by Chris Levers, *New Yorker* 85, no. 28 (September 14, 2009).

9. Angiegirl, "Interview."

10. Lo, "Interview."

11. Diana Peterfreund, "Worldbuilding Q&A," Official Website of Diana Peterfreund, http://www.dianapeterfreund.com/worldbuilding-qa/.

12. Diana Peterfreund, "Unicorn Research," Official Website of Diana Peterfreund, http://www.dianapeterfreund.com/books/unicorns/research/.

13. Diana Peterfreund, "What I've Been Busy With," Official Website of Diana Peterfreund, http://www.dianapeterfreund.com/category/plot -board/.
14. Lo, "Interview."
15. Peterfreund, "Rampant Spoiler Thread."
16. Angiegirl, "Interview."
17. Diana Peterfreund, "Short Fiction," Official Website of Diana Peterfreund, http://www.dianapeterfreund.com/books/short-fiction/.

Bibliography

Peterfreund, Diana. *Rampant*. New York: HarperTeen, 2009.
———. *Ascendant*. New York: HarperTeen, 2010.
Review of *Natural History of Unicorns* by Chris Levers. *New Yorker*, September 14, 2009.
Suhr, Elmer G. "An Interpretation of the Unicorn." *Folklore* 75, no 2 (1964): 91–109.

20

Killer Demons: The Demon's Lexicon Trilogy by Sarah Rees Brennan

Sarah Rees Brennan's demon hero was inspired by a television documentary on a wolf who brought up two human children and was killed by two hunters who thought the children were in danger from her. Brennan wondered what a demon might be like if it were brought up as a human, and Alan and Nick came to her, their relationship defining their characters.[1] Which is more important, nature or nurture, who you are or how you are brought up? Could an emotionless, evil creature without a voice be taught loving emotions, how to speak, how to live as a human, a brother, a son, a friend? With those questions, Nick, the demon put into the body of a baby at his birth, and Alan, his older brother, who is determined to bring up his little brother as a boy, not a demon, were born. Brennan was also able to work the story of the documentary into the last chapter of the book.

But in order to make this mismatched pair work, Brennan had to create a magical world to put them in. Her favorite genre is YA urban fantasy, because it gives the magic a realistic frame and setting. Nick and Alan have to worry about demons and magicians, but they also have to worry about leaky sinks, Nick's grades in school, and how to pay the rent.[2] These details set them squarely into a realistic world, easy to identify with, where magic is just part of everyday life. The first two sentences in *The Demon's Lexicon* demonstrate this juxtaposition clearly: "The pipe under the sink was leaking again. It wouldn't have been so bad, except that Nick kept his favorite sword under the sink."[3]

She knew she wanted all kinds of magical creatures in the story, but she had to define her demons first. Researching, Brennan decided to take the bits and pieces of demonology that she liked and craft them together to create her world. Sumerians believed that demons were creatures made of fire, while humans were made of earth.[4] They weren't evil, just powerful and very different from humans.[5] She also stole from the Elizabethan view of demons as creatures of the air, using the air spirit Ariel (from Shakespeare's *The Tempest*) as an example. At one point Ariel says that if he were human, his heart would break because of the suffering humans go through—a powerful being who is enslaved, unable to feel emotions, yet knowing that if he could, he would.[6] How close is that to actually feeling love—or loss, or loneliness, or pity?[7] When Nick tries to "act human," following up on Mae's instructions, he wants to do the right thing, yet sometimes has to ask to make sure he hasn't made another mistake. When he comforts Mae, holding her close as she sobs, he checks with her to make sure that this is what she wants. It is not the action of a being who is both emotionless and unfeeling, but of one who wants to give the exact thing that she needs at that moment. Nick may be a demon, but he is pulled toward being a human as well.

Brennan also invented magicians, powerful beings who make deals with demons to get more power and give demons a chance to possess people,[8] which is always fatal. They sacrifice humans without a thought, because they are not magical, and therefore unimportant. Alan and Nick have been on the run from magicians for their entire lives. Brennan based these magicians on German tracts from the fifteenth century that said that magicians call up demons who give them power over humans, great beauty, power over the elements, and enormous wealth—and her magicians have all of that, and more.

Magicians live in groups, or Circles, that help them increase and focus their power. These Circles are generally named after a stone or rock, because an actual circle of those stones is the center of their power. The various Circles are in competition with each other, each wanting to be the largest and most powerful. The leaders of these Circles—Black Arthur, Gerald, and Celeste—are portrayed as twisted, scheming, and evil, perhaps cases of absolute power corrupting absolutely, or perhaps the effects of dealing with demons for so many years.

But the magicians are not the only ones who can use magic. There are many different kinds of magic in Brennan's world; many different kinds of people practice it. Magic is used to show danger, love, music, language,[9] and for making a profit,[10] which is the point of the Goblin Market, a gathering place for all kinds of magical people. Based on the Christina Rosetti poem "The Goblin Market,"[11] it is a traveling fair where once a month all kinds of wonderful, magical things are sold. The poem is about dangerous goblins who entice young women to buy their fruit and enter their enchanted world for one evening, whereupon they spend the rest of their lives longing to return. The poem's lyrical verses seem to weave a magical spell around the reader, enticing and haunting. But while there are no goblins in Brennan's Market, it is still tempting and dangerous to the innocent or the unwary.

Brennan created the Market because she had to have a place for Nick and Alan to buy the weapons they needed to fight the magicians. At the Goblin Market, you can barter—money isn't the only way to purchase something. That's how Alan is able to buy the talismans to protect him, Nick, Mae, and Jamie, and the knives and swords he and Nick use to fight with, because guns don't always work against magicians. Tourists come and pay dancers for dangerous dances inside magical circles to call up demons who answer questions truthfully, but never pleasantly. (Demons always tell the truth, and the more painful it is to hear, the more they like it.) Nick is one of the best dancers at the market, and he and Alan depend on the money he makes there.

Tourists go to the Market for more than to question demons—there are all kinds of magic to buy—fever fruit that the dancers eat that takes away every inhibition, lanterns to put in the window and call lost or wandering loved ones home, chimes to play your favorite songs, charms to protect the wearer from evil, or curses against an enemy, or a light of love, that glow only for one's true love.[12] The magic workers of the Market live on what the tourists pay to have a chance to touch and hold the magic they find there.

The Goblin Market exists because Brennan's fantasy world is neither open (everyone knows about the magic) nor closed (only those who are magical or are loved by a magical person know about the magical part of the world), but halfway between.[13] Magic exists, and if someone wants to take the time to investigate and uncover the secret, he or she will be able to find the magic and shop at the Goblin Market. So some humans never know about the magic, and others look for it and find it. It is always there, waiting for them to discover it.

The trilogy is set in England, because Brennan was living there at the time she wrote it. When she got the idea for the story she had just been on a ghost tour of Exeter, and as a result, she saw the place as a creepy, frightening city where it was entirely possible that dark magic could reach out and grab the unsuspecting passerby. London is an old city, with all the secrets of generations, and so it seemed like a logical place to continue the story. While doing research, Brennan made trips to the various settings in the trilogy; once she was mistaken for a health inspector in a Salisbury pub because of the notes she was making about it,[14] and another time she was mistaken for a suicide jumper on the Millennium Bridge, when she climbed onto the bridge supports to see if they would hold up Nick during his duel on the bridge. The security guard who pulled her down was sure she was going to jump.[15]

Brennan had to do research on the fight scenes to make sure they were realistic, and she even took fencing and archery lessons to learn how Nick and Alan would move and attack. She also has a friend who works for a museum, who made it possible for her to see weapons not usually seen by the public, some of which made it into the books.[16]

Once the magic and the settings were decided on, Brennan had to create realistic characters to populate them. She decided early to write about sibling relationships, because almost everyone has siblings and can empathize with the joys and the problems that they create. Siblings are sometimes like friends, sometimes like enemies; people you feel responsible for and yet didn't choose to have in your life.[17] But they are also people who are hard to push out of your life, no matter how much you sometimes want to.

She thought of Nick and Alan first, their opposing natures, their lightness and darkness. But that was too simple—good guy and bad guy. She also wanted to turn those characters inside out, so while Nick is definitely a bad boy on the outside and Alan is the geeky good guy that everyone loves, when the reader gets to know them better, it is easy to see that Alan is a liar and a murderer, willing to betray his brother for his idea of the greater good, while Nick always tells the absolute truth, means what he says, is trying very hard to be human, and is very undemonic.[18] Nick is supposed to be an emotionless demon, but his human veneer seems to be having an effect on him, as does the love of the people surrounding him.

Alan is attractive, kind, intelligent, the kind of guy parents will always approve of, but he is also ruthless, determined, certain that his way is the only right way, and a flawless liar. He is willing to do anything at all to get what he wants, including manipulating those he knows care about him, without any consideration of their pain when they discover what he's done. It would be all too easy to get sucked into trusting him or falling in love with him. So Brennan has actually created two characters who are both dangerous and morally corrupt, but in very different ways. She has switched the archetypes, so that the hero is villainous and the villainous monster is very close to human.[19]

Brennan also wanted to give her readers a glimpse inside Nick, because while YA novels about a bad boy are easy to find, not many of them show him from inside his own head or give any clues about who he is and why he acts the way he does. She wanted to know what it would be like to get into the head of a demon.[20] Writing the first volume from Nick's perspective allowed her to do this. He is puzzled by who he is and why he is different from his brother and the other people he knows. He doesn't feel emotions and doesn't like to be touched, unless it is his idea. He has no trouble flirting or dancing with girls who are attracted by his dark good looks, yet flinches away whenever Alan reaches to ruffle his hair. He is puzzled by the things that other people think are important, things he sees as irrelevant. He doesn't want to get close to other people, and he really doesn't have any idea what human love is. He didn't learn to talk until he was four, and he still has trouble expressing what he thinks and feels. Fighting, using his body, is what he enjoys most. Practicing for hours relaxes him, and his swords and his knives are a part of him. The sword is always with him in a sheath down his spine, the hilt hidden under his long hair, his knives strapped to his body and arms.

But Nick also shows his love for Alan, even though he can't describe it, or even admit to it. He wears his talisman because Alan wants him to, even when it is painful and scars his chest where it rests. Alan wants him to go to school, and so Nick does, even though reading is difficult for him and it's hard for him to make friends. There are two halves of his life—the home life, with demons and magic and a mother who hates him, and the school life, where he tries to hide how he struggles in class, hangs with the other bad boys, and works part time fixing cars. When Mae and Jamie, whom he knows from school, come to the Ryves home looking for help with a demon mark, those two worlds collide, and Nick's life changes in ways he could never have predicted. He hates that they know about both halves of his life, hates that they endanger his brother, and hates that his brother seems driven to help them.

When Nick's true demon nature is revealed during the final scenes of the first volume, it explains many of the things Nick has found puzzling about himself and those around him. He leaves his body behind to explore his full demonic powers, yet when he remembers that he left Alan vulnerable to the Obsidian Circle magicians, he returns to his body without hesitation, removing the demon's mark on Alan, and waiting beside him until he wakes up. Alan may have set him free, but he still feels the human pull of Alan's love and of the home that they have created together. This same scenario ends the second book as well—Nick and Alan play out the roles that have become so familiar to them, frequently at odds, yet always together. Alan loves Nick, in spite of what he is, and although Nick doesn't seem to be aware of it, he loves Alan just as deeply. When he finds out Alan has made plans to betray him, he doesn't care about anything that Alan might do to him, if Alan will just not leave him, no matter what. And Alan never will.

Since Alan was four, he has been his brother's caretaker. It was Alan who named Nick, taught him how to speak, made sure he went to school, and did everything he could to let Nick know that he was loved and cherished. When he played football, he wanted Nick there to watch him. And on the night his father died, and Nick forgot to wear his talisman, Alan gave him his own, and so was vulnerable to the magicians who attacked them.

But Alan has his darker side, also. Their life has taught him to lie extremely well, to be charming, to persuade or manipulate people to do what he wants, to make them see in any situation what he wants them to see. He is harsh and ruthless in his defense of Nick and his mother, willing to do anything necessary to take care of them. His handicap makes it difficult to use a sword, but he has a gun and several knives on him at all times. He is a skilled marksman, and Nick proudly says, "My brother never misses."

Mae and Jamie are the other two main characters in the first volume. They come to Alan and Nick for help when Jamie has a third-tier demon's mark, leaving him vulnerable to the magicians and demons, able to be easily possessed. Their arrival also coincides with Alan's receiving a first-tier mark, allowing him to be tracked by magicians who control the demon that made it. This sets Nick against them, since they have helped put Alan in danger. Mae is desperate to get help for her little brother and persuades Alan to do whatever he can. Alan is vulnerable because she is his latest crush (or so Nick thinks). He agrees to help them by taking them to the next Goblin Market to see if the mark can be removed.

Jamie is in Nick's class at school, and Mae is a year older. Neither of them likes him very much, his cold and scary demeanor keeping them at a distance. In fact, at first Jamie is so terrified of Nick that he doesn't talk much when he's around, something Nick appreciates. However, this changes as Jamie gets to know both of the brothers, and his snarky comments elicit equally snarky responses, adding to the humor of the book. Brennan says that Jamie is the character who is easiest to write because he talks like she does, and all she has to do is just write down what she'd say in the same situation.[21]

In many ways, Mae is like Alan in the intensity of her desire to look after her brother. Their parents are divorced, their mother is a workaholic who doesn't have a clue how to relate to her kids, and they are essentially bringing up themselves—one reason why Jamie was so easy for the demon to mark. Once Mae finds out about the mark, she will stop at nothing to have it removed.

Mae is not aware that Jamie has magical powers, although he's been aware that he's different for years. He has kept it a secret for fear of what she and their parents would think if they knew. He's been far more open about being gay, and he came out to them several years before the first volume begins. Brennan is aware that she may create some controversy by putting an openly gay character in her books, but has been pleased by readers' responses to the character. She's also been pleased by the response to Alan as a handicapped character.[22]

Jamie is determined that he not be judged just on his sexual identity, but on who he is and what he can do. Nevertheless, he is softhearted almost to a fault, ready to believe what anyone says, especially if he cares about them, making him easy to manipulate. He has an almost pathological fear of weapons, and his attempts to escape Nick's training at throwing knives leads to some of the more humorous scenes in the books. Drawn to Alan when he and Mae first meet the brothers, Jamie connects more with Nick as he gets to know him better, even agreeing to Nick's suggestion that they be friends, even though Nick isn't exactly sure what that means or how to do it. But as their relationship develops, Jamie comes to realize that Nick will have his back, always. Whatever happens, Nick will be there to rescue him.

Other characters also spring from the page fully fledged, moving from minor to major characters as the story develops. Gerald, who inherits the Obsidian Circle, hides his vicious and greedy nature behind a soft-spoken and charming exterior; Celeste, leader of the Aventurine Circle, is also scheming and determined to make her circle the most powerful; Sin, the beautiful dark-skinned dancer who will inherit the Market, and through whose eyes the final volume of the series is seen; Merris, who sets many things in motion as the Leader of the Market and keeps many things secret; and Matthias, the pied piper of the Market, who creates magic through music, and is one of the characters that Brennan is most fond of.[23]

Brennan stays in touch with her readers, and the Demon's Lexicon world extends far beyond the books. She has a blog that she's been writing for many years and uses to promote the books through giveaways and contests, to respond to readers' questions, and to ask what they'd like to see in future books. She posts links to the short stories she's written about the Demon's Lexicon world[24] and has also posted a number of "cookies," or monthly excerpts from *Demon's Surrender*,[25] in the year leading up to the publication date. An online contest on how to best promote *Demon's Surrender* produced some creative projects from her readers, including several videos, a list of cocktails to go with the eight main characters, and a song written and sung by a young woman to show the importance of love and loving even when it is risky to do so.[26] Her blogger's ID is Sirael, and this is how she describes her song, which is posted on YouTube: "With normal people, it's instinctual and natural to believe that they value other[s], that they have morals, and that they understand the social contract. With Nick, you can't assume any of that. Alan, Jamie, and Mae have all seen the supernatural violence that Nick is capable of, but they still actively and voluntarily decided to trust him anyway." (Click on the "Show More" link under the video window to see the complete description).[27] The song ends with these words:

> That smile like a knife is still a smile.
> And that gaze of ice cuts through the haze.
> That heart buried deep is still a heart,
> Even when you don't know what to say.
> 'Cause I can't move the mountains,
> I can't boil the seas,
> But I can be for you
> What you need me to be. . . .
> When you look for me
> I'll be right here.[28]

Notes

1. Rebecca L. Sutton, "Q&A with Sarah Rees Brennan, author of *The Demon's Lexicon*," *Coldwater High eZine* (blog), July 26, 2010, http://fallen archangelnews.blogspot.com/2010/07/q-with-sarah-rees-brennan-author -of.html.
2. Sarah Rees Brennan, "FAQ," Sarah Rees Brennan, http://sarahrees brennan.com/faq/.
3. Sarah Rees Brennan, *The Demon's Lexicon*, Simon & Schuster (Margaret K. McElderry, 2009), 1.
4. Sutton, "Q&A."
5. "Sarah Rees Brennan," Simon & Schuster, http://authors.simonand schuster.com/Sarah-Rees-Brennan/46599925/interview.
6. "Sarah Rees Brennan."
7. Sutton, "Q&A."
8. Brennan, "FAQ."
9. Travis P., "Interview + Giveaway with Sarah Rees Brennan," *Inked Books* (blog), July 20, 2010, http://inkedbooks.blogspot.com/2010/07/ interview-giveaway-with-sarah-rees.html.
10. Nikki, "Author Interview: Sarah Rees Brennan," *YA Reads* (blog), August 18, 2009, http://www.yareads.com/author-interview-sarah-rees -brennan/author-interviews/1805.

11. Christina Rossetti, "Goblin Market," Reflections: Leon Malinofsky, http://plexipages.com/reflections/goblin.html.

12. Sarah Rees Brennan, "Guest Post with Sarah Rees Brennan & Contest: The Goblin Market," *The Book Butterfly* (blog), July 8, 2010, http://thebook butterfly.com/2010/07/guest-post-with-sarah-rees-brennan.html.

13. Brennan, "Guest Post."

14. "Sarah Rees Brennan."

15. Write Away, "An Interview with Sarah Rees Brennan," Just Imagine, 2010, http://www.justimaginestorycentre.co.uk/node/1265349903.

16. Travis, "Interview."

17. "Sarah Rees Brennan."

18. Sutton, "Q&A."

19. Sutton, "Q&A."

20. Write Away, "Interview."

21. Sutton, "Q&A."

22. Travis, "Interview."

23. Sutton, "Q&A."

24. Sarah Rees Brennan, short stories of various dates, *Sarah Tells Tales* (blog), http://sarahtales.livejournal.com/tag/short%20story.

25. Sarah Rees Brennan, Cookie stories, *Sarah Tells Tales* (blog), http://sarahtales.livejournal.com/tag/cookies.

26. Sarah Rees Brennan, "The Promotion Notion: Winners & Awesomeness (i.e., Everyone)," *Sarah Tells Tales* (blog), April 19, 2011, http://sarah tales.livejournal.com/tag/contest.

27. Sirael, *Song for Nick*, video, April 6, 2011, http://www.youtube.com/watch?v=nuo2eB0wzZI.

28. Sirael, *Song for Nick*.

Bibliography

Brennan, Sarah Rees. *The Demon's Lexicon*. Simon & Schuster (Margaret K. McDerry), 2009.

———. *The Demon's Covenant*. Simon & Schuster (Margaret K. McDerry), 2010.

———. *The Demon's Surrender*. Simon & Schuster (Margaret K. McDerry), 2011.

Afterword:
Looking Back, Looking Ahead

We have come to the end of our story, the fork in our road. There are fewer piles of books on the dining room table, and without all the books on the sofa, there's room for myself and two cats once again. But there's still one question that remains to be answered: What now? Where have we come from, and what have we learned? Supernatural creatures are constructs and tools that teens can use to understand themselves and their worlds better and help them make the decisions that will guide them through those worlds. Who am I? What do I believe? What's the right thing to do? Feeling like an outsider is a common experience for a teen, and discovering that immensely powerful monsters can feel that way as well helps them not only identify with the monster, but also realize that perhaps others feel like outsiders as well. And who wouldn't like to have supernatural powers to display when enemies approach? Monsters have one foot in the real world, and one foot in the supernatural world. Teens have one foot in the world of childhood, and one foot in the world of adulthood. Monsters are rejected and hunted, looked at with suspicious eyes because of the way they look or behave. Teens' appearance and behavior are always suspicious to some adults, who look at them as if *they* might be the monsters. No wonder teens identify with these creatures!

Yes, they are scary, and they do scary things. But they are also the person sitting next to you, in class, at the movies, on the train or the bus—not all that scary, after all. And sometimes the monsters are created by the very people that fear them—making something monstrous out of someone who just wants to be himself or herself. Learning about someone or something that is frightening can reduce the fear and replace it with understanding. I hope these particular monsters aren't so scary any longer, now that you know them better.

And now we go on to human monsters, who are in many ways far more frightening than supernatural monsters are. What can they teach us, and what lessons can we learn from them? What makes them tick, and why are they so monstrous? The bully, the abuser, the addict, the toxic teen or adult—what created them and why, and how can they be dealt with? *They Hurt, They Scar, They Steal, They Kill: The Psychological Meaning of Human Monsters in Young Adult Literature* is the logical next project.

Appendix: Booklists

Angels

Angelfire Trilogy (ongoing)

Mouton, Courtney Allison. *Angelfire*. New York: Katherine Tegan Books, 2011.

Angel Star Series (ongoing)

Murgia, Jennifer. *Angel Star*. Potomac, MD: Lands Atlantic Publishing, 2010.
——. *Lemniscate*. Potomac, MD: Lands Atlantic Publishing, 2011.

Fallen Angel Series (ongoing)

Terrell, Heather. *Fallen Angel*. New York: HarperTeen, 2010.
——. *Eternity*. New York: HarperTeen, 2011.

Fallen Series (ongoing)

Kate, Lauren. *Fallen*. New York: Delacorte Press, 2009.
——. *Torment*. New York: Delacorte Press, 2010.
——. *Passion*. New York: Delacorte Press, 2011.

Halo Trilogy (ongoing)

Adornetto, Alexandra. *Halo*. New York: Feiwel & Friends, 2010.
———. *Hades*. New York: Feiwel & Friends, 2010.

Hush Hush Series (ongoing)

Fitzpatrick, Becca. *Hush Hush*. New York: Simon & Schuster, 2009.
———. *Cresendo*. New York: Simon & Schuster, 2010.
———. *Silence*. New York: Simon & Schuster, 2011.

Internal Devices Series (ongoing)

Clare, Cassandra. *Clockwork Angel*. New York: Margaret K. McElderry, 2011.
———. *Clockwork Prince*. New York: Margaret K. McElderry, 2011.

Kissed by an Angel Series (ongoing)

Chandler, Elizabeth. *Kissed by an Angel*. New York: Simon Pulse, 1995.
———. *The Power of Love*. New York: Simon Pulse, 1995.
———. *Soulmates*. New York: Simon Pulse, 1995.
———. *Evercrossed*. New York: Simon Pulse, 2011.

Mercy Series (complete)

Lim, Rebecca. *Mercy*. New York: Hyperion, 2011.
———. *Exile*. New York: Hyperion, 2012.

Mortal Instruments Series (ongoing)

Clare, Cassandra. *City of Bones*. New York: Margaret K. McElderry. 2007.
———. *City of Ashes*. New York: Margaret K. McElderry. 2008.
———. *City of Glass*. New York: Margaret K. McElderry. 2009.
———. *City of Fallen Angels*. New York: Margaret K. McElderry. 2011.

Stand-Alone Titles

Clifford, Leah. *A Touch Mortal*. New York: Greenwillow Books, 2011.
Hand, Cynthia. *Unearthly*. New York: HarperTeen, 2011.

Howe, N. *Angel in Vegas: The Chronicles of Noah Sark.* Somerville, MA: Candlewick Press, 2009.

Pearce, Bryony. *Angel's Fury.* Glasgow, UK: Egmont Books, 2011.

Demons

Demonata Series (complete)

Shan, Darren. *Lord Loss.* New York: HarperCollins, 2005.
——. *Demon Thief.* New York: HarperCollins, 2006.
——. *Slawter.* New York: HarperCollins, 2006.
——. *Bec.* New York: HarperCollins, 2006.
——. *Blood Beast.* New York: HarperCollins, 2007.
——. *Demon Apocalypse.* New York: HarperCollins, 2008.
——. *Death's Shadow.* New York: HarperCollins, 2008.
——. *Wolf Island.* New York: HarperCollins, 2008.
——. *Dark Calling.* New York: HarperCollins, 2009.
——. *Hell's Heroes.* New York: HarperCollins, 2009.

Demon Envy Series (complete)

Lynn, Erin. *Demon Envy.* New York: Berkley Trade, 2007.
——. *Speed Demon.* New York: Berkley Trade, 2008.

Demon Princess Series (ongoing)

Rowen, Michelle. *Reign or Shine.* New York: Walker Books for Young Readers, 2009.
——. *Reign Check.* New York: Walker Books for Young Readers, 2010.

Demon Trappers Series (ongoing)

Oliver, Jana. *The Demon Trapper's Daughter.* New York: St. Martin's Griffin, 2011.
——. *Soul Thief.* New York: St. Martin's Griffin, 2011.

Personal Demons Trilogy (ongoing)

Descrochers, Lisa. *Personal Demons.* New York: Tor Teen, 2010.
——. *Original Sin.* New York: Tor Teen, 2011.

Prophecy of the Sisters Series (complete)

Zink, M. *Prophecy of the Sisters*. New York: Little, Brown, 2009.
——. *Guardian of the Gate*. New York: Little, Brown, 2010.
——. *Circle of Fire*. New York: Little, Brown, 2011.

Renegade Spirit Series (complete)

Jenkins, Jerry, and Perrodin, John. *The Tattooed Rats*. Nashville, TN: Thomas Nelson, 2006.
——. *Demon's Bluff*. Nashville, TN: Thomas Nelson, 2007.
——. *Seclusion Point*. Nashville, TN: Thomas Nelson, 2008.

Waking Trilogy (ongoing)

Randall, Thomas. *Dreams of the Dead*. New York: Bloomsbury USA, 2009.
——. *Spirits of the Noh*. New York: Bloomsbury USA, 2011.

Stand-Alone Titles

Enthoven, Sam. *The Black Tattoo*. New York: Razorbill, 2006.
Jenkins, A. M. *Repossessed*. New York: HarperTeen, 2007.
Johnson, Maureen. *Devilish*. New York: Razorbill, 2006.
Kaye, Marilyn. *Demon Chick*. New York: Henry Holt, 2009.
Lewis, Richard. *The Demon Queen*. New York: Simon & Schuster, 2008.
Nayeri, Daniel, and Nayeri, Dina. *Another Faust*. Somerville, MA: Candlewick Press, 2009.
Pullman, Philip. *Count Karlstein, or the Ride of the Demon Huntsman*. London: Transworld Children's Hardbacks, 2002.
Taylor, Laini. *Lips Touch: Three Times*. New York: Arthur A. Levine Books, 2009.

Shapeshifters

Claire de Lune Series (ongoing)

Johnson, Christine. *Claire de Lune*. New York: Simon Pulse, 2010.
——. *Nocturne*. New York: Simon Pulse, 2011.

Crescent Series (complete)

Deen, Jordon. *Crescent*. Castroville, TX: Black Rose Writing, 2010.
———. *Half Moon*. Castroville, TX: Black Rose Writing, 2011.
———. *Full Moon*. Castroville, TX: Black Rose Writing, 2012.

Dark Divine Series (ongoing)

Despain, Bree. *Dark Devine*. New York: Egmont USA, 2009.
———. *Lost Saint*. New York: Egmont USA, 2010.
———. *Savage Grace*. New York: Egmont USA, 2011.

Dark Guardians Series (complete)

Hawthorne, Rachel. *Moonlight*. New York: HarperTeen, 2009.
———. *Full Moon*. New York: HarperTeen, 2009.
———. *Dark of the Moon*. New York: HarperTeen, 2009.
———. *Shadow of the Moon*. New York: HarperTeen, 2010.

Dragon Diaries Trilogy (ongoing)

Cooke, D. *Flying Blind*. New York: NAL Trade, 2011.
———. *Winging It*. New York: NAL Trade, 2011.

Keisha'ra of the Den of Shadows Series (complete)

Atwater-Rhodes, Amelia. *Hawksong*. New York: Delacorte Press, 2003.
———. *Snakecharm*. New York: Delacorte Press, 2004.
———. *Falcondance*. New York: Delacorte Press, 2005.
———. *Wolfcry*. New York: Delacorte Press, 2006.
———. *Wyvernail*. New York: Delacorte Press, 2007.

Lonely Werewolf Girl Series (unknown)

Millar, M. *Lonely Werewolf Girl*. Berkeley, CA: Soft Skull Press, 2008.
———. *Curse of the Wolf Girl*. Berkeley, CA: Soft Skull Press, 2010.

Mistwood Series (ongoing)

Cypess, Leah. *Mistwood*. New York: Greenwillow Books, 2010.
———. *Nightspell*. New York: Greenwillow Books, 2011.

Moondog Trilogy (complete)

Garfield, Henry. *Moondog*. New York: Simon Pulse, 1995.
———. *Room 13*. New York: Simon Pulse, 1995.
———. *Tartabull's Throw*. New York: Simon Pulse, 2001.

Once in a Full Moon Series (ongoing)

Schreiber, Ellen. *Once in a Full Moon*. New York: Katherine Tegan Books, 2011.
———. *Magic of the Moonlight*. New York: Katherine Tegan Books, 2011.

The Raven Duet Series (ongoing)

Bell, Hilari. *Trickster's Girl*. New York: Houghton Mifflin 2011.

Shifters Series (complete)

Vincent, Rachel. *Stray*. Don Mills, ON: Mira, 2007.
———. *Rogue*. Don Mills, ON: Mira, 2008.
———. *Pride*. Don Mills, ON: Mira, 2009.
———. *Prey*. Don Mills, ON: Mira, 2009.
———. *Shift*. Don Mills, ON: Mira, 2010.
———. *Alpha*. Don Mills, ON: Mira, 2010.

Sisters Red Series (unknown)

Pearce, Jackson. *Sisters Red*. New York: Little, Brown, 2010.
———. *Sweetly*. New York: Little, Brown, 2011.

13 to Life Series (ongoing)

Delany, Shannon. *13 to Life*. New York: St. Martin's Griffin, 2010.
———. *Secrets and Shadows*. New York: St. Martin's Griffin, 2011.
———. *Bargains and Betrayals*. New York: St. Martin's Griffin, 2011.

Stand-Alone Titles

Bennett, Holly. *Shapeshifter*. Vancouver, BC: Orca Book Publishers, 2010.
Block, Francesca Lia. *The Frenzy*. New York: HarperTeen, 2010.
Bruchac, Joseph. *Bearwalker*. New York: HarperCollins, 2007.

Cooper, Louise. *Sleep of Stone.* New York: DAW, 1993.
Davis, Heather. *Never Cry Werewolf.* New York: HarperTeen, 2009.
Dunkle, Clare B. *By These Ten Bones.* New York: Henry Holt, 2005.
Garfield, Henry. *My Father the Werewolf.* New York: Atheneum, 2005.
Gray, Claudia. *Fateful.* New York: HarperCollins, 2011.
Jennings, Patrick. *The Wolving Time.* New York: Scholastic, 2005.
Jinks, Catherine. *The Abused Werewolf Rescue Group.* New York: Harcourt Children's Books, 2011.
Johnson, Kathleen Jeffrie. *A Fast and Brutal Wing.* New York: Roaring Brook Press, 2004.
Landon, Dena. *Shapeshifter's Quest.* New York: Dutton Children's Publishing, 2005.
Larbalestier, Justine. *Liar.* New York: Bloomsbury USA, 2009.
Nobleman, Marc Tyler, and Bradford Kendall. *Werewolf High.* New York: Stone Arch Books, 2009.
Reisz, Kristopher. *Unleashed.* New York: Simon Pulse, 2008.
Shusterman, Neal. *Red Rider's Hood.* New York: Dutton Juvenile, 2005.
Windsor, P. *The Blooding.* New York: Scholastic, 1996.

Unicorns

Black, Holly, and Justine Larbalestier, eds. *Zombies vs. Unicorns.* New York: Margaret K. McElderry, 2010.
Coville, Bruce, ed. *A Glory of Unicorns.* New York: Scholastic, 1998.
Humphreys, Cris C. *Hunt of the Unicorn.* New York: Alfred A. Knopf Books, 2011.

Vampires

Alex Van Helsing Series (ongoing)

Henderson, J. *Vampire Rising.* New York: HarperTeen, 2010.

Bite Me Series (ongoing)

Francis, Melissa McKenzie. *Bite Me!* New York: HarperTeen, 2009.
———. *Love Sucks!* New York: HarperTeen, 2010.

Blood and Lace Series (complete)

Locke, Joseph. *Vampire Heart*. New York: Bantam Books, 1994.
———. *Deadly Relations*. New York: Bantam Books, 1994.

Blood Coven Series (complete)

Mancusi, Marianne. *Boys That Bite*. New York: Berkley Trade, 2006.
———. *Stake That!* New York: Berkley Trade, 2006.
———. *Girls That Growl*. New York: Berkley Trade, 2007.
———. *Bad Blood*. New York: Berkley Trade, 2010.
———. *Night School*. New York: Berkley Trade, 2011.
———. *Blood Ties*. New York: Berkley Trade, 2011.

Bloodline Series (complete)

Cary, Kate. *Bloodline*. New York: Razorbill, 2005.
———. *Reckoning*. New York: Razorbill, 2007.

Bloodlines Series (ongoing)

Mead, Richelle. *Bloodlines*. New York: Razorbill, 2011.

Blood Ninja Series (ongoing)

Lake, Nick. *Blood Ninja*. New York: Simon & Schuster, 2009.
———. *Blood Ninja II: Revenge of Lord Oda*. New York: Simon & Schuster, 2010.

Chronicles of Blood Series (complete)

Cross, Gary. *Plague of the Undead*. Rosedale, Auckland: Penguin Global, 2010.
———. *Empire of the Undead*. Rosedale, Auckland: Penguin Global, 2010.
———. *Swarm of the Undead*. Rosedale, Auckland: Penguin Global, 2011.

Cirque du Freak: The Saga of Darren Shan Series (complete)

Shan, Darren. *A Living Nightmare*. New York: Little, Brown, 2002.
———. *The Vampire's Assistant*. New York: Little, Brown, 2002.

———. *Tunnels of Blood*. New York: Little, Brown, 2002.
———. *Vampire Mountain*. New York: Little, Brown, 2002.
———. *Trials of Death*. New York: Little, Brown, 2003.
———. *Vampire Prince*. New York: Little, Brown, 2003.
———. *Hunters of the Dusk*. New York: Little, Brown, 2004.
———. *Allies of the Night*. New York: Little, Brown, 2004.
———. *Killers of the Dawn*. New York: Little, Brown, 2005.
———. *Lake of Souls*. New York: Little, Brown, 2005.
———. *Lord of the Shadows*. New York: Little, Brown, 2006.
———. *Sons of Destiny*. New York: Little, Brown, 2006.

Crave Series (ongoing)

Metz, Melinda, and Laura J. Burns. *Crave*. New York: Simon & Schuster, 2010.
———. *Sacrifice*. New York: Simon & Schuster, 2011.

Crusade Series (ongoing)

Holder, Nancy, and Debbie Viguié. *Crusade*. New York: Simon Pulse, 2010.
———. *Damned*. New York: Simon Pulse, 2011.

Evernight Series (ongoing)

Gray, Claudia. *Evernight*. New York: HarperTeen, 2008.
———. *Stargazer*. New York: HarperTeen, 2009.
———. *Hourglass*. New York: HarperTeen, 2010.
———. *Afterlife*. New York: HarperTeen, 2011.
———. *Fateful*. New York: HarperTeen, 2011.

Half-Blood Vampire Novels (Colby Blanchard series) (complete)

Robar, Serena. *Braced2Bite*. New York: Berkley Trade, 2006.
———. *Fangs4Freaks*. New York: Berkley Trade, 2006.
———. *Dating4Demons*. New York: Berkley Trade, 2007.

House of Night Series (ongoing)

Cast, P. C., and Kristin Cast. *Marked*. New York: St. Martin's Griffin, 2007.
———. *Betrayed*. New York: St. Martin's Griffin, 2007.

———. *Chosen*. New York: St. Martin's Griffin, 2008.
———. *Untamed*. New York: St. Martin's Griffin, 2008.
———. *Hunted*. New York: St. Martin's Griffin, 2009.
———. *Tempted*. New York: St. Martin's Griffin, 2009.
———. *Burned*. New York: St. Martin's Griffin, 2010.
———. *Awakened*. New York: St. Martin's Griffin, 2011.
———. *Destined*. New York: St. Martin's Griffin, 2011.
———. *Fledgling Handbook 101*. New York: St. Martin's Griffin, 2010.
———. *Nyx in the House of Night*. New York: St. Martin's Griffin, 2011.
———. *Dragon's Oath*. New York: St. Martin's Griffin, 2011.

Immortals Series (complete)

Noel, Alyson. *Evermore*. New York: St. Martin's Griffin, 2009.
———. *Blue Moon*. New York: St. Martin's Griffin, 2009.
———. *Shadowland*. New York: St. Martin's Griffin, 2009.
———. *Dark Flame*. New York: St. Martin's Griffin, 2010.
———. *Night Star*. New York: St. Martin's Griffin, 2010.
———. *Everlasting*. New York: St. Martin's Griffin, 2011.

Intertwined Series (ongoing)

Showalter, G. *Intertwined*. Don Mills, ON: Harlequin Teen, 2009.
———. *Unraveled*. Don Mills, ON: Harlequin Teen, 2010.
———. *Twisted*. Don Mills, ON: Harlequin Teen, 2011.

Morganville Vampires Series (ongoing)

Caine, Rachel. *Glass Houses*. New York: NAL Jam, 2006.
———. *The Dead Girls' Dance*. New York: NAL Jam, 2007.
———. *Midnight Alley*. New York: NAL Jam, 2007.
———. *Feast of Fools*. New York: NAL Jam, 2008.
———. *Lords of Misrule*. New York: NAL Jam, 2009.
———. *Carpe Corpus*. New York: NAL Jam, 2009.
———. *Fade Out*. New York: NAL Jam, 2009.
———. *Kiss of Death*. New York: NAL Jam, 2010.
———. *Ghost Town*. New York: NAL Jam, 2010.
———. *Bite Club*. New York: NAL Jam, 2011.
———. *Last Breath*. New York: NAL Jam, 2011.

Night Runner Series (ongoing)

Turner, Max. *Night Runner*. New York: St. Martin's Griffin, 2008.
———. *End of Days*. New York: St. Martin's Griffin, 2010.

Otherworldlies Series (ongoing)

Kogler, Jennifer Anne. *Otherworldlies*. New York: HarperTeen, 2008.
———. *Siren's Cry*. New York: HarperTeen, 2011.

Peeps Series (completed)

Westerfeld, Scott. *Peeps*. New York: Razorbill, 2005.
———. *Last Days*. New York: Razorbill, 2006.

The Principal Series (complete)

Sumner, M. C. *The Principal*. New York: HarperCollins, 1994.
———. *The Substitute*. New York: HarperCollins, 1994.
———. *The Coach*. New York: HarperCollins, 1994.

Pulse Series (ongoing)

Gow, Kailin. *Pulse*. Calgary, AB: The EDGE, 2010.
———. *Life's Blood*. Calgary, AB: The EDGE, 2010.
———. *Blood Burned*. Calgary, AB: The EDGE, 2010.
———. *Blue Blood*. Calgary, AB: The EDGE, 2011.
———. *Blood Bone*. Calgary, AB: The EDGE, 2011.
———. *Pulse Papers*. Calgary, AB: The EDGE, 2011.
———. *Brotherhood of Blood*. Calgary, AB: The EDGE, 2011.

Rancour Chronicles (complete)

McCann, James. *Rancour*. Vancouver, BC: Simply Read Books, 2005.
———. *Pyre*. Vancouver, BC: Simply Read Books, 2007.

The Saga of Larten Crepsley Series (prequel to Cirque du Freak series) (ongoing)

Shan, Darren. *Birth of a Killer*. New York: Little, Brown, 2010.

Shivers Series (ongoing)

Storm, Derek. *Vampire Island*. Northport, AL: Family Vision Press, 1993.

Stoker Sisters Series (complete)

Gow, Kailin. *Daughters of Dracula*. Calgary, AB: The EDGE, 2010.
————. *Angels and Hunters*. Calgary, AB: The EDGE, 2010.
————. *Sisters of the Strigois*. Calgary, AB: The EDGE, 2011.

Strange Angels Series (complete)

St. Crow, Lili. *Strange Angels*. New York: Razorbill, 2009.
————. *Betrayals*. New York: Razorbill, 2009.
————. *Jealousy*. New York: Razorbill, 2010.
————. *Defiance*. New York: Razorbill, 2011.
————. *Reckoning*. New York: Razorbill, 2011.

Sucks to Be Me Series (completed)

Pauley, Kimberly. *Sucks to Be Me: The All-True Confession of Mina Hamilton, Teen Vampire*. Renton, WA: Mirrorstone, 2008.
————. *Still Sucks to Be Me: The All-True Confession of Mina Hamilton, Teen Vampire*. Renton, WA: Mirrorstone, 2010.

Vamped Series (unknown)

Diver, Lucienne. *Vamped*. Woodbury, MN: Flux, 2009.
————. *Revamped*. Woodbury, MN: Flux, 2010.

Vampire Academy Series (complete)

Mead, Richelle. *Vampire Academy*. New York: Razorbill, 2007.
————. *Frostbite*. New York: Razorbill, 2008.
————. *Shadow Kiss*. New York: Razorbill, 2008.
————. *Blood Promise*. New York: Razorbill, 2009.
————. *Spirit Bound*. New York: Razorbill, 2010.
————. *Last Sacrifice*. New York: Razorbill, 2010.

Vampire Beach Series (complete)

Duval, Alex. *Bloodlust*. New York: Simon Pulse, 2006.
———. *Initiation*. New York: Simon Pulse, 2006.
———. *Ritual*. New York: Simon Pulse, 2007.
———. *Legacy*. New York: Simon Pulse, 2007.

Vampire Diaries: The Hunters Series (ongoing)

Smith, L. J. *Phantom*. New York: HarperTeen, 2011.

Vampire Diaries: The Return Series (complete)

Smith, L. J. *Nightfall*. New York: HarperTeen, 2009.
———. *Shadow Souls*. New York: HarperTeen, 2010.
———. *Midnight*. New York: HarperTeen, 2011.

Vampire Diaries: Stefan's Diaries Series (complete)

Smith, L. J. (author), Kevin Williamson (TV show developer), and Julie Plec
(TV show developer). *Origins*. New York: HarperTeen, 2010.
———. *Bloodlust*. New York: HarperTeen, 2011.
———. *Craving*. New York: HarperTeen, 2011.

Vampire High Series (complete)

Rees, Douglas. *Vampire High*. New York: Delacorte Press, 2003.
———. *Sophomore Year*. New York: Delacorte Press, 2010.

Vampire Hunters Series (complete)

Hill, William. *Vampire Hunters*. Middleburg, FL: Otter Creek Press, 1998.
———. *Vampire Hunters Stalked*. Middleburg, FL: Otter Creek Press, 2006.

Vampire Kisses Series (ongoing)

Schreiber, Ellen. *Vampire Kisses*. New York: Katherine Tegan Books, 2003.
———. *Kissing Coffins*. New York: Katherine Tegan Books, 2005.
———. *Vampireville*. New York: Katherine Tegan Books, 2006.
———. *Dance with a Vampire*. New York: Katherine Tegan Books, 2007.

——. *Coffin Club*. New York: Katherine Tegan Books, 2008.
——. *Royal Blood*. New York: Katherine Tegan Books, 2009.
——. *Love Bites*. New York: Katherine Tegan Books, 2010.
——. *Cryptic Cravings*. New York: Katherine Tegan Books, 2011.

Vampire Princess of St. Paul Series (ongoing)

Hallaway, Tate. *Almost to Die For*. New York: NAL Trade, 2010.
——. *Almost Final Curtain*. New York: NAL Trade, 2011.
——. *Almost Everything*. New York: NAL Trade, 2012.

Vampire Queen Series (ongoing)

Maizel, Rebecca. *Infinite Days*. New York: St. Martin's Griffin, 2010.

Vamps Series (unknown)

Collins, Nancy. *Vamps*. New York: HarperTeen, 2008.
——. *Night Life*. New York: HarperTeen, 2009.
——. *After Dark*. New York: HarperTeen, 2009.

Stand-Alone Titles

Atwater-Rhodes, Amanda. *Persistence of Memory*. New York: Delacorte Press, 2008.
Black, Bekka. *iDrakula*. Naperville, IL: Sourcebooks Fire, 2010.
Black, Holly, and Theo Black. *The Poison Eaters and Other Stories*. Easthampton, MA: Big Mouth House, 2010.
Block, Francesca Lia. *Blood Roses*. New York: Delacorte Press, 2008.
——. *Pretty Dead*. New York: HarperTeen, 2009.
Cast, Kristin, et al. *Kisses from Hell*. New York: HarperTeen, 2010.
Cast, P. C., ed. *Immortal: Love Stories with Bite*. Dallas, TX: BenBella Books, 2008.
——. *Eternal: More Love Stories with Bite*. Dallas, TX: BenBella Books, 2010.
Conrad, Liza. *High School Bites: The Lucy Chronicles*. New York: NAL Trade, 2006.
Cusick, Richie Tankersley. *Vampire*. New York: Simon Pulse, 1991.
Datlow, Ellen, and Terri Windling, eds. *Teeth: Vampire Tales*. New York: HarperTeen, 2011.

Doyle, D. *Hunters' Moon*. New York: Berkley Books, 1994.

Hahn, Mary Downing. *Look for Me by Moonlight*. Boston, MA: Clarion Books, 1995.

Jablonski, Carla. *Thicker Than Water*. New York: Razorbill, 2006.

Jenkins, A. M. *Night Road*. New York: HarperTeen, 2008.

Jinks, Catherine. *The Reformed Vampire Support Group*. Boston, MA: Harcourt Children's Books, 2009.

Jones, Patrick. *The Tear Collector*. New York: Walker Books for Young Readers, 2009.

Marrone, Amanda. *Uninvited*. New York: Simon Pulse, 2007.

———. *Slayed*. New York: Simon Pulse, 2010.

McKinley, Robin. *Sunshine*. New York: Berkley Books, 2003.

Meehl, Brian. *Suck It Up*. New York: Delacorte Press, 2008.

Moore, Peter. *Red Moon Rising*. New York: Hyperion, 2011.

Noyes, Deborah, ed. *The Restless Dead: Ten Original Stories of the Supernatural*. Somerville, MA: Candlewick Press, 2007.

Onge, Caissie. *Jane Jones: Worst. Vampire. Ever.* New York: Ember, 2011.

Rex, A. *Fat Vampire: A Never Coming of Age Story*. New York: Balzar + Bray, 2010.

Robinson, A. M. *Vampire Crush*. New York: HarperTeen, 2010.

Rowen, Michelle, and Richelle Mead. *Vampire Academy: The Ultimate Guide*. New York: Razorbill, 2011.

Somtow, S. P., and Gary Lippincott. *The Vampire's Beautiful Daughter*. New York: Antheneum, 1997.

Summers, Tamara. *Never Bite a Boy on the First Date*. New York: HarperTeen, 2009.

Taylor, Drew Hayden. *The Night Wanderer: A Native Gothic Novel*. Richmond Hill, ON: Annick Press, 1997.

Telep, Trisha, ed. *The Eternal Kiss: 13 Vampire Tales of Blood and Desire*. Philadelphia, PA: Running Press Kids, 2009.

Van Diepen, Allison. *The Vampire Stalker*. New York: Point Books, 2001.

Wilde, Terry Lee. *The Vampire . . . in My Dreams*. Macon, GA: Samhain Publishing, 2008.

Zombies

Forest of Hands and Teeth Trilogy (complete)

Ryan, Carrie. *Forest of Hands and Teeth*. New York: Delacorte Press, 2009.

———. *Dead-Tossed Waves*. New York: Delacorte Press, 2010.

———. *The Dark and Hollow Places*. New York: Delacorte Press, 2011.

Megan Berry Series (ongoing)

Jay, Stacey. *You Are So Undead to Me.* New York: Razorbill, 2009.
———. *Undead Much?* New York: Razorbill, 2010.
———. *My So-Called Death.* New York: Razorbill, 2010.

Stand-Alone Titles

Ashby, Amanda. *Zombie Queen of Newbury High.* New York: Speak, 2009.
Black, Holly, and Justine Larbalestier, eds. *Zombies vs. Unicorns.* New York: Margaret K. McElderry, 2010.
Fischer, Rusty. *Zombies Don't Cry: A Living Dead Love Story.* St. Charles, IL: Medallion Press, 2011.
Ford, Michael Thomas. *Z.* New York: HarperTeen, 2009.
Golden, Christopher. *Soulless.* New York: MTV, 2008.
Harris, Carrie. *Bad Taste in Boys.* New York: Delacorte, 2011.
James, Brian. *Zombie Blondes.* New York: Feiwel & Friends, 2009.
Selzer, Adam. *I Kissed a Zombie and I Liked It.* New York: Delacorte Press, 2010.
Van Lowe, E. *Never Slow Dance with a Zombie.* New York: Tor Teen, 2009.

Index

About the Author

Joni Richards Bodart received her PhD in library science from Texas Woman's University. She also holds an MLS and an MA in psychology. Prior to joining the San José State University as a full-time faculty member in 2006, she taught as a part-time faculty member for three years. She has also taught for Emporia State University and the University of Denver. Dr. Bodart also speaks regularly at school and public library workshops and conferences.

In addition to controversial literature and monster literature, her research interests include the need in LIS education for youth librarianship coursework on the culture of adolescents and their developmental psycho-social needs; how to create a "third place" for teens at public libraries; how the changes in technology (i.e., web pages, blogs, social networking software) have impacted the ways YA authors communicate with their readers; and the impact this interaction has on their writing.

Dr. Bodart has published twenty books on YA literature, including two series on booktalking, which are considered to be the standard for the field. Her books for Scarecrow Press include *The World's Best Thin Books: What to Read When Your Book Report Is Due Tomorrow* (2000) and *Radical Reads: 101 YA Novels on the Edge* (2002). *Radical Reads 2: Working with the Newest Edgy Titles for Teens* (2009), which focuses on the newest and most controversial fiction titles for teens, is designed to help librarians and teachers use and defend these important titles.

Dr. Bodart is the winner of the 2010 Scholastic Library Publishing Award, formerly the Grolier Award, given annually to a librarian whose "extraordinary contributions to promoting access to books and encouraging a love of reading for lifelong learning exemplifies outstanding achievement in the profession."

CPSIA information can be obtained at www.ICGtesting.com
Printed in the USA
BVOW031745031111

275068BV00002B/6/P